# of mice and miracles:
An American Educator's Story

Frederick J. Day

Published by 2DonnBooks, United States in 2014
Editor: F. M. Donnell
Consulting Editor: John Donnell
Printed in the United States

Text copyright © 2014 by Frederick J. Day
Notre Dame 1961-62 wrestling team photo, used courtesy of *Dome* yearbook
Photograph of Dick Martin climbing the steps at
Sainte-Anne-de-Beaupré used by permission of photographer Jim Welsford
All other photos courtesy of the Martin family
Graphic layout © 2014 by Catherine Hébert

All publishing rights reserved. No part of this publication may be reproduced or transmitted in any form or by any means, electronic or mechanical, including photocopy, recording, or any information storage and retrieval system, without permission in writing from the publisher, except in the case of brief quotations embodied in critical articles or reviews.

Requests for permission to make copies of any part of this work should be addressed to:
2DonnBooks
11354 Links Drive
Reston, Virginia 20190

E-mail: francie@2DonnBooks.com

Title: *Of Mice and Miracles: An American Educator's Story*
Author: Frederick J. Day
First U.S. edition 2014

p.cm. Summary:
Memoir of Richard "Dick" Martin, a Catholic educator and coach for 50 years.
Biographical indexes

I. Biography of Martin, Richard J. – nonfiction
1. Notre Dame University – United States
II. Catholic Education
1. High School Educator
2. Administrator
III. Youth Sports
1. High School Coaching – High School Wrestling
IV. Personal Enlightenment and Spiritual Growth
1. Willie Mays   2. Mother Teresa
[B]

ISBN 978-0-9770893-4-5

2DonnBooks
11354 Links Drive
Reston, Virginia 20190
www.2DonnBooks.com
Esse quam videri

Cover photograph: Richard J. "Dick" Martin outside Bishop O'Connell High School, Arlington, Virginia, 1968.

Cover design by Hung Pham, Washington, D.C.
Back cover design by Catherine Hébert, Vail, CO

*For my sister, Marzie Day McCoy,
always a survivor,
who chooses to follow the sun.*

If one listens closely, the Dick Martin of 2014 sounds much like a current-day Morrie Schwartz, the subject of Mitch Albom's *Tuesdays with Morrie*. It wasn't always that way. Those who knew Martin in his earlier years might well marvel at the transformation. Many have contributed to that transformation, most especially Martin's parents, Dr. James Martin and Mary Elizabeth Martin, his sisters Dolly and Mary Jane, his brothers Jimmy and Bill, and his daughters, Kelly, Kimberley and Kerry. Each played a significant role in Martin's progression toward enlightenment. Each deserves special recognition.

Kerry, Martin's youngest daughter, once told her father, "I so respect the depths to which you have changed yourself." In addition to Kerry, Kelly and Kimberley, many others witnessed the process of growth that Dick Martin has undergone. For the most part, the friends and contemporaries who knew Martin most intimately and who could best attest to the change have passed away. Therefore, this account of Martin's life and his experiences is necessarily based largely on Martin's recollections. The history books and family scrapbooks have helped to supplement those recollections. So have the observations made while listening to Martin's classroom lectures. However, the account of the mice and the miracles and other events related in this book are based almost exclusively on information provided by Martin himself.

Of Mice and Miracles

"Hope lies in dreams, in imagination and in the courage of those who dare to make dreams into reality."

–Jonas Salk

Table of Contents

Warm-up		1
Chapter 1.	Twenty-eight Steps	3
Chapter 2.	Saturday Afternoon Thoroughbreds	14
Chapter 3.	"Be A Good Boy"	26
Chapter 4.	Five Fingers of Structure	36
Chapter 5.	The Toast of Mt. Lebanon	43
Chapter 6.	Notre Dame's Smallest Quarterback	50
Chapter 7.	The Influence of a Revolutionary	65
Chapter 8.	Fighting the War on Poverty	72
Chapter 9.	Expunging the Bureaucrat	87
Chapter 10.	Touchdown Twins	93
Chapter 11.	The Imposing Figure of Father McMurtrie	100
Chapter 12.	"Will Anybody Stop O'Connell?"	111
Chapter 13.	Four Glasses of Bourbon	123
Chapter 14.	Professor of Love	128
Chapter 15.	Yes, There Really Is A Kalamazoo	134
Chapter 16.	Mice, Mischief, and Miracles	151
Chapter 17.	The Leprechaun and the Priest	162
Chapter 18.	Tissues, Issues, and Lip Gloss	166
Chapter 19.	Peering Into Eternity	171
Overtime		176
Appendices:	Biographical Timeline	i
	Roster of Players	iii
About the Author		

Warm-up

Daniel Klein, author of *Travels with Epicurus,* writes, "A man's face tells the truth about him; the face a man acquires is the result of the choices he has made and the experiences that followed from those choices. It is the face he has earned, and its raw beauty is in the fully lived life it expresses."

In a sense, Richard Martin's face is at odds with his story. Seventy-three years in the making, Martin's face bears no noteworthy blemishes or scars. His countenance gives evidence of neither extraordinary hardship nor perplexing choices. The only suggestion of hidden pain is the halfway smile that often appears. Student and athlete, coach and athletic director, teacher and principal, Martin has played a number of roles during his lifetime. One is inclined to think that his face should reveal more evidence of the struggle.

In younger years, Martin displayed little tendency toward either patience or gentleness. Innately gifted as an athlete, Martin possessed little inclination toward reflection. At age 13, he could be feisty and combative. At 16, he was twice brought before a juvenile court judge for underage drinking. At age 21, he dismissed his steady girlfriend of four years in a fit of jealousy, never to speak with her again. Maturity was late in coming.

How does one grow? What is it that causes a youth of little discipline and restraint to grow into a reflective and thoughtful educator? At what point does one embrace a philosophy of life and living that is founded in love?

In Martin's case, coaches and mentors were helpful. However, mentors cannot alone account for the growth. For Martin, the example of others, the caring exhibited by Willie Mays, the encouragement of a selfless professor named Tom Stritch, were instructive. Ultimately, though, maturity seems to have come from the wisdom gained of experience and, most prominently, the experience that comes from loving and losing family members and friends. With each new disappointment and each new loss of a loved one, Martin grew. He learned, even more, how precious the gifts of family and friendship are. With growth came a remarkable capacity for love and longing, as well as a special facility for passing on what he had learned about love and the human condition to others.

Of Mice and Miracles is the story of Martin's maturation, sometimes in fits and spurts, into a man with a gift for teaching others the importance of love.

Chapter 1
Twenty-eight Steps

In 1945, James Martin, a physician from Mt. Lebanon, Pennsylvania, traveled to the Basilica of Sainte Anne-de-Beaupré in Quebec, Canada seeking help—not for himself but for his youngest son. Richard Martin, known as "Dick" to his family, was four years old and suffering from nephrosis, a disease of the kidneys. The nephrosis caused abnormal levels of protein to be released in the boy's urine, resulting in swelling in his face, abdomen and limbs. A Catholic priest had already administered the sacrament of last rites to the boy. Quietly religious, Dr. Martin prayed for a miracle. According to custom, those who came to the Basilica of Sainte Anne-de-Beaupré seeking a cure would walk on their knees from the foot of the steps that led up to the plaza in front of the basilica until they reached the plaza—twenty-eight steps in total. Standing at the lowest step, James Martin knelt down. He then proceeded to climb the steps on his knees until he reached the plaza.

The Basilica of Sainte Anne-de-Beaupré stands majestically alongside the Saint Lawrence River. The basilica was built in honor of Saint Anne, the grandmother of Jesus and the patron saint of Quebec. Initially, the site served as a shrine to Saint Anne. The first reported miracle at the site occurred in 1658 during construction of the shrine. One of the workers, a man named Louis Guimond, suffered from debilitating rheumatism. According to legend, after Guimond had placed three stones upon the foundation for the shrine, he was healed of his ailments. As word of the cure spread, visitors began flocking to the shrine. Over the years, the shrine was expanded several times to accommodate the crowds. Construction of the present-day basilica was completed in 1926. Each year since, upwards of 500,000 people have traveled to the site. Many have entered the basilica on crutches and, when departing, are able to leave their crutches behind.

Dick Martin was born on February 1, 1941. Dr. Martin was then already a well-established physician in the Pittsburgh area. Years earlier, the elder Martin had moved the family to Mount Lebanon, Pennsylvania, from Avella, a coal-mining community located twenty-five miles to the west. Situated six miles south of Pittsburgh, Mount Lebanon had been a quiet farming community until the street cars arrived. In 1901, the City of Pittsburgh completed the construction of steel rails to Mount Lebanon Township. Almost overnight, Mount Lebanon was transformed into a streetcar suburb.[1]

When young Martin's illness was first diagnosed in 1945, he spent nine weeks in Pittsburgh's Saint Joseph Hospital. It was the same facility where his father served as chief of staff. Doctors placed the boy on a special diet consisting predominantly of soups and other liquids. At mealtimes, the hospital nuns would feed Dick by spooning his soup through the vertical restraining bars of his hospital bed. Physicians administered the measles vaccine to him as part of an experimental program. The vaccine seemed to produce some benefit. When the medical staff had done all they could, James Martin checked his son out of the hospital and brought him home.

In Pittsburgh and elsewhere, physicians were at a loss when attempting to treat nephrosis. The disease was a hot topic in the medical journals of the day, especially because the majority of those who fell victim to nephrosis were children. Anecdotal evidence of the effects of nephrosis abounded. In some children, the disease attacked suddenly.[2] In others, the nephrosis developed more gradually. Children afflicted with the disease were routinely placed on a high-protein, low-sodium diet. In some cases, the nephrosis went into remission. In other cases, the nephrosis proved fatal.[3]

Having exhausted all medical options, Dr. Martin decided to embark on the pilgrimage to Quebec. Dr. Martin was prompted by Saint Anne's reputation as "the great wonder worker," a saint who intervened in a special way for those seeking her intercession. Possessed of a faith that accepted miracles as an indispensable component of life, Dr. Martin held out great hope that his son might be healed. Through that faith, Dr. Martin readily embraced the humility that he felt was necessary to approach Saint Anne on one's knees.

Dr. Martin was a well-respected physician in Mt. Lebanon and a man of influence in the community. As one of the few medical doctors in Mt. Lebanon, Dr. Martin was accorded an exalted status. Mt. Lebanon authorities reserved a special parking place for him directly in front of the family home on Overlook Drive, a block of space marked by bright yellow paint. The Mt. Lebanon police were quick to ticket anyone who dared park in Dr. Martin's space.

Well-rounded in his medical training, Dr. Martin was equally at ease delivering babies, treating cancer patients, or operating to repair broken bones and ruptured tendons. Nonetheless, Dr. Martin readily recognized the limits of both his profession and his own capabilities. He never presumed to think of himself as a miracle worker. A devout Catholic, Dr. Martin firmly believed that miracles were the unique province of the heavenly Father.

Dr. Martin's own story was something of a miracle. Born in Syracuse, New York in 1898, James Martin was one of six children in his family. Sometime after the birth of the sixth child, James's father succumbed to meningitis. Suddenly, James's mother was the sole support for her children. Her job as a cleaning woman left her without enough money to feed all her children. With the family in dire straits, James and his next oldest brother went to live in a Syracuse orphanage.

James's mother worked to save money for the day that she could bring her two eldest sons home from the orphanage. When James was nearing college age, he and his brother moved out of the orphanage and back with the family. Shortly thereafter, James enrolled at Syracuse University, working an assortment of odd jobs to pay the tuition and expenses. After receiving his undergraduate degree, James enrolled in the University of Pittsburgh Medical School. Money was a constant struggle. As a medical student, James possessed only one pair of pants. On those occasions when he was laundering his clothes, he would have to wait indoors until his pants were washed and dried before going outside.

After earning his medical degree, James married his fiancée, Mary Elizabeth Clair. Children soon followed. Jimmy, the oldest child, was born in 1928. Katherine, who went by the nickname "Dolly," arrived in 1930. Mary Jane was born in 1934, Bill in 1936. Dick, the youngest, arrived in 1941. Even after earning his medical degree, James remained a driven man. He aspired to be a surgeon. To accomplish that goal, he would have to spend two years as a resident in an out-of-state hospital. In the early 1940s, with the infant Dick and his four older siblings at home, Dr. Martin accepted a position as a surgical resident at Chicago's Cook County Hospital. For the better part of two years, Dr. Martin lived in Chicago, traveling home only for holidays and occasional weekends to visit his family.

By 1945, Dr. Martin had completed his surgical residency and returned to his job at Saint Joseph Hospital. Shortly thereafter, he learned that his son was suffering from nephrosis. The disease was known to be a killer, with no proven remedy. One of the accepted treatments of the day was penicillin. It was suspected, though never confirmed, that exertion in any form would exacerbate the symptoms. For that reason, though he was old enough for kindergarten, Dick stayed out of school for the entire year after coming home from the hospital.

At home, a family ritual developed. Dolly, Mary Jane, Jimmy and Bill would take turns holding their younger brother down while Dr. Martin injected Dick with penicillin. At the time, the use of penicillin to kill bacteria was still in its infancy. The so-called "miracle drug" had first been isolated from mold in 1929.[4] The chance discovery of a unique mold on an ordinary cantaloupe in a Peoria, Illinois grocery store in the early 1940s had led to the development of higher-yielding penicillin molds. The drug soon became available on a widespread basis. To young Dick, the penicillin needle looked to be as big as the bore of a cannon. The mere sight of the needle caused him to squirm relentlessly. Dick's mother, Mary Elizabeth, both caring and nurturing, would usually refrain from helping out when the penicillin was being administered. She had seen her son suffer greatly. She found it difficult to watch as her youngest child recoiled at the sight of the penicillin needle.

On his good days, when it was warm, Dick would venture out to the front porch of the family's home on Overlook Drive. The four-year-old came to know every nook and every corner of that porch. By the time Dick was old enough for first grade, the doctors pronounced him cured. They could find no hint of the nephrosis. To some, it was the effect of the penicillin; to others, it was the power of prayer. One way or another, Dr. Martin sensed the hand of God in his son's cure, whether in the developments that had given rise to the availability of penicillin or in the intervention of Saint Anne, or both. Among child-age victims of nephrosis, remission would occur with some frequency, but the disease was not easily vanquished. The probability of the symptoms returning was high. To Dr. Martin, if there was a miracle, it lay in the fact that, for the remainder of Dick's elementary school days and into high school, his son never experienced any residual effects from the nephrosis and never had a relapse.

With the cure confirmed, Dick no longer had to watch other children walk to school and wonder why he was confined to home. Freed from the boundaries of the front porch, Dick attended first and second grade at Lincoln Elementary. The public school was closer to home than St. Bernard School, a Catholic grade school situated farther out on Washington Road. By the third grade, however, Dick was strong enough to walk longer distances and so transferred to St. Bernard's.

From the time he started elementary school, athletics consumed Dick's time and energy. Dick's class at St. Bernard School included several talented athletes. Denny Phillips was the best of the group, excelling in every sport he played. Harold "Bud" Vogel was tall and had good speed for a tight end. Fullback Jackie Smith was strong and powerful, a workhorse. Howard "Butch" Breinig, known as "the Tank," was short in stature but possessed a bull-like physique and an inherent toughness that caused others to leave him alone. Dick was the shortest of the bunch. Nonetheless, he could throw a football a long way, with accuracy. Coaches of the St. Bernard football team were heard to say that there was magic in the way Dick handled a football. When positioned at quarterback, he was adept at hiding the ball, making it difficult for opponents to tell whether he had shuffled the ball to one of his running backs or was carrying it on a quarterback keeper. When Dick and his friends were not playing football or basketball, they followed Pittsburgh's professional teams, the Pirates in baseball and the Steelers in football. They also followed professional boxing, an interest heightened by the fact that one-time world champion welterweight boxer Fritzie Zivic lived within shouting distance of the Martin home.

On the playground, Dick's passes to halfback Denny Phillips mimicked the passes from Steelers quarterback Jim Finks to Lynn Chandnois. Dick's spirals to end Bud Vogel became a less heralded version of the Finks-to-Elbie Nickel combination. Dick had a special claim to the role of Jim Finks. Though much smaller in stature, Dick could rifle the ball in a manner similar to Finks. More importantly, however, Finks was an occasional guest at the Martin home. No other kid could boast of having Finks as a visitor.

When his schedule permitted, Finks played poker on Friday nights at the Martin house. Drafted by the Steelers out of the University of Tulsa in 1949, Finks ascended to the team's starting quarterback position in 1952. He would not relinquish the job until his retirement after the 1955 season. In retirement, Finks liked to joke that his tenure with the Steelers was memorable only because he was the quarterback whom the Steelers kept in 1955 when they cut future Hall-of-Famer Johnny Unitas.[5] However, Finks was a competent quarterback who occasionally showed flashes of brilliance. He threw a league-leading twenty touchdown passes in 1952 and, in the process, earned Pro Bowl honors. He also excelled as a baseball player, moonlighting as a catcher in the Cincinnati Reds' farm system during the summers of 1950 and 1951.

Dr. Martin had formed a friendship with Steelers owner Art Rooney. Sundays during football season were a special treat for young Dick. Rooney had arranged for Dr. Martin to get box seats for the Steelers' home games. Dick and his father would attend Mass early on Sunday morning and then drive to St. Joseph Hospital so Dr. Martin could check in on his patients. Dick had heard people remark that Dr. Martin possessed a soothing bedside manner. During the Sunday trips to the hospital, Dick would witness firsthand his father's gentleness and caring. Dick watched with awe as patients found both encouragement and cheer in Dr. Martin's words. When Dr. Martin had finished his hospital rounds, Dick and his father would drive to Forbes Field in time for the 2:00 p.m. games.

Throughout his childhood and early teens, Dick gave little thought to matters of life and death. He never consciously pondered the gift of life that had been bestowed. He was alive and able to throw a football.

That was enough. In a predictably teenage twist on René Descartes' observation, "I think, therefore I am," Dick's mantra was akin to "I throw a football, therefore I am alive." Depth of thought did not begin to emerge until he was well along in his high school years. However, as Dick matured, his recovery from nephrosis remained in memory. He was well aware that many child-age victims of nephrosis did not live to see their teenage years. He came to believe that there was a purpose behind his recovery.

Dr. Martin would emphasize, frequently, that the purpose of life was to help others. Dick's own experience of being confined to the porch as a child—of being isolated from others—provided a useful context to his father's sense of a purposeful life. Over time, Dick came to see that if his mission in life was to help others, he could best do so by working with children and working with those who are themselves isolated.

At times, the relationship between Dick and his father was subject to a tension that seemed to arise from Dr. Martin's stern demeanor. On one occasion, Dick was injured while attempting to tackle a ballcarrier during an elementary school football practice. The ballcarrier dragged Dick for a few yards, at which point the player's cleats got caught in Dick's mouth, loosening two of Dick's front teeth. When ice packs failed to stem the flow of blood, Father John McCarren, the associate pastor at St. Bernard Church, drove Dick to Dr. Martin's office for treatment. With palpable hesitation, Dick climbed the steps leading to his father's suite. He was never sure how his father would react. Often, Dr. Martin seemed to dispense an extra dose of tough love. This time was no exception. Dick's father saw the remnants of blood and asked, "What happened to you?" Dick told of the collision on the practice field. More physician than father, Dr. Martin replied, "You're going to have to wait. I've got patients to take care of."

There were times when Martin's father could be a funny man, especially when entertaining Rooney, Finks, and the Steelers' backup quarterback, Ted Marchibroda. Dr. Martin could tell a story with ease. He made Rooney laugh. In other settings, however, Dr. Martin would sometimes come off as humorless, a man not given to frivolity. Most often, Dr. Martin seemed to be engaged in serious pursuits, befitting his role as a leader in the Mt. Lebanon community. Among other accomplishments, he had been instrumental in establishing the Mt. Lebanon Knights of Columbus Council 3084, serving as the inaugural grand knight of the Council. The Knights of Columbus, a Catholic fraternal organization devoted to fellowship and service to others, seemed an especially fitting focus for Dr. Martin's charitable instincts. The founder of the Knights, a Catholic priest named Michael McGivney, had devoted much of his life to caring for children who were either without parents or were confined to orphanages. On occasion, Father McGivney would agree to serve as the guardian for children in New Haven, Connecticut in order to prevent them from being sent to orphanages.

As a young boy, Dick Martin found that his father's interest in sports provided an effective means of easing their relationship. An ardent fan of boxing, Dr. Martin would often take Dick to the Toner Institute, a home for boys in Mt. Lebanon under the care of the Capuchin Franciscan Fathers. The Franciscans raised funds for the orphanage by scheduling boxing matches among the boys and inviting paying customers. Dr. Martin was particularly impressed by a Toner Institute boxer who fought under the name "Razzle Dazzle" Ritz. The younger Martin would soon become a "Razzle Dazzle" fan as well.

If "Razzle Dazzle" Ritz served as a common bond between father and son, it was football that cemented the relationship. When Dick was eleven years old, the Pittsburgh Steelers played a charity exhibition game against the Detroit Lions in Dr. Martin's hometown of Syracuse. Dick's parents and the five Martin children drove to Syracuse that weekend to visit relatives. The day before the game, Dr. Martin stopped off at a Syracuse hotel to meet Rooney. To Dick's delight, Rooney arranged to have Dick and his father ride in the Steelers' bus from the hotel to the stadium before the game.

Buddy Parker was the coach of the Detroit Lions at the time. It was Parker's custom, before each game, to walk around the perimeter of the field when the stadium grandstands were still empty. For the Lions-Steelers game in Syracuse, Dick accompanied Parker on his walk around the field.[6] As the two completed their circuit, Leon Hart, a rugged end on both offense and defense for the Lions, came out of the players' tunnel and stepped onto the field. Hart was a mountainous man and winner of the 1949 Heisman Trophy, an award given annually to the most outstanding player in collegiate football. Parker stopped walking long enough to introduce Dick to Hart. Standing six-foot-four and weighing 240 pounds, Hart had earned All-American honors three times at the University of Notre Dame, an all-male Catholic college in South Bend, Indiana known for its football prowess.[7]

Hart's name had become ingrained in collegiate football lore primarily as the result of a single play in Notre Dame's 1948 game against the University of Southern California. Taking a short pass from his quarterback, Frank Tripucka, Hart ran 40 yards to the end zone—breaking eight tackles along the way—to spur Notre Dame to victory. During Hart's four years of football at Notre Dame, his teams never lost a game and won the national championship three times. Hart's exploits continued after he reached the pros in 1950. In 1951, his second season with the Lions, Hart was named All-Pro on both offense and defense, the last player in the history of the National Football League to earn that distinction.

Dick was familiar with Hart's Heisman and with his All-Pro honors. However, it was the size of Hart's hands that made the biggest impression on the eleven-year-old. Years after the fact, Dick remembers Hart as possessing the biggest hands he had ever seen. When the two shook hands, Hart's right hand completely enveloped Dick's hand.

With his son by his side, Dr. Martin served as the Steelers' team physician for the exhibition game against the Lions. The sideline was not a useful vantage point for watching the game, but it did allow Dick to witness, up close, the rigors of professional football. He watched as his father examined an injury to the leg of Steelers tackle Ernie Stautner. "You're fine," Dr. Martin told Stautner, who, though small for a lineman, would be enshrined in the Pro Football Hall of Fame in 1969. Dr. Martin knew well that with mangled fingers, numerous fractures to his nose, fractures to both shoulders and a host of cracked ribs, Stautner was never really "fine." Several other Steelers were injured during the game. Dr. Martin patched them up as well. Dick learned that, in other respects also, pro football was not a delicate world. He couldn't help but listen as Pittsburgh's players cursed their opponents, cursed the officials and, on occasion, cursed their own teammates.

Dr. Martin was not inclined to be a man of leisure. When not working at his office, Dr. Martin could be found providing needed medical treatment for Pittsburgh's indigent population and organizing charity events on behalf of the Knights of Columbus. Friends were fond of saying that the Hippocratic Oath served as merely a starting point for the beliefs that governed Dr. Martin's life. The larger inspiration, it was said, came from Saint Vincent de Paul, who had spent years treating the wounds and illnesses of lowly convicts in 17th century France. It was common knowledge that Dr. Martin would accept payment in kind when patients lacked the resources to pay his bills. On one occasion, Dr. Martin negotiated with a cancer patient, a carpenter named McVeigh, for construction of a two-locomotive train set at the Martin home in lieu of payment. When Dr. Martin died, the family found that he had purposely refrained from collecting $40,000 in bills from patients who were of lower income.

Each year, Dr. Martin allowed himself one extended break from his schedule. In August, he and the family would pack their belongings and drive to Ocean City, New Jersey for a month-long vacation at the Southern Hotel, a facility owned by a family friend. For Dick, summers in Ocean City were relaxing and enjoyable. He swam in the ocean by day and sampled the boardwalk amusements by night. He and his family consumed Taylor pork rolls and birch beer in the hours after dinner. Summers became even more enjoyable in 1955 when Dr. Martin purchased a small summer retreat in Ocean City for $19,000. The home was two blocks from the oceanfront residence of actress Grace Kelly, later to become Princess Grace of Monaco.

It was in Ocean City that Martin got his first job—working as a car washer at a local gas station. Martin's brother Bill, older and possessing a more polished résumé, landed a job setting up beach umbrellas for the oceanfront families, among them Grace Kelly.

For Dick Martin, life in the late 1940s and early 1950s was comfortable. He rarely gave any thought to the nephrosis that had threatened his life and preoccupied his family in his early years. Even the monstrous needles became a distant memory. Endowed with more athletic ability than most of his contemporaries, Martin excelled on the playgrounds and ball fields. For a sports-minded child growing up in the shadows of Forbes Field, the home of the football Steelers and the baseball Pirates, little else mattered.

[1] Mount Lebanon would experience another transformation, not nearly as dramatic, in 1975 when the town changed the official spelling of its name to "Mt. Lebanon."

[2] Writing in *The Journal of the American Medical Association* in June 1945, David Hoehn, M.D. reported on a three-year old Caucasian boy who was suddenly beset with severe swelling in his lower extremities. Dr. Hoehn noted that, when the boy was admitted to the hospital, his scrotum was the size of a grapefruit. Physicians concluded that the boy was suffering from nephrosis. Dr. Hoehn expressed the belief that the boy's condition probably resulted from excessive exposure to Sta-Way insect repellent. David Hoehn, M.D., "Nephrosis Probably Due to Excessive Use of Sta-Way Insect Repellent," *The Journal of the American Medical Association*, vol. 128, 16 June 1945, 513.

[3] In the modern era, where nephrosis leads to kidney failure, patients may have to resort to dialysis. Dialysis is not a treatment for nephrosis but rather a means of replacing the kidney function in cases where nephrosis has ravaged the kidneys to the point that they no longer effectively remove waste and regulate the composition of the blood. Dialysis did not come into widespread use until the 1960s.

[4] The onset of World War II in 1939 spurred hurried research into methods for producing penicillin in large quantities. Initially, the primary penicillin research and production facility was located in London. In 1941, the facility was moved to the United States to prevent it from being destroyed by the barrage of bombs that the Germans were dropping on England. On the battlefield, penicillin brought hope. The drug prevented harmful bacteria from forming new cell walls, effectively killing off the bacteria. With penicillin, the incidence of wounded soldiers dying from infection declined markedly.

[5] The Steelers' second-string quarterback in 1955 was Ted Marchibroda from the University of Detroit. The third quarterback on the roster was Vic Eaton, a rookie from the University of Missouri. In addition to playing quarterback, Eaton had experience as a punter and punt returner. His versatility likely contributed to the team's decision to keep him on the roster and release Unitas. Eaton lasted only one season in the National Football League. He punted 66 times for the Steelers in 1955, averaging 38.2 yards per punt. He also returned 23 punts for a total of 73 yards.

[6] Parker was superstitious and unpredictable, a man of many idiosyncrasies. After coaching the Lions for seven seasons, he spent eight more years as head coach of the Steelers. One year, after the Steelers had lost a preseason game, Parker put his entire team on waivers. The commissioner's office called Parker and told him that he could not expose all his players to the waiver process. Parker responded, "Why not? They all stink." *Recollections of former Pittsburgh Steelers running back Dick Hoak.*

[7] The University of Notre Dame became co-educational in 1972. Today, the composition of the student body is approximately 53 percent male and 47 percent female.

Chapter 2
Saturday Afternoon Thoroughbreds

Sister Mary Flavia, head of the cafeteria at St. Bernard Grade School, was one tough nun. Sister Flavia cooked the food that was offered to St. Bernard's students each lunchtime, 25 cents a meal. When students failed to eat all of their vegetables, Sister Flavia took it as a personal insult. Under her watch, no students left the cafeteria with food on their plates. Sister Flavia was wise to all the tricks. She would stand by the trash cans as students exited and shake each empty milk carton before it was thrown away. Any student caught concealing unwanted vegetables in his or her milk carton faced harsh consequences. Sister Flavia would empty the carton and require the student to consume every last lima bean, even if soaked in milk. With milk cartons removed as a viable option, students took to stuffing tasteless vegetables in their pockets, an alternative vastly more appealing than having to eat them.

Stern by nature, Sister Flavia never went out of her way to cultivate a following among the students at St. Bernard School. She demanded the respect of the students, but cared little about whether the students liked her. To the contrary, the manner in which she carried out her duties as lunchroom "cop" seemed designed to keep the students from developing any affinity for her at all. In that sense, Sister Flavia was much like Father Joseph Lonergan, the long-time pastor at St. Bernard Catholic Church. Father Lonergan possessed a natural reserve in the presence of students, a stiffness that seemed to ward off any visible demonstrations of affection.

The Most Reverend Hugh C. Boyle, the venerable bishop of the Diocese of Pittsburgh, appointed Lonergan to serve as pastor at St. Bernard Church in 1943. Lonergan was a man of simple tastes. When he first took up residence at St. Bernard, he used a spare Army cot as his bed. He steadfastly refused to allocate parish funds to renovate his living quarters, preferring to spend the money for facilities that would benefit either St. Bernard's students or the nuns teaching at the school. Standing prominently in Lonergan's living quarters at St. Bernard Church was a statue of Saint Jean Vianney, the 19th century French clergyman who is regarded as the patron saint of parish priests. Saint Jean Vianney lived modestly and was given to self-mortification. Lonergan followed his lead.

Lonergan had been ordained as a priest in 1911 at the age of 29. With less than six months as an ordained cleric, Lonergan assumed the position of pastor of St. Charles Borromeo Church in Sutersville, Pennsylvania. Sutersville lay in the heart of the Western Pennsylvania coal region, ten miles from the city of McKeesport. Lonergan's arrival in Sutersville coincided with the period of the "Westmoreland Coal Wars." The coal wars consisted of repeated clashes between coal miners intent on organizing into labor unions and "Coal and Gas Police" hired by the coal companies to thwart unionization. Spurred by the encyclicals of Pope Leo XIII and Pope Pius XI affirming the dignity of workers, Lonergan made his church's facilities available to the workers for organizational meetings. He watched with anger as the coal companies fired his parishioners from their jobs in the mines in retribution for having attended union meetings. In 1923, Lonergan was appointed the pastor of St. Paulinus Church in Clairton, Pennsylvania. Many of the parishioners of St. Paulinus worked in the Clairton Mill. As pastor, Father Lonergan used his position to help Clairton's workers organize under the banner of the United Steel Workers of America.

Lonergan was 60 years old when he took on the position as pastor at St. Bernard. He quickly directed his energies toward the children of the parish, especially the boys who played football. The aging priest saw football as a means of promoting the development of boys whom he thought of as "thoroughbreds." In Lonergan's rather simplistic view of the world, the "thoroughbreds" were distinct from and superior to the boys who were inclined to join organizations such as the Boy Scouts. From the time of Lonergan's arrival in Mt. Lebanon in 1943 until his death in 1959, football reigned supreme at St. Bernard School. When Lonergan hired male teachers for the school, his focus was primarily on football and, secondarily, on academics. Lonergan's preference was to employ former University of Notre Dame football players as coaches at St. Bernard. Lonergan's fascination with the "Fighting Irish" was due, in part, to the fact that his father, Luke Lonergan, had studied at Notre Dame.[8] Near the end of Martin's time at St. Bernard, Lonergan enticed former Notre Dame quarterback Bernie Powers to join the school's staff. On paper, Powers was a teacher. There was no doubt, however, that his tenure at the school depended on his ability to coach football. Lonergan's introductory words to Powers were sparse and direct. "I pay for performance," he told Powers, "not excuses." The message was clear: Father Lonergan wanted a winner on Saturday afternoons.

Lonergan outfitted the St. Bernard team in gold pants and blue jerseys patterned after the Notre Dame uniforms. He paid for the St. Bernard coaches to travel to South Bend to observe spring football practices under Irish head coach Frank Leahy. When a key St. Bernard assistant coach received an offer to work at a manufacturing plant for $335 a month, Lonergan countered by bumping the coach's pay to $350 a month. During Lonergan's time at St. Bernard, his football teams won 180 games and lost 19, with 6 ties. As he made clear in a commentary that appeared in the St. Bernard Church bulletin on September 10, 1950, he had little use for "the sluggard, the shirker, the coward, the scatterbrain, the dolt."[9] Lonergan wanted only boys of character and dedication on the St. Bernard football team.

Lonergan believed that the best way to transform a boy into a man was through competition, discipline, and the hard knocks of football. From a competitive standpoint, Lonergan's methods worked; the school produced winners. From 1949 to 1953, the "Bernies" won 30 consecutive games. In pursuit of victory number 31, St. Bernard School hooked up with Resurrection School in the latter part of the 1953 season. The game pitted the two most powerful squads in the South Hills Catholic Grade School League. At the time, Dick Martin was in St. Bernard's seventh-grade class. In football, he was the first-string quarterback for the seventh-grade team and an occasional backup during the eighth graders' games.

Interest in the St. Bernard-Resurrection game was at a feverish pitch. Onlookers anticipated a close contest. By late in the third quarter, however, it was apparent that St. Bernard's winning streak was over. Resurrection had put up 20 points while holding St. Bernard scoreless. The Bernies' head coach, Raymond Pulaski, showed his frustration, pulling all of his starters. St. Bernard's eighth graders each took a seat on the bench, turning the game over to Dick and his seventh-grade classmates. Dick knew the drill. He ran a 28-sweep and sent halfback Denny Phillips darting around the end. He called on his bruising fullback, Jackie Smith, and let Smith plow straight ahead. When Phillips and Smith tired, Dick would call his own number and sneak forward behind the blocking of his aptly named center, Ray Blockinger. Late in the fourth quarter, Dick rolled out and hit Bud Vogel with a pass in the Resurrection end zone for St. Bernard's only score of the game. When the final gun sounded, Resurrection walked off the field with a 33-6 victory.

The loss to Resurrection was the only blight on St. Bernard's record for 1953. The team closed out the season with six wins against the one loss and finished in a tie with Assumption School for first place in the South Hills League. As with other seventh graders, Dick had seen only spot duty during the season, completing five passes in eight attempts for 80 yards. Prospects for the following year looked good, however, as fellow seventh graders Denny Phillips and Jackie Smith excelled in their limited opportunities in the backfield. For the season, Phillips ran for 59 yards on fourteen carries, averaging 4.2 yards per run. Smith averaged more than six yards per carry, gaining 105 yards in 17 attempts. Smith was one of the most physical players in the league. He was also Dick's best friend. Smith possessed a mischievous sense of humor and a flair for pinning appropriate, often ironic, nicknames on others. To Smith, Martin was always "Beaver," a tribute to Dick's two prominent front teeth.

On March 14, 1954, the seventh and eighth graders on St. Bernard's 1953 team assembled for one last time to attend the school's Monogram Banquet. In keeping with the exalted status of grade school football in Pittsburgh, three members of the Pittsburgh Steelers attended the Monogram Banquet: Jim Finks, fullback Fran Rogel, and head coach Joe Bach. Later that same year, on October 9, Dick's older brother, Jimmy, took Dick to see the Notre Dame-University of Pittsburgh contest in Pittsburgh. Dick watched as Notre Dame shut out Pitt by a score of 33-0. After the game, Jimmy took his younger brother to meet Notre Dame's head coach, Terry Brennan. Jimmy, a Notre Dame graduate, had been friends with Brennan ever since the future coach had played halfback for the Irish from 1946 to 1948.[10] After meeting Brennan, Dick also had the opportunity to meet one of his heroes, Notre Dame quarterback Ralph Guglielmi, later a quarterback for the Washington Redskins.

It was around this same time that Dick learned, in dramatic fashion, that heroes were not confined to the football field. More than most of his fellow students, Dick understood the significance of the research that Dr. Jonas E. Salk had undertaken in the early 1950s to combat the crippling childhood disease, poliomyelitis. Dr. Salk had graduated from the New York University School of Medicine, but his interest was in the field of research and not in practicing medicine. He aspired to help humankind in general rather than single patients. Following medical school, Salk spent two years in residency at Mount Sinai Hospital in New York.[11] By 1947, Dr. Salk was running his own laboratory at the University of Pittsburgh School of Medicine. It was there that he developed a vaccine that offered the promise of eradicating polio. From his home base in nearby Mt. Lebanon, Dick's father took particular interest in Dr. Salk's work. Dr. Martin arranged for the students at St. Bernard School to participate in what came to be known as the Francis Field Trial, a program that involved 1.8 million children from 44 states in a test application of the vaccine. Dick and the other Martin children also learned of Salk's selflessness. His work had the potential to earn him millions. However, he declined to seek a patent on the vaccine. It was Salk's hope that by relinquishing his rights to the patent, he could make the vaccine available more quickly to children throughout the world.[12]

As the 1954-55 school year approached, Dick looked forward to competing for the starting quarterback position on St. Bernard's team. He was well aware, however, that St. Bernard's new head coach, Bernie Powers, was looking for a taller quarterback. Even after adding a couple of inches in seventh grade, Dick still measured well short of five feet. He was adept, even deceptive, at handling a football. His quickness and ball-handling skills, however, could not compensate for his lack of height. When St. Bernard's season started, Powers installed Ned

Doran as the quarterback. Doran was taller than Dick and equally athletic, though perhaps not as accurate a passer as Martin.

Doran led the team to an undefeated season. Martin saw limited duty as the second-string quarterback, filling in occasionally when Doran needed a rest. In early November of 1954, St. Bernard went up against a powerful team from Assumption School for the Catholic League championship. Matt Zecony and Dick Teresi were Assumption's best players. Both would go on to play for the University of Iowa after finishing their high school careers. Coach Powers was concerned that Assumption's team might be too big and too experienced for St. Bernard. Others who followed scholastic sports were inclined to agree. In the first three quarters, however, Doran led the Bernies to three touchdowns. Entering the fourth quarter, St. Bernard led 19-13. Midway through the quarter, Doran went down with an injury. Powers summoned Martin to replace him. Taking the field in front of some 5,000 fans, Dick worked with a full-house backfield of Phillips, Smith, and halfback Lee Wells. Unlike Martin, his three backfield mates had played almost the entire game. They were noticeably tired. Passing sparingly, Dick marched the team down the field, alternating hand-offs to Phillips and Wells with shovel passes to Smith. Near the Assumption ten-yard line, Martin handed off to Phillips, who ran in for the score, giving St. Bernard a 25-13 lead. For the point after, Dick called on his fullback, Jackie Smith, to carry the ball. Smith erupted. "Beaver, don't call my number," he screamed. Exhilarated after his first extended action of the season, Martin yelled at Smith, "You're not as tired as the other guys." The team broke huddle. Dick pitched the ball to Smith, low and wobbly. Smith picked the pigskin off his shoelaces and stumbled into the end zone for the extra point.

St. Bernard walked off the field with a convincing 26-13 victory and the league championship. Dr. Martin, tears in his eyes, met his son as St. Bernard's players boarded the team bus for the return trip to school. "Congratulations," the elder Martin said to his son. The quarterback beamed.

During his years as a student at St. Bernard, Dick hung out most often with the athletes in his class and, more often than not, with his buddy Jackie Smith. Off the football field, Smith was distinguished primarily by his aversion to any form of self-discipline. On one occasion, after Dick and Jackie had finished playing a game of pickup basketball on St. Bernard's blacktop court, Smith went off alone, looking for a diversion. A short time later, Dick noticed a stream of smoke rising in the distance. He learned that the smoke was from a fire at an abandoned house. Arson was suspected. The police investigated and determined that Jackie Smith was responsible. Juvenile court proceedings followed, and Smith was sentenced to two weeks at Pittsburgh's Thorn Hill Reform School.

The incident sent ripples throughout the St. Bernard community. The nuns at St. Bernard had a reputation as strict disciplinarians, adept at dealing with students who failed to eat their lima beans or who flouted the prohibition against shooting squirt guns. Arson was way out of their league. In the insulated world of St. Bernard Grade School, Smith's conduct generated profound shock. The incident prompted Father Lonergan to give St. Bernard's students a small card containing homespun guidance on avoiding trouble with the law. "Be sure you go out with the right companions," Father Lonergan's card advised. On occasions when trouble occurred, the card instructed students to "get away fast, keep your mouth shut, and talk to no one but your lawyer." To ensure that the students knew what to do during times of difficulty, the priest's final prescription advised the students to "keep this card in your pocket and read it five times every day."[13]

Dick and his classmates knew that Father Lonergan was merely trying to help them stay out of trouble. Even so, the pastor's advice was the source of some amusement, especially the segment that recommended talking only to one's lawyer. Dick knew few details regarding Jackie Smith's case in juvenile court. He knew even less about what lawyers did. The world of lawyers and courts was far removed from the common experiences of Dick and most of his St. Bernard classmates. Those who knew Jackie Smith were not surprised that he would be involved in burning a vacant house. Some who knew Dick may have been surprised that "Beaver" was not a party to the arson. Dick was generally regarded as an overachiever in athletics and an underachiever in most other pursuits. He studied when the mood struck him, but preferred throwing a ball to opening a book. For a time, Miss Bruning, an especially attractive woman and Dick's favorite teacher, seemed to inspire Dick to study with more than his usual diligence. For the most part, however, Dick was indifferent to any teaching not delivered by Miss Bruning.

The youthful Martin was not one to start fires in vacant buildings. Neither, however, was he inclined to keep Father Lonergan's "get away fast" card in his pocket, let alone read it five times a day. If the football team's Monogram Banquet represented the high point of Beaver Martin's years at St. Bernard, the low point would come during the eighth-grade basketball season. On a pleasant spring evening in Mt. Lebanon, Dick was feeling privileged. He and several of his basketball teammates had been invited to a party at the home of a classmate named Nancy. Dick knew that the evening was destined to be fun and maybe a bit naughty. A single parent, Nancy's mother provided the students with cigarettes. Dick and his classmates provided the laughter and a festive atmosphere. The parties made Nancy's mother feel young and made the eighth graders feel mature beyond their years.

Nancy's party ended without incident. Before the night got too late, Dick and his teammates went home. All was quiet until the following week. In the middle of Monday basketball practice, Coach Powers blew his whistle in the shrillest manner possible. Powers called the team over to the sideline and instructed them to sit in the stands. The exchange was brief and mostly one-sided. Powers informed the boys that he had heard about the weekend party. One by one, Powers interrogated his basketball players. "Were you there?" he asked each player in succession. Dick and most of his friends on the team admitted to having been at the party. "That house is condemned," Powers told the team. If the literal meaning of "condemned" did not quite fit the context, there was no mistaking the message being conveyed. Dick and his teammates understood that they were not to visit Nancy's house ever again.

The interrogation finished, Powers advised the boys that they would all have to go to confession—no exceptions. The team marched en masse to the church. All fifteen basketball players knelt in the pews and prepared for confession. One by one, each player entered the confessional and confessed to having attended a party where there were cigarettes, girls and questionable conduct. Most were unsure about which of the ten commandments had been violated. For some, the fourth commandment admonition to honor one's father and mother seemed to be implicated. Clearly, the party was not an activity their parents would condone. Others opted for the sixth commandment, thinking they may have engaged in unwholesome thoughts. For his part, Dick simply knew that he had done something wrong. He also knew that he had to conceal his involvement from his father. Dick feared that his father's reaction would be one of unbounded rage.

Dr. Martin had always attempted to inspire his children to avoid wasting their time and talents. He frowned on frivolous pursuits and aimless activities. Each child in the Martin family was well aware that their father placed great credence in the admonition contained in the Gospel of Saint Luke, "Much is required from the person to whom much is given."[14] Having grown up in poverty, Dr. Martin made every effort to ensure that his children would have the advantages in life that he himself had lacked as a child. To Dr. Martin, obligation came hand in hand with opportunity. Wasting time and effort on frivolous pursuits was not to be tolerated. Dick knew well that the weekend party, at once scandalous in appearance and presenting abundant temptation, would be anathema to his father.

Athletically, if not in other ways, Dick had been blessed with more gifts than his two older brothers. Though short in stature, Dick possessed instincts that allowed him to react quickly and intuitively to the flow of his football and basketball games. Childhood friends marveled at Dick's hand-and-eye coordination and, just as often, cursed his uncanny ability to return serves in table tennis that were seemingly out of reach. So, when Dr. Martin considered the talents bestowed on his youngest son, it was Dick's ability to compete in sports that often drew Dr. Martin's admiration. Dr. Martin was confident, also, that despite Dick's lackluster grades at St. Bernard and in his early years of high school, his son possessed the intelligence to do well in school. Dr. Martin readily accepted, and even welcomed, Dick's fascination with sports, particularly football. For Dr. Martin, the time that his son spent on Mt. Lebanon's playing fields was one facet of developing his natural talents. Conversely, Dr. Martin would be infuriated that his son had wasted precious hours at an aimless weekend party.

Eight days after the party at Nancy's house, during a Sunday Mass attended by Dick and his parents, Father Lonergan made reference to the eighth-graders' party in his sermon. The pastor decried the permissiveness in society and, in particular, the prevailing climate in which teenagers felt it was acceptable to engage in adult conduct at parties. When Father Lonergan first broached the topic in his sermon, Dick began to squirm, as did several teammates sitting in adjacent pews.

Back at home after Mass, Mrs. Martin asked Dick whether he had attended the party. If it had been his father posing the question, Dick would have attempted to avoid a direct answer, out of fear for his father's wrath. With his mother asking the question, Dick did not hesitate to tell the truth. He admitted to being at the party and then pleaded, "Mom, please don't tell Dad."

It was not the first time that Dick had sought his mother's help in hiding bad news from his father. Martin's father was the disciplinarian in the family; his mother was the healer. Mary Elizabeth Martin patiently allowed her husband to set the rules for the household. She recognized, however, that Dr. Martin had little tolerance for mischief. As a civic leader and prominent member of the Mt. Lebanon community, he seemed to hold his children to a higher standard than did most parents. Dr. Martin expected excellence, if not perfection. The standards he imposed made no allowance for attending parties at "condemned" houses. When his children did misbehave, Dr. Martin reacted swiftly and unsparingly. When provoked to anger, Dr. Martin was a man to be feared.

When Dick admitted that he had been at the party, Mrs. Martin was disappointed but realistic. She knew the classmates whom Dick considered to be friends. She would have preferred that Dick keep his distance from Jackie Smith. Aside from Jackie, however, Mrs. Martin was comfortable with Dick's friends. She knew that if Denny Phillips, Bud Vogel, Lee Wells and others were going to attend a party, Dick was likely to accompany them. Her son's inclination to follow his friends caused little concern for Mrs. Martin. She was confident that, in almost all cases, Denny, Bud, and Lee functioned as positive influences on her son.

There was risk for Dick's mother in hiding the news of the party from her husband. Dr. Martin had long thought that his wife was overly tolerant of their children's shortcomings. Mary Elizabeth knew well that her husband would react with anger if he learned that she had deliberately concealed Dick's presence at the party from him. It was a risk that Mrs. Martin accepted, the price of being a protective mother.

Quiet by nature, Mary Elizabeth was not one to publicly challenge her husband. Nonetheless, on matters that she considered important, she held her ground with tenacity. The days following local, state, and national elections proved to be particularly interesting times in the Martin household. A staunch Republican, Dr. Martin would regularly ask his wife how she had voted. To the amusement of Dick and his siblings, their mother steadfastly refused to reveal her candidates of choice.

When it came to politics, Mrs. Martin considered it her civic duty to resist her husband's subtle attempts to influence her vote. She valued the right to cast her votes freely—and frequently for the Democratic ticket. Similarly, when it came to her role as a parent, she did not hesitate to shield her children from Dr. Martin's outbursts. For his part, Dick admired and greatly appreciated his mother's assertion of independence. He knew well that what Mary Elizabeth considered to be exercising her prerogative as a mother, Dr. Martin would likely view as defiance, if not betrayal. Dick found inspiration in his mother's resolve.

Later in life, Dick's mother would experience severe rheumatoid arthritis. Routine movements of her arms and legs would produce great pain. Often she relied on a walker and a cane when traveling outside her home. Martin never heard her utter a word of discouragement. She endured the pain without complaint. Time and again, he would look at his mother and reach the same conclusion. She was, he thought, the most courageous woman he had ever known.

During his years at St. Bernard Grade School, Martin gained a reputation as an average student and an above-average athlete. Though not exceptionally diligent in his studies, he did well enough that his academic record never became a concern at home. When sufficiently motivated, Martin performed well in the classroom. And though he rarely consumed the lima beans served up by Sister Mary Flavia, he was sufficiently crafty to find ways to dispose of the lima beans without detection.

Saturday Afternoon Thoroughbreds

[8] The University of Notre Dame athletic teams have been referred to as the "Fighting Irish" since at least the 1920s. One oft-repeated story is that the nickname developed after a disgruntled member of the Notre Dame football team criticized the play of his teammates during halftime of the 1909 Notre Dame-University of Michigan football game. The player is said to have yelled, "What's the matter with you guys? You're all Irish and you're not fighting worth a lick." According to legend, newspapermen picked up on the comment. After Notre Dame rallied in the second half to defeat Michigan, sportswriters wrote that the "Fighting Irish" were victorious.

[9] Steigerwald, John. *Just Watch the Game (Again)*. Canonsburg, PA: Little M Productions, 2011.

[10] The 25-year-old Brennan was named as head coach at Notre Dame in 1954, succeeding Frank Leahy. Brennan had an impressive résumé as a player, having led Notre Dame in receiving and scoring in both 1946 and 1947. However, he had little coaching experience. The Notre Dame job was Brennan's first shot as a head coach. When asked if he was too young to be coach of the Fighting Irish, Brennan responded, "Oh, I don't know. I'll be 26 in a few months."

[11] It was said that "to intern [at Mount Sinai] was like playing ball for the New York Yankees . . . only the top men from the nation's medical schools dared apply." David M. Oshinsky, *Polio: An American Story*, Oxford University Press (2006).

[12] Famed television journalist Edward R. Murrow once asked Dr. Salk who owned the patent to the polio vaccine. Salk replied, "There is no patent. Could you patent the sun?" George Johnson, "Once Again, A Man With A Mission," *The New York Times*, 25 November 1990.

[13] In his handout, Father Lonergan recommended the following measures for avoiding trouble: "(1) Be sure you go out with the right companions; (2) Be sure you go to the right places; (3) Be sure that what goes on there is right." When students saw trouble coming, Father Lonergan advised them to "(1) Be sure you get away as fast as you can; (2) Be sure you see nothing; (3) Be sure you hear nothing; (4) Be sure you keep your mouth shut; (5) Be sure you talk to no one but your lawyer."

[14] Luke 12:48.

Chapter 3
"Be A Good Boy"

Dick Martin couldn't believe his good fortune. Barely 15 years old and still in his freshman year of high school, he had managed to gain the acquaintance of a Mt. Lebanon High senior, Steve Yeager, who had access to a clandestine party apartment. It was an unusual arrangement. Yeager, then 18 years old, had combined some of his own savings with contributions from other students and rented the apartment. Yeager made no pretense of using the apartment as his residence. His sole purpose for renting it was to have a place where he could relax and entertain friends without the knowledge of his parents. Martin would sometimes join classmate Butch Breinig and others for beer parties at the apartment. Together, and no less so when alcohol-fueled, Breinig and Martin could be a rowdy, tough pair. Late one evening, the two found themselves sitting side-by-side in a closet at the apartment, with a party going full blast. The two were singing, off-key and loudly. They heard a knock on the door. "Who's there?" someone yelled. "Howdy Doody," came the reply, "open the damn door!"

When Steve Yeager opened the door, Howdy Doody was nowhere to be found. There was, however, a contingent of Mt. Lebanon police officers. The police entered the apartment, pulled Martin and Breinig out of the closet, and rounded up the other participants. As Martin exited the apartment, he spied a laundry chute that was used to drop clothes from the upper floors of the apartment building to the basement laundry room. Hoping to avoid notice, Martin started to climb the laundry chute. An observant patrolman ordered Martin to freeze. The police then herded Martin and his companions into a cavernous paddy wagon.

This time, not even his mother's protective instincts could shield Martin from his father's wrath. Once the police escorted Martin and his friends into the police station, the officer on duty asked them for their home telephone numbers. Martin and all of his friends—except the ever feisty Breinig—provided their numbers. When the officer on duty demanded to know Breinig's home phone number, he professed not to know it. "What do you mean, you don't know it?" the officer bellowed. Breinig responded, "I never call my own house."

The phone call to the Martin home was quick. Martin's father was quicker. He arrived at the police station at midnight, sporting his customary three-piece suit, a bow tie, his natty Homburg hat, and a look of fierce agitation. The police moved aside to allow Dr. Martin to pass. The physician marched directly to his son's holding cell, opened the door, and commanded, "Stand up!" The younger Martin rose to his feet. He had a good idea of what was coming—a robust slap to the cheek.

Even after the apartment beer bust, Martin continued his youthful encounters with alcohol. During his sophomore year of high school, Martin typically got together with friends on at least a couple of Friday evenings each month to drink. Sometimes, it would be just Martin and Jackie Smith. The two would bring a quart of beer to the hills on the outskirts of Mt. Lebanon and drink. Occasionally, they branched out into whiskey. On New Year's Eve of 1956, Martin and friends opened a fifth of Penny whiskey—as cheap a drink as could be found in Mt. Lebanon. Over the course of a couple of hours, Martin consumed a third of the bottle. Feeling more of a buzz than usual, Martin consumed a couple of raw eggs in an effort to sober up. He then staggered up the steps to his home. Once inside the house, Martin waddled past the dining room where his father was playing poker with friends, climbed the stairs to his bedroom, and hastened into bed.

Dr. Martin sensed something was wrong. He entered Martin's bedroom and lowered his nose to a position just inches from his son's nose. Martin expected a tongue-lashing from his father, if not more. The doctor spoke only three words, however. "Go to sleep," he told his son. To Martin's surprise, there were no further repercussions, not that evening and not the next day. His father never mentioned the incident.

At the time, a popular view attributed underage drinking to the rebellious attitude that was common among teenagers. The landmark 1955 movie, *Rebel Without A Cause*, fueled that view. Starring Hollywood idol James Dean, *Rebel Without A Cause* told the story of Jimmy Stark, a teenager who had been arrested for drunk and disorderly conduct. Stark was rebellious to his core. Martin, however, was hardly a disciple of Jimmy Stark. The fifteen-year-old's drinking arose from more subtle causes. Martin often felt as if he was in a continual struggle with what he referred to as the "the tyranny of expectations." Many in the Mt. Lebanon community viewed Dr. Martin as having been "anointed." He was a surgeon and community leader, angel to the impoverished, the doctor who delivered more than half of the babies born each year to Mt. Lebanon's families, a man with his own designated parking place sanctioned by the town hall, a poker pal of local legend Art Rooney.

The younger Martin knew it was unlikely that he would ever become a surgeon or deliver a baby. He would never get to play poker with Art Rooney or engage in small talk with the starting quarterback of the Pittsburgh Steelers. In his more pensive moments, Martin thought that he might never measure up. It was in those more pensive moments that Martin often turned to drinking. Shortly before James Dean's untimely death in a 1955 automobile accident, Dean had issued a quote that has lingered as a mantra to his followers, "Dream as if you'll live forever. Live as if you'll die today." With a glass of beer in his hand, Martin found it easier to dream as if he would live forever. For brief moments, drinking helped to ease the burden of having to walk in his father's footsteps.

In his sophomore year, Martin reported to the school gym for tryouts for the Mt. Lebanon junior varsity basketball team. George "Lampy" Lamprinakos, a coach and member of the Mt. Lebanon High faculty, noticed Martin working out on the court with the other sophomores. Kindly and insightful, Lamprinakos could see that basketball did not hold much promise for a high school kid who stood only four-foot-seven. Nonetheless, Lamprinakos admired the kid's moxie. He saw touches of raw athleticism too. "Come here, son," Lamprinakos said to Martin during a break, "I don't think basketball is your sport." Lamprinakos told Martin that he was starting a wrestling team at the school. "I think you would make a good wrestler," Lamprinakos said.

Mr. Lamprinakos asked Martin to come to the wrestling room. When Martin arrived downstairs, the coach picked out an opponent of comparable weight, introduced him to Martin, and directed the two boys to start wrestling. Martin and the other boy wrestled for a couple of minutes, during which Martin was able to throw his opponent down to the mat at will. Later, while Martin was toweling off in the locker room, he overheard an exchange between two other wrestlers. "Lampy says Martin is a natural," one wrestler commented. For Martin, lingering out of sight in the locker room, the casual remark became a turning point—toward belief in himself.

Martin lost interest in basketball and began to put his time and energy into wrestling. Now he had a reason for staying in shape. Drinking beer, once a welcomed diversion, had become a deterrent, an impediment to his dreams of excelling in wrestling. For the 1956 season, Martin and his teammates wrestled a junior varsity schedule. Their real work would begin the following year, when they would compete at the varsity level. Over the spring and summer of 1957, Martin began to put in miles of endurance running. He spent less time with Jackie Smith and fewer evenings in conversation on the hills of Mt. Lebanon.

Wrestling provided the ideal outlet for Martin's competitive nature. He had more than held his own in his one year of competitive wrestling, compiling a record of eight wins against two losses. He was confident that, with work, he could excel. Unlike basketball, wrestling did not place a premium on height. Unlike football, wrestling afforded Martin the opportunity to compete within a specified weight class; heavyweights competed against heavyweights, lightweights against lightweights. Martin, whose weight during wrestling season fluctuated from 105 pounds to 110 pounds, competed in the 112-pound class as a junior and senior. Wrestling rewarded superior strength and quickness but not girth.

Midway through his sophomore year, Coach Lampy had warned Martin that he would not be able to continue wrestling unless he improved his grades and stayed away from the wrong crowd. At the time, he was working on a firmly entrenched "F" in Mrs. Nesbitt's geometry class. On the verge of losing a key member of his team, Lamprinakos took Martin to see Mrs. Nesbitt. As was his style, Lamprinakos didn't pull any punches. "If you change that 'F' to a 'D,'" he told Mrs. Nesbitt, "Dick will bring it up to a 'C' by the end of the year." The teacher was receptive. Martin got his "D," allowing him to stay on the wrestling team. He then met for a tutorial session with classmate Lee Wells, a student for whom geometry posed little challenge. With the insights from Wells and the continual encouragement of Lamprinakos, Martin was able to earn a "C" for the remainder of the year.

As the autumn of 1957—Martin's junior year of high school—approached, Martin took delight in the progress he had made. Under the tutelage of the man whom Martin referred to as "Mr. Lamp," Martin had blossomed into a savvy wrestler and a tireless competitor. He was winning most of his matches. Martin liked nothing better than to come home from school after a match and tell his mother, "I won, Mom!" Invariably, his mother would respond with a magnificent smile. He found inspiration in his mother's reaction. With Lampy's encouragement, Martin was also becoming a capable student. After a victory on the wrestling mat, Lampy would approach Martin and ask, "Isn't that a great feeling?" Then Lampy would turn the subject to Martin's studies. "You can have the same feeling in your classes if you work at being a good student," he would tell Martin. Mr. Lamp provided Martin with the direction that he needed. His mother's approving smiles provided the inspiration for him to keep on working. He would soon become one of the top ten wrestlers in his weight class in the State of Pennsylvania.

Martin was strong for his size. He was also blessed with exceptional quickness. Not many other scholastic wrestlers in his weight class possessed a similar combination of strength and quickness. Throughout his high school career, Martin would encounter no more than one or two opponents in his weight class who could match him in strength. One of his most memorable matches came against a wrestler named Darryl Wilson. Wilson, nicknamed "the Squirrel," was considered to be as strong as Martin. Their match was billed as "The Squirrel vs. The Beaver." Fittingly, the match ended in a 1-1 draw. Wilson, though strong, did not have Martin's quickness. Although Martin did not win the match, he was elated to have held his own against Wilson. It was a performance that Martin's father might have enjoyed. Dick hoped that someday he would have an opportunity to wrestle with his father in the stands.

For Dr. Martin, there would not be enough time. He never had the opportunity to watch his son in a competitive wrestling match. On the morning of December 10, 1957, the doctor suffered a severe heart attack. Within the span of an hour, a member of the staff at Mt. Lebanon High School summoned Martin from class. Martin went home immediately and then rushed to the hospital. Martin's mother, brothers and sisters were there. One by one, the children went in to see their father. Dr. Martin was encased in a plastic tent and taking oxygen, amid a labyrinth of tubes. As Dick walked to his father's bedside, James Martin reached his hand out of the tent and grasped Dick's hand. "Be a good boy," his father said. The tone of his father's voice took Dick by surprise. He sensed a feeling of resignation. The man who had always been larger than life and the anchor of the family, the man who healed others, had been betrayed by his own body. Death came shortly thereafter.

So much meaning was embodied in Dr. Martin's words, "Be a good boy"—the last words that Dick would hear his father speak. Martin understood the implication. His father's words were both guidance and command. Martin was well aware of the conduct that his father expected. First and foremost, in Martin's mind, he was to take care of his mother and make her proud. Beyond that, Martin knew there could not be any more episodes involving the Mt. Lebanon police.

Dr. Martin was 59 years old when he died. The news of his death was broadcast over Pittsburgh's TV channel 4. The television broadcast mentioned, briefly, Dr. Martin's charitable work in the Pittsburgh community. In the days that followed, Martin would gain a glimpse of his father's life that was largely unknown to him. He learned that, if his father seemed to be perpetually in a hurry, it was for good reason. Martin knew that his father earned his livelihood at St. Joseph Hospital. He didn't know that his father spent hours each month treating low-income patients at several of the more than thirty hospitals that dotted Allegheny County.

On the day of his father's funeral, family friends came up to Dick and told him that he was "the man of the house now." That much was true, if only because Martin's two older brothers, Jimmy and Bill, were both gone from the family home and living on their own. "What am I supposed to do now?" Martin asked his mother. Long the rock of the family, Martin's mother exuded calm. "Just remember to do what your father taught you," his mother said.

Dr. Martin's death brought an end to summer vacations in Ocean City. Martin's mother quickly sold the summer home. Gone also was the link to Art Rooney and the Steelers. Four days after Dr. Martin's death, Rooney and his Steelers were to travel to Washington, D.C. to take on the Redskins at Griffith Stadium. Nonetheless, Rooney made time to serve as a pallbearer at the funeral Mass held for Dr. Martin in Mt. Lebanon. Football would wait.

Martin missed his father's presence and the wisdom that came with it. Dr. Martin had consistently encouraged his son to dream of greatness and to pursue his dreams with a bona fide sense of commitment. For a time, the young Martin had dreamed of achieving success on the football field. In some ways, it was not an idle dream. Throughout his time in elementary school, Martin could throw a football farther and with greater precision than most of his St. Bernard classmates. Lack of height was seemingly the only thing holding him back. Dr. Martin encouraged his youngest son's visions of glory. Indeed, when Martin's father would get together with Rooney, Finks and others for Friday night poker, the physician would delight in telling stories of his son's football prowess. Martin's father would tell Rooney, "Dick is going to be the next quarterback at Notre Dame."

For Dick, there were regrets. He knew that wrestling offered him the opportunity to achieve a level of success that was comparable to what his father had once envisioned for him on the football field. Yet Martin had never told his father that Coach Lampy considered him to be a natural at wrestling; he had never so much as hinted at how much he enjoyed the sport. Martin knew his father's views on nutrition and health. He knew his father would have bristled at the expectation that wrestlers would limit their consumption of food so they could come in to a match at or under their weight limit. Martin was wary of his father's views on nutrition, fearing that his father might demand that he quit wrestling.

Martin's progression from an aimless student as a freshman to a star wrestler as a junior had earned him a certain cachet at Mt. Lebanon High. A perky and very pretty girl named Nancy Rhoades took particular notice. Martin caught his first glimpse of Nancy when, in his junior year, he was playing ping pong at the Mt. Lebanon recreational center, down the hill from the high school. A friend said to Martin, "There's a girl in the next room whom you might be interested in. She has an interest in you." Martin thought the notion was preposterous. "What are you, crazy? I don't know her," he replied, and continued playing ping pong. The notion was not as far-fetched as Martin had presumed. Later in the evening, when Nancy headed for the door to go home, she glanced at Martin surreptitiously. Martin noticed. "There is an interest there," he thought to himself. During his conversations with female students, Martin was still the undersized and slightly insecure "Beaver." Eventually, however, he summoned the nerve to ask Nancy Rhoades out on a date. To his surprise and delight, she accepted. It was the start of a four-year relationship.

In Martin's senior year at Mt. Lebanon, he wrestled Henry Hissrich from Shaler High School in a packed gymnasium for the 112-pound district championship. Hissrich took Martin down in the first period, causing the Shaler fans to break out in a frenzy of cheers. Martin recovered, however, and controlled the match the rest of the way. He defeated Hissrich 4-2, delighting the Mt. Lebanon fans who were in attendance. With the gymnasium spotlight focused directly on Martin, the referee raised Martin's arm in triumph. The "Beaver" from Mt. Lebanon was district champion.

The victory earned Martin the right to compete in the Western Pennsylvania Interscholastic Athletic League regionals. At the weigh-in preceding the regional semi-finals, Martin sized up his opponent, a boy named Dugan. Dugan was unknown to Martin, but was about the same height. Dugan appeared to be quite muscular; Martin thought his opponent might have the advantage in strength. Early in the match, Martin built up a 4-0 lead. Comfortably ahead, he allowed himself a peek at the adjacent mat. There he saw Arthur "Bucky" Maughan of Canonsburg High School, the much-heralded winner of 70 consecutive dual wrestling matches.

Located twelve miles southwest of Mt. Lebanon, the borough of Canonsburg had produced the renowned singing talents, Perry Como and Bobby Vinton. In the years from 1957 to 1959, however, Bucky Maughan was nearly as well-known in Canonsburg as the two crooners. He was widely acknowledged to be the best wrestler in western

Pennsylvania, if not the entire state. Maughan would go on to wrestle at Moorhead State College in Minnesota, where he won the 1963 National Collegiate Athletic Association championship in the 115-pound class.

Martin's quick glance at the adjacent mat proved disastrous. He now found himself fending off two competitors: Dugan on the mat and Maughan in his head. Martin knew that if he could hold the lead in his match with Dugan, he would have to go up against Maughan. Doubt began to seep into Martin's thoughts; the prospect of wrestling Bucky Maughan was fueling anxiety. Perhaps sensing Martin's distraction, Dugan quickly reeled off four straight points. The match was tied. Dugan was now the aggressor; Martin was on his heels. With the match deadlocked, the referee, Mr. Babyiak, issued Martin a warning for stalling. The warning took Martin by surprise. Stalling was a technical violation, akin to the delay of game penalty in football but without a clock to measure the delay. The rules required a wrestler to be assertive. Beyond that, there was little guidance. Martin knew there were referees who refused to penalize wrestlers for stalling, thinking the rule to be too arbitrary. Clearly, Mr. Babyiak was not in that mold. Now Martin had to be careful. A second stalling violation would give a point—and the match—to Dugan.

Martin knew and liked Mr. Babyiak. During the summer, the official doubled as a tutor. Nancy Rhoades was one of his students. The thought occurred to Martin that maybe Babyiak was going overboard to maintain the appearance of impartiality. As the match continued, Martin knew he was thinking too much: of Bucky Maughan and his unbeaten streak; of Mr. Babyiak and his role as Nancy's tutor; of the fine line between being assertive and stalling. Random thoughts tumbled haphazardly in Martin's head. He knew he had lost the athlete's sharp edge, the focus. The timing was terrible. Again, Babyiak penalized Martin for stalling. Quietly, his senior season of wrestling came to an end.

Dugan, not Martin, met up with Maughan in the 112-pound finals. Maughan defeated Dugan handily, holding his opponent without a single point. Maughan then advanced to the state tournament, where he went undefeated and walked away with the Pennsylvania state championship.

"Be A Good Boy"

As a teen, Martin used alcohol to have some fun, bolster his confidence, and lessen the stress of trying to fulfill his father's expectations. The untimely death of his father came just as Martin, then a high school junior, was committing his time and talent to wrestling. In June 1959, as Martin stood poised to graduate from high school, he could still feel the sting of his father's death. In quiet moments, he would feel sadness. For the most part, however, his final three years of high school were a time of triumph. He had left the Howdy Doody incident far behind. He no longer needed alcohol to bolster his self-esteem. Martin had grown. He had been able to provide consolation and comfort for his mother. He walked through the school halls with the confidence of a champion. Under the watchful eye of Coach Lamprinakos, he had found his sport. Consistent with his father's final request, Martin had become "a good boy."

Chapter 4
Five Fingers of Structure

Upon graduation from high school, Martin hoped to compete in wrestling at the collegiate level. Cliff Keen, coach of the 1948 U.S. Olympic wrestling team and the one-time president of the National Wrestling Coaches Association, tried to lure Martin to the University of Michigan. Keen, who had coached the Michigan wrestlers for more than 30 years, dangled a very attractive offer of scholarship money in the form of a grant-in-aid.[15] Martin was intrigued; his mother was not. "You know where your father always wanted you to go," his mother told him.

Dr. Martin had made it clear to all his children that he expected them to pursue a college education. In succession, each had enrolled in college and completed the requirements for a bachelor's degree. Jimmy, the first-born, graduated from Notre Dame. The next in line, Dolly, gained her degree from the University of Pittsburgh. Mary Jane graduated from the University of Michigan, and Bill from Villanova. The Martin family was unique for the times. In the 1940s and through the end of the 1950s, less than 10% of all adults who were twenty-five years of age or older possessed college degrees.[16]

The University of Notre Dame wasn't exactly a family tradition. Martin's father had, in fact, studied pre-med at Syracuse University and later obtained his medical degree from the University of Pittsburgh. However, Martin's father was an avid Fighting Irish football fan, which had motivated Martin's older brother, Jimmy, to attend Notre Dame. Dr. Martin expected his youngest son to follow suit.

Notre Dame was established in 1844 as an institution of higher learning for young Catholic males. The essential purpose was to provide a fertile environment for learning in an atmosphere that would protect the morals of the students. A secondary objective was to provide an educational facility where Catholic students would be free from the prejudices they might otherwise encounter as a minority group at a non-denominational college or university. In its early years and up until the 1970s, Notre Dame put considerable effort into protecting the morals of its students. For the most part, women were excluded from campus. There were evening bed checks. On weekdays, students were required to turn out their bedroom lights by 10:00 p.m. Attendance at daily religious services was encouraged, if not required.

Gaining admission to Notre Dame proved to be a challenge for Martin. Initially, the university rejected his application. Martin was disappointed but not surprised. For his four years of high school, his academic ranking stood at 256th out of a class of 585 students. Unlike Michigan, Notre Dame had no particular interest in attracting a promising wrestler with mediocre grades. When Notre Dame's letter of rejection arrived, Martin's brother Jimmy wasted little time in responding. Academically, Jimmy had done well at Notre Dame. He was convinced that his brother could succeed too. Jimmy called an old acquaintance, Father Edmund Joyce, executive vice president of the university. "Father, why isn't my brother getting into Notre Dame?" Jimmy asked. His arguments flowed easily. "Six of his friends from Mt. Lebanon all got in, and he has grades that are just as good," Martin's brother told Joyce. Jimmy neglected to point out that his argument was based on a limited sample; the comparison applied only to Martin's grades during his senior year of high school.

Eventually, Notre Dame did reverse its decision. Martin received a letter from Father Charles Sheedy, Dean of the College of Arts and Letters, stating that the university would admit Martin on probationary status, so Martin packed his bags for South Bend, Indiana. It was September 1959. Even as he packed his clothes and furnishings, Martin had mixed emotions. Part of him wanted to stay in Mt. Lebanon, close to his girlfriend of almost two years, Nancy Rhoades. Nancy, however, had promised to send him a letter every day. With the comfort of that promise and with an ample supply of writing paper for his use in writing return letters, Martin gave Nancy a final kiss and told her he would see her at Thanksgiving.

Once on the Notre Dame campus, Martin met with Father Sheedy to discuss his academic program. The priest told Martin, "We have the toughest history program in the United States. There's a lot of reading. Your reading scores are bad. I don't think you are going to make it." Father Sheedy required Martin to take a remedial reading course. Martin had plenty of company; there were 74 other freshmen in the class. Like Father Sheedy, the remedial reading instructor made little effort to instill confidence. "Three-fourths of you will not be here in January," the instructor told the students. Even before the meeting with Sheedy and the session with the reading instructor, Martin was homesick. Afterward, he was both homesick and scared.

If Father Sheedy viewed it as his responsibility to inject fear, Father Joseph Hoffman readily took on the task of enforcing the penal code. One day, early in Martin's first semester in South Bend, he went to the dining hall for dinner immediately after wrestling practice. Thirsty from practice, Martin took three glasses of milk. He knew the dining hall rules limited students to two glasses, but he thought his circumstances justified an exception.

Father Hoffman thought otherwise. "So who do you think you are, taking three milks?" Father Hoffman railed. "Father, I'm sorry," Martin responded, "my name is Dick Martin. I was very thirsty. I was just coming off wrestling practice, and I needed another glass of milk." Father Hoffman replied, "You are only allowed two, and you know it. You are going to be punished for this."

Father Hoffman barred Martin from the dining room for two weeks. In addition, Hoffman told Martin that, for the duration of those two weeks, he would not be allowed inside his dormitory during the hours from 6:00 a.m. to 10:00 p.m., weekends included. Each day while the ban was in place, Martin ate his meals at the on-campus snack shop, *The Huddle*, at his own expense. When not in class or at wrestling practice, Martin spent the daytime hours camped out in the library or with classmates who lived in other dorms. When he needed books for a mid-day class, he would rely on friends to throw the books down from the fourth-floor window of his Keenan Hall dormitory room.

The severity of the punishment left Martin baffled, angry and discouraged. For reasons that he could not comprehend, Father Hoffman seemed to find satisfaction in being vindictive. Martin had come to Notre Dame expecting to benefit from one of the finest academic traditions in the nation. The environment that he encountered, however, was shockingly reminiscent of the St. Bernard lunchroom patrolled by Sister Flavia. Martin had never heard of any comparable punishments being imposed on other Notre Dame students. He mused to himself and others, "I can't be the first person to sneak an extra milk."

In November 1959, Martin went back to Mt. Lebanon for the Thanksgiving recess, convinced that Notre Dame was not a good fit. With Nancy 373 miles away, Martin found the adjustment to South Bend to be difficult. Academically, he was doing well in his Spanish, philosophy and history of Western Europe courses and getting passing grades in his English composition and general mathematics classes. The treatment that he had received from Father Hoffman had left a bitter aftertaste, however.

There was also the matter of the weather. The winter wind whipped through the school's prairie campus, depositing a chill that seemed never to ease. The 1962 edition of *Dome*, Notre Dame's yearbook, contained an apt photographic essay that focused on the rigors of the winter months in South Bend. The text accompanying the photographs read, "The incomparable Northern Indiana weather. With its monsoons. And early winters. Snow from Thanksgiving to Easter. Then the late spring thaw and all but impassable sidewalks. Finally warm days return; windows open, studies suffer, and again even South Bend seems bearable."[17] If Martin had been asked to write the text for the photographic essay, he would have condensed the description of the weather to eight words: "Cold. Snowy. Windy. Nasty. Want to go home."

Martin spent long periods with Nancy over the Thanksgiving break. Much of their talk focused on alternatives for college. Increasingly, Martin found himself wondering whether he should return to Notre Dame. When Martin expressed his concerns to his mother, she urged him to talk to Father McCarren, the associate pastor at St. Bernard Church. Perceptive and thoughtful, McCarren projected self-confidence and a sense of calm. Martin knew that Father McCarren cared deeply about the students who had passed through St. Bernard School. He also knew that he could depend on McCarren for insight and wisdom.

Father McCarren arranged to see Martin on the Saturday following Thanksgiving. After listening to Martin's account of his first three months in South Bend, Father McCarren took over the conversation. "Dick," he said, "you need structure." McCarren cupped his right hand and pressed all five fingers against the surface of his desk. He emphasized that all five fingers had to bear the weight. McCarren then proceeded to lift his index finger, subjecting the other fingers to untoward stress. Without structure, McCarren said, Martin would have a difficult time focusing on his studies, as if he were trying to cope without using all five fingers.

It was not the message that Martin wanted to hear. He would have liked to remain in Mt. Lebanon, close to Nancy. Martin told Father McCarren about his difficulties in dealing with individuals such as Father Hoffman. McCarren urged patience. He suggested that Hoffman was an aberration and that there were plenty of faculty members who would provide structure through encouragement instead of harassment. Emboldened by his talk with Father McCarren, Martin decided to return to South Bend.

Martin's first year at Notre Dame coincided with the historic campaign by John Fitzgerald Kennedy to capture the nomination as the Democratic candidate in the 1960 presidential election. The election was to take place on November 8, 1960. Kennedy was the first Roman Catholic to seek the U.S. presidency since Alfred E. Smith, then Governor of New York, in 1928. As had happened decades earlier when Smith secured the Democratic nomination, Kennedy's candidacy raised concerns that the Catholic Church might seek to dictate U.S. foreign and domestic policy if Kennedy were to be elected.

As the spring semester of 1960 progressed, Martin and his friends found themselves paying greater attention to the political arena. In April, the university staged a mock convention to select the Democratic Party nominee for president. Befitting the occasion, the university president, Rev. Theodore Hesburgh, delivered a speech at the mock convention, as did Democratic U.S. Senator Frank Church of Idaho. John Kennedy was the clear winner of the mock convention, garnering 934 delegate votes, compared with 501 votes for the runner-up, Senator Lyndon B. Johnson of Texas. The real Democratic convention took place from July 11 to July 15 in Los Angeles. Notre Dame's mock convention provided a reliable foretaste of the actual event. On the third day of the Los Angeles convention, Kennedy secured the Democratic nomination with a total of 806 votes, compared with 409 for the second-place finisher, Johnson.

Throughout his first two years at Notre Dame, the two constant sources of satisfaction for Martin were his relationship with Nancy and the success that he experienced in wrestling. He could count on receiving a letter from Nancy nearly every day and, in turn, wrote letters to her almost every day. Martin loved Nancy's letters for both the content and the penmanship. Her style of writing was unmistakably feminine. If penmanship can be said to be charming, the manner in which Nancy formed her characters was exactly that. The content was exactly what Martin needed; she cheered his successes in the classroom and on the wrestling mat.

Martin's freshman year of wrestling consisted of training and occasional scrimmages with members of the varsity. At the time, National Collegiate Athletic Association regulations prohibited freshmen from competing as members of a varsity team. One day during a team practice session, Martin went up against Irish senior Gerry Sachsel, who, like Martin, competed at 123 pounds. Sachsel was a standout wrestler from New Jersey, one of the best in the history of Notre Dame wrestling. He had made a name for himself because of his agility and quickness and had gone undefeated in dual matches in his three years as a member of the Notre Dame varsity.

Less than a minute into his scrimmage against Sachsel, Martin sensed the reason for Sachsel's success. He was quick—quicker than Martin, quicker than anyone whom Martin had ever wrestled. Nonetheless, Martin held his own. In the course of the match, Martin tried to hold Sachsel down with one arm. Sachsel was too crafty and strong, however. He jumped up in the air and came down on Martin's arm and snapped it, dislocating Martin's elbow. Up to that point, the scrimmage was thought to be even.

As far back as the football practice at St. Bernard School during which two of Martin's front teeth were knocked loose, Dick had subscribed to the code which found honor in a hard-earned sports injury. Among Notre Dame wrestlers, his dislocated elbow brought a form of distinction. It was a sign of how close Martin had come to defeating the invincible Gerry Sachsel. Martin would write to Nancy of his near victory over Sachsel, describing the sensation of narrowly losing to the best wrestler on the team, but downplaying the injury.

Long after graduating from Notre Dame, Martin had occasion to call Gerry Sachsel to discuss plans for an upcoming reunion of the wrestling team in South Bend. By then, Sachsel was back in his home state of New Jersey, where he headed up a high school wrestling program. After getting Sachsel on the telephone, Martin said, "This is Dick Martin, do you remember me?" Sachsel responded, "Damn right, I remember you. You damn near beat me."

In June 1960, after final exams, Martin hurriedly packed his belongings and headed back home to Mt. Lebanon. Over the course of his freshman year, he had come to the realization that, with persistence, he could succeed at Notre Dame. It was this lesson that he would take forward with him. He had encountered and survived a series of opponents far tougher than Gerry Sachsel—Father Hoffman, the South Bend winter, and a rigorous academic workload. The structured environment at Notre Dame, if not appealing to Martin, was at least becoming tolerable.

---

[15] A grant-in-aid is a promise of money to be used to offset the cost of enrolling at a college or university. It is similar to a scholarship but usually imposes fewer requirements on the athlete in terms of maintaining eligibility to participate in the sport and maintaining a specified grade level.

[16] Camille L. Ryan and Julie Siebens, *Report: Educational Attainment in the United States*, U.S. Census Bureau (February 2012).

[17] *Dome*, 1962, p. 7.

Chapter 5
The Toast of Mt. Lebanon

On the Monday following Martin's first varsity wrestling match, Denny Phillips, a halfback on the Notre Dame football team and Martin's friend since their days at St. Bernard School, came bounding up the stairs of the University's Rockne Memorial Building, heading for the handball courts. Phillips was taking two steps at a time, a man in a hurry. He encountered Martin walking down to the locker room, having just finished wrestling practice for the day. Phillips saw Martin coming in his direction and broke into a big smile. "Way to go, Martz, you beat Purdue!" Phillips yelled out.

There would soon be even more smiles. Martin followed his victory against Purdue with wins over opponents from Miami University of Ohio and Western Michigan University. Over the Thanksgiving recess of 1960, Martin and his teammates traveled to Illinois for a match against the University of Illinois at Navy Pier,[18] one of eight dual matches on the schedule that season.[19] Martin did not disappoint. He won his match against Navy Pier, showered and dressed, and slipped on his Notre Dame jacket. He told a teammate or two that he was going home for the holiday. Upon leaving the University of Illinois facilities, situated near downtown Chicago, Martin stuck out his thumb in the hope of hitching a ride to Interstate Route 94. The Notre Dame jacket was his ticket to free passage. He knew that, in and around Chicago, drivers were quick to stop when they saw a hitchhiker sporting the Notre Dame insignia.

It was late afternoon and snowing heavily. The weather was ill-suited for traveling, especially for a man on foot. The extended forecast called for more snow. Martin had good reason, however, not to let the weather slow him down; he wanted to see Nancy. Martin found a ride that took him to the entrance to Interstate 94. As Martin stood on the

Interstate, a trucker who was heading east saw him and hit the brakes. Martin hustled to catch up, opened the door to the tractor trailer and slid into the cab.

As Martin traveled to Pittsburgh in the frosty 18-wheeler, Coach Tom Fallon and the rest of the Notre Dame wrestlers were en route back to South Bend. Martin knew the station wagon in which they were riding, though cramped, was at least warm. In contrast, crunched up in the passenger seat of the semi, Martin felt little heat coming from the vents. The sight of the snowflakes piling up on the bottom edge of the truck's windshield made it seem even colder. The anticipation of seeing Nancy, however, made the cold tolerable.

Tom Fallon made little effort to endear himself to the members of Notre Dame's wrestling team. His expertise lay in coaching tennis. He performed his work as coach of the wrestling team without conviction, more administrator than mentor. Though providing little in the way of either coaching or leadership, Fallon knew insubordination when he saw it. He had not known of Martin's plan to return to Mt. Lebanon. He would not have given his approval in any event. Martin's detour caused him to miss two team practices. Fallon was irate, Martin unrepentant. Had he been on scholarship, Martin would have felt a greater obligation to adhere to Fallon's rules. However, at the time, Notre Dame did not award scholarships for wrestling. Martin had never sought out many liberties, but he was insistent on returning home at Thanksgiving, as did the students who were not athletes.

When Fallon first encountered Martin after the Thanksgiving recess, the coach expressed his displeasure loudly. "I did what I did," Martin answered, "just give me my punishment." Martin found himself running extra laps around the campus golf course for a week and then returned to Fallon's good graces.

Martin won each of his first six matches as a sophomore, a fact that was trumpeted in both the Notre Dame newspaper, *The Observer*, and in the Pittsburgh papers. During a trip home for the Easter break, Martin stopped in at the local Green Lantern Bar with friends. The place was packed with Notre Dame fans. There were toasts all around to Martin and his winning streak.

At the end of the season, Martin and his teammates traveled to

Cleveland to compete in the Intercollegiate Individual Independent Interstate Tournament. More commonly referred to simply as the "4-I," the tournament was a national event for college teams not affiliated with an established collegiate conference. A total of 62 schools were represented in Cleveland, with some 360 individual wrestlers competing.

For both Martin and fellow sophomore Eddie Rutkowski, the expectations were high. Good friends away from the mat, Martin and Rutkowski were polar opposites athletically. At 6' 1" and a solid 198 pounds, Rutkowski had been a standout high school quarterback in Kingston, Pennsylvania. He competed as a heavyweight in wrestling. Scrawny in comparison and eight inches shorter, Martin had closed out his career in organized football in unceremonious fashion—the backup quarterback for his eighth-grade team. At Notre Dame, Rutkowski played defensive back and quarterback, excelling at both positions. He would later sign with the Buffalo Bills of the American Football League and play six seasons in the pros as a wide receiver, kick returner, and quarterback.

Martin went to Cleveland not knowing whether he would wrestle at 117 pounds or in his standard weight class, 123 pounds. Toledo University's 27-year-old Dick Wilson, the reigning 123-pound Pan American champ, was considered a lock for a 4-I title in either of these weight classes. Martin had never competed against Wilson before, nor had he ever met him. However, Wilson was a legend in wrestling circles. He was significantly older than Martin, having served in the U.S. Army before entering college. He was a two-time member of the U.S. Olympic team, competing in 1956 in Melbourne and in 1960 in Rome. He had wrestled at 114 pounds in Rome, where he was the captain of the U.S. wrestling squad.[20]

For the 4-I Tournament, it was uncertain whether Wilson would compete in the 123-pound class or the 117-pound class; the scale would make that determination. At the weigh-in, Wilson checked in at 123 pounds, Martin at 121 pounds. Fallon and Martin conferred. "Do you want to win this tournament?" Fallon asked Martin. Both agreed that Martin had to avoid an encounter with Wilson.

With Wilson set to compete at 123 pounds, Martin had four hours to sweat off four pounds. For once, the math came to him easily—one pound per hour. The standard trick for a wrestler who needed to sweat off weight was to put on a rubber suit and run laps. Martin took that trick to the extreme and then added an additional measure of his own design. He donned three overlapping layers of sweats and put on three rubber suits over the sweats. He then ran laps around the indoor swimming pool for 45 minutes. After he had finished his running, teammates rolled him up in a wrestling mat, his head extending out of the mat, so he could sweat off some more weight.

The unorthodox regimen worked. When Martin next weighed in, he tipped the scales at 116.5 pounds, allowing him to compete in the 117-pound class. Martin was delighted. He no longer had to worry about facing Wilson. He was also in a good position to win the 117-pound title. There was extra incentive to do well. Nancy Rhoades and her mother had traveled to Cleveland for the tournament. In Martin's mind, he would win the title for Notre Dame, of course, but also for his mother back home in Mt. Lebanon, and for Nancy.

Martin fell short of the title but acquitted himself well. He made it to the finals before losing in double overtime, 2-1, to Dan Finlay of Marquette. The second-place finish earned Martin a berth in the NCAA championships, which would be held in Oklahoma. Rutkowski also qualified for the nationals. For different reasons, both Martin and Rutkowski declined the invitations to Oklahoma. Martin would have had to maintain his weight at 117 pounds for the two weeks prior to the NCAA's, a daunting challenge. Rutkowski chose to remain in South Bend and devote his time to working out for football.

Martin looked to be a mainstay of the Notre Dame wrestling team for the next two years. Beyond Martin and Rutkowski, there was not much depth. When commenting on the 1960-61 wrestling season, the Notre Dame yearbook, *Dome*, summed up the team's efforts with the heading, "Wrestlers Hampered by Lack of Veterans." The *Dome* reported, "the 'greenness' showed and the matmen trudged through the early season at a 1-6 walk. But the picture was not entirely bleak: at 123, Dick Martin had won all his dual meets."[21] Away from wrestling, Martin gradually came to realize that, for every Father Sheedy or Father Hoffman, there was a member of the faculty who chose to nurture rather than intimidate. Unsure of his post-college plans, Martin delayed choosing a major until the beginning of his junior year. He had little interest in the English or business programs. Fortunately, two innovative professors, Thomas Stritch and Edward Fischer, were at the point of launching a new major in the area of communication arts. Their intended focus was journalism writing, TV production writing, movie production, and script writing. As the long-tenured chairman of Notre Dame's Department of Journalism—from 1946 to 1970—Stritch brought unique expertise to the classroom. He was an accomplished writer, having authored several books dealing with mass media. Fischer's expertise lay in movie production. He was an international figure in the study of movies and films and served as a juror at the Venice International Film Festival. Martin settled on communication arts as his major, hoping that he might later find a job in radio and television work.

Stritch, in particular, offered a most appealing contrast to Father Hoffman. Stritch had originally been a professor of English and American literature. He was a fixture at Notre Dame, a beloved "bachelor don," who maintained permanent living quarters in an apartment in Notre Dame's Lyons Hall. The unique living arrangement allowed Stritch to serve as a mentor to students during evenings and weekends, outside the classroom walls. Well after midnight, he could often be found in deep discussions with students regarding history, politics, literature, and on occasion, his ambivalence toward Notre Dame football.

As Father Sheedy had predicted, Martin struggled with his academic load in his freshman year. It was not, however, the courses in history that caused concern. With grading on a 6.0 scale, Martin consistently recorded 4.0 in his history classes. It was a required freshman mathematics course that, initially, posed his greatest challenge. In the first semester of his freshman year, Martin managed only a 2.0 in math, good enough to get academic credit but not with much room to spare. With the aid of a tutoring program designed for athletes and extra help in the evenings from his math professor, Martin brought that mark up to 3.0 for the second semester.

As Martin's comfort level in South Bend increased, his grades improved. He signed up for a challenging course in U.S. history in the first semester of his sophomore year and took home a 5.0. Another 5.0

in philosophy sent Martin's grade point average up to the 80th percentile midway through his sophomore year. During the last two years of his college career, Martin's class ranking rose steadily. His classroom performance was validated each time he and his roommates had to bid for living quarters for the succeeding year. The University based the pecking order in the selection of dormitory rooms on grade point average. When two or three students agreed to be roommates for a given year, priority would be assigned according to the grade point average of the student with the best academic ranking. It was always Martin's GPA that landed his roommates and himself priority in the room selection process.

In March 1962, as his junior year raced to a close, Martin looked ahead with confidence to his senior year. His junior year of wrestling had not gone as well as he had hoped. He was sidelined by injury early in the year. The *Dome* reported, "Dick Martin, a star at 123-pounds last year, and Fred Morelli, leader in the 137-pound category, were hurt in the early part of the season, and missed five matches apiece."[22] However, Martin was still able to wrestle in enough matches to again earn a varsity letter.

Martin was flourishing. His grades were climbing, his wrestling portfolio included an invitation to the NCAA championships, and Father Hoffman was a distant memory. Most importantly, each day's mail brought another encouraging letter from Nancy.

Nancy was then working as a secretary at the Gulf Oil Company headquarters in Pittsburgh. Her encouragement was vital to Martin's success, both athletically and academically. The relationship was his bedrock, his motivation for doing well. It was also his hope for the future. Nancy and Martin talked of someday marrying and having children. Their relationship had progressed to the point that they had even discussed the names they would give to their future children.

Nonetheless, for Martin, there were lingering doubts. He was uneasy with what seemed to be an ever-widening gap between his situation and Nancy's. He was still in school; Nancy was in the business world, earning a respectable salary, working toward financial stability, and mingling with Gulf Oil executives. There was no doubt that men would give Nancy a second look when she walked by. The thought fed

Martin's insecurity. He wanted Nancy to stay by his side forever. He wondered, however, how she would respond if a rising young Gulf Oil accountant or engineer showed an interest in her.

If Nancy was going to break up with him, he hoped she would do it during the summer months while he was home from school. His worst fear was to receive a letter in the mail from Nancy telling him that she no longer wanted a steady relationship. Martin knew well that the effect of a long-distance breakup would be devastating. "Don't break up with me when I'm at school," he would tell Nancy.

By the end of his junior year at Notre Dame, it was clear that, on or off the wrestling mat, Martin was a competitor. After being told he would have trouble passing Notre Dame's history courses, Martin achieved marks that were worthy of commendation. If competing at the 4-I Tournament required Martin to lose four pounds in four hours, he would find a way to shed the weight. In both academics and in wrestling, Martin thrived on competition. In his relationship with Nancy, however, he would not tolerate any competition.

---

[18] For a period of twenty years, 1946-1965, the University of Illinois maintained a campus at a structure on the Chicago shoreline of Lake Michigan known as Navy Pier. The structure was a 3,300-foot long pier that was built in 1916, primarily to serve as a cargo facility for freighters on Lake Michigan. During World War II, the pier was converted into a Navy training site. With the end of the war, the training facility was taken over by the University of Illinois. The pier is now a popular tourist attraction.

[19] A dual match is the name given to a wrestling match in which one school competes solely against another school, for example, Notre Dame vs. Purdue. In high school wrestling competition, there may also be three-way matches, in which three schools compete simultaneously. In a three-way match, a wrestler from one school would initially take on a wrestler from the second school and then, in the same venue, wrestle his opponent from the third school. Dual and tri-matches are to be distinguished from tournaments, in which a number of schools meet at the same venue to compete for a title or championship.

[20] In 1964, Wilson qualified for the U.S. Olympic team a third time and competed in Tokyo, where he again served as captain of the U.S. wrestling team.

[21] *Dome* Yearbook, vol. 52 (Notre Dame, IN, 1961), 284.

[22] *Dome* Yearbook, vol. 53 (Notre Dame, IN, 1962), 290.

Chapter 6
Notre Dame's Smallest Quarterback

In the summer of 1962, Neil Sedaka's classic tune, "Breaking Up Is Hard To Do," reached Number 1 on the Billboard Hot 100. Gene Pitney was working on the melody for "Only Love Can Break A Heart," anticipating a September release. On a warm summer evening, Martin called Nancy. The day had been sunny. Nancy told Martin that she had spent the afternoon at the nearby Dormont swimming pool relaxing with a girlfriend. The news was unsettling to Martin, as if Nancy's intent in going swimming was to meet other men. Abruptly, Martin drove to Mt. Lebanon Boulevard. He needed to talk. Nancy got into his car. Asserting her independence, Nancy suggested that it might be good for both of them to date others. Martin wouldn't hear of it. "I don't want to see you again," he told her, "get out of the car."

Martin's impulsive response ended the conversation on that summer evening. Nancy got out of Martin's car, slammed the door, and walked away. The love of Martin's young life disappeared into the night.

Martin never knew with certainty what had prompted Nancy to suggest that they begin to date others. Possibly, he thought, she wanted to focus more on pursuing opportunities for developing her business career. He also wondered whether Nancy had begun to cultivate friendships at Gulf Oil that offered the potential for romantic involvement. Martin knew for sure, however, that his feelings of insecurity had introduced a degree of awkwardness into his relationship with Nancy. He needed the assurance that Nancy would always be there for him. He needed to know that when other men looked at her, she would not feel the attraction. For reasons that she kept to herself, Nancy was unable or unwilling to give Martin the assurances that he demanded.

He would come to realize that the events of that evening had called for a meaningful conversation with Nancy to discuss the terms of their future relationship. It was not a conversation that Martin would have welcomed. He was not even sure that he could have calmly engaged in such a conversation, given his emotional attachment to Nancy and his tendency to jump to hasty conclusions. Martin viewed Nancy's suggestion that they date others as a rejection. With the passage of years and an increase in maturity, he would come to see that Nancy's suggestion might have been an opportunity for growth.

Bereft of Nancy's company, Martin saw no reason to remain in Mt. Lebanon for the summer. He recounted the breakup to his mother and told her that he was planning to get away. In need of time to sort things out, he wanted both a diversion and an escape. He hooked up with Willie McCorkel, a longtime friend, and the two drove to Ocean City, New Jersey to spend the rest of the summer near the beach.

In quiet moments at the New Jersey shore, Martin would often replay his last conversation with Nancy. He was haunted by his irrevocable last words; emptiness filled his head and his heart. He thought of how indelible last words tended to be. It had been four years since his father had issued his deathbed directive, "Be a good boy." Martin thought of the irony: last words could inspire; they could haunt. Martin's words to Nancy had removed any possibility of reconciliation. He would never speak to her again after that evening. He saw her once at a dance, but only from a distance. The caring, the closeness were irretrievably gone.

Without Nancy's support and companionship, Martin hit unfathomable depths. His spirit was wounded. He came to doubt everything in his world, including his desire to wrestle. Upon his return to South Bend for his senior year, Martin gave up wrestling and, with it, the honor of serving as team captain. His teammates asked him to reconsider his decision; he told them that his heart wasn't in wrestling any more. He focused his time and energy elsewhere, largely on his studies and Saturday beer nights, the camaraderie of his classmates, and working out in the weight room.

There were days when Martin would walk the campus feeling all alone, knowing that Nancy was really gone. He would think of her and wonder what she was doing. Even when he was feeling sad, however, Martin knew his situation could be so much worse. He was 21 years old, energetic and poised to receive his college degree from a respected university. Martin did not have to worry about finances. His father had left both mother and son with sufficient assets for the future. Unlike some of his classmates, Martin never fretted about how he would come up with money to pay his tuition.

The Notre Dame of the 1960s tended to be an insular community. For a 21-year-old senior with ample money and no significant academic hurdles remaining, there were few pressing concerns. Martin and his classmates were shielded from the more perplexing problems of society by a youthful nonchalance. Martin was vaguely aware of the political crises that were creating havoc in distant locations. It was a time when armed East German border guards would routinely shoot at residents of Communist-controlled East Berlin who tried to scale the Berlin Wall and flee to West Berlin.[23] Martin and his friends might read about the Berlin Wall or the high-stakes jockeying by the United States and the Soviet Union for nuclear weapon supremacy. However, these were not matters to which they gave much thought. They were more apt to spend their time discussing the 1962 Heisman Trophy candidates or the movies of Hollywood bombshell Marilyn Monroe, star of *Gentlemen Prefer Blondes* and *Some Like It Hot*, who had died from an apparent overdose of sleeping pills one month before the start of Martin's senior year.

During Martin's four years in South Bend, some students began an organized effort to respond to the needs of poverty-stricken residents of other countries, forming an organization they named the Council of the International Lay Apostolate. The council provided an outlet for students who were interested in working on-site in the slum areas of Latin America. During the 1962-63 school year, twenty-three Notre Dame students and two priests went to work among the poor and uneducated in Lima, Peru and the towns of Tacambaro and Aguascalientes in Mexico. The students and priests showed the townspeople sanitary measures, taught them basic life skills, and worked to rehabilitate their housing structures. After returning to Notre Dame, the students presented seminars aimed at educating other students regarding the social situations they had encountered during their work.[24]

Even with the presence of the Council of the International Lay

Apostolate on campus, Notre Dame's students lived an isolated existence for the most part. The editors of the 1963 edition of *Dome*, the yearbook for Martin's graduating class, looked to history to explain the "seclusion" that seemed to characterize the Notre Dame experience. "Historically," the *Dome* stated, "coming to America generally as poor immigrants, scorned and discriminated against as a 'foreign' minority, American Catholics developed leanings towards seclusion, both social and mental."[25] If Martin and his classmates tended to be insular and somewhat narrow in focus, the *Dome* suggested, there was an historical context, if not a justification, for that attitude.

Even so, there were times when world events intruded on campus life in a way that could not be ignored. On Monday, October 22, 1962, Martin was eating dinner with friends in the North Dining Hall. The football season was barely four weeks old, and the mood on campus was downcast. Two days earlier, the Fighting Irish had lost to Michigan State, 31-7. It was the team's third consecutive loss after an opening day 13-7 win over the University of Oklahoma. As Martin sat in the dining hall, the loud speaker suddenly began to broadcast an urgent speech by President Kennedy regarding the threat posed by the Soviet Union's installation of medium-range ground-to-ground ballistic missiles in Cuba.

Nikita Khrushchev, the Soviet Premier, and Andrei Gromyko, the Soviet Foreign Minister to the United States, had steadfastly maintained that the missiles were defensive in nature. Their sole purpose, the Soviet leaders said, was to protect Cuba in the event of an attack. U.S. reconnaissance photographs showed those assertions to be false. As Kennedy took to the airwaves on October 22, there were much weightier concerns on the Notre Dame campus and throughout the United States than college football. The so-called "Cuban missile crisis" was the closest the world had ever come to nuclear war. General Anatoly Gribkov, the Soviet Army Chief of Operations, would later state, "Nuclear catastrophe was hanging by a thread… and we weren't counting days or hours, but minutes."[26]

In his October 22 address to the nation, Kennedy announced that the United States had imposed a naval blockade of the island of Cuba, termed a "quarantine," to prevent any shipments by water into or out of Cuba. The President promised the nation that "any hostile move anywhere in the world against the safety and freedom of peoples to whom we are committed, including in particular the brave people of West Berlin, will be met by whatever action is needed."[27] Over the span of the next six days, the tension continued to build. Finally, on October 28, Khrushchev agreed to dismantle the Soviet missile sites and return the missiles to the Soviet Union. In exchange, Khrushchev received tacit agreement that the United States would refrain from invading Cuba.

With the crisis resolved, the students at Notre Dame, Martin among them, returned their attention to school and to their musings about Marilyn Monroe and, especially, to the Fighting Irish football team.[28] Martin had grown up with Notre Dame football as a backdrop to his childhood. His father had recited stories about the gridiron heroics of Notre Dame's players, particularly Coach Knute Rockne's famed "Four Horsemen" of 1924—quarterback Harry Stuhldreher, right halfback Don Miller, left halfback Jim Crowley, and fullback Elmer Layden. Even in years when Notre Dame did not have a backfield of equivalent talent, Rockne's enduring legacy often seemed sufficient to lead the Irish to victory.

During Martin's first two years at Notre Dame, the football team went from mediocre to bad. The Irish were 5-5 in 1959 and then endured a dismal 2-8 season in 1960. In 1961, 165-pound halfback Angelo Dabiero would spearhead a revival of sorts. Dabiero had been a favorite of Notre Dame boosters since early in his sophomore season. When Dabiero would carry the ball at home games, public address announcer Moose Krause would intone over the loud speaker, "Angelo Dabiero is the ballcarrier. He's five-feet-eight, 165 pounds, and he's only a soph-o-more." Krause would give full effect to the middle "o" in "sophomore," lingering over it as if the vowel deserved to be isolated on center stage. In 1960, head coach Joe Kuharich installed Dabiero, then a junior, as the featured back. Dabiero responded with 325 rushing yards in 80 carries, leading all Notre Dame ballcarriers. He would do even better in 1961.

Kuharich's squad began the 1961 season, Martin's junior year, with three consecutive wins. In the opener against Oklahoma, the Irish demonstrated little in the way of a passing game, attempting only eight passes for the entire game. However, Dabiero's flashy running propelled Notre Dame to a 19-6 victory. Dabiero totaled 176 yards in 11 carries, including a run of 51 yards for a touchdown. *Sports Illustrated* reported that Dabiero "ran through Oklahoma like a berserk water bug."[29] He played a key role in each of the next two games, leading the Irish to victories in a squeaker over Purdue, 22-20, and a 30-0 rout of the University of Southern California. The luck of the Irish quickly evaporated, however, as Notre Dame totaled only 27 points in its next three games, losing to Michigan State, Northwestern, and Navy. A year that had begun with promise ended in disarray as Notre Dame closed out the season with crushing defeats at the hands of Iowa and Duke.

By 1962, the university and its board of trustees had tired of Kuharich's losing ways and replaced him with Hugh Devore, a man looked upon with fondness and trust. Devore had coached the Fighting Irish to seven wins during the 1945 season while serving as an interim replacement for head coach Frank Leahy, who was on active duty with the U.S. Navy.[30] At roughly the same time that Leahy was relinquishing the head coaching position to Devore, a quirky professor of philosophy named Father Thomas Brennan was solidifying his reputation as a campus legend in South Bend. Brennan had graduated from Notre Dame in 1923 and entered the seminary after graduation. By 1931, then an ordained priest, he was back at the university as a professor of philosophy, with a bent for teaching logic.

Indefatigable and an irrepressible optimist, Brennan was a favorite among students, in and out of class. His popularity was such that he was selected to deliver the commencement address at the class of 1944 graduation exercises, an honor that placed him in a category with other noted commencement speakers, including Dr. William Mayo, cofounder of the Mayo Clinic, who addressed the class of 1936; Joseph P. Kennedy, the former ambassador to Great Britain, who spoke to the class of 1941; and J. Edgar Hoover, Director of the Federal Bureau of Investigation, the commencement speaker in 1942.

There were, however, limits to Brennan's popularity; his fan base did not include many basketball referees. Brennan was the official chaplain to the Notre Dame basketball team. He attended most of the team's home games, occupying a seat on the team bench. If Brennan's schedule permitted, he would also travel with Notre Dame's basketball team when it played games away from South Bend. Whether at home or away, Brennan would take a seat next to the Notre Dame players and unleash a constant stream of criticism for what he perceived to be bad calls. Sportswriter Frank Deford once observed that Brennan and Notre Dame basketball coach Johnny Dee would perform a "good cop/bad cop" routine during games. "And the *priest* is the bad cop," Deford wrote.[31] According to Deford, during one game in Evansville, the head referee grew tired of Brennan's running commentary. The ref walked over to the Irish bench, pointed to Father Brennan, and threatened to give him a technical foul for mouthing off too much. "Hey, Father," the ref said, "you call the Mass, and I call the game."[32] When Martin arrived at Notre Dame in the fall of 1959, Father Brennan was 61 years old and no longer a full-time professor. His official title was professor emeritus; however, he continued to hold legendary status on campus—renowned for his multiple roles as part jock, part jester, and full-time mentor. He was an enthusiastic bowler, golfer, and pickup basketball player and served as chaplain for the basketball and football teams. When Warner Bros. released the movie *Knute Rockne, All American* in 1940, Brennan attended the world premiere, held in South Bend. He kept the program from that movie in his personal papers until the day he died.

During his long and illustrious career as a professor and fixture on the Notre Dame campus, Brennan had earned the nickname "88 Brennan." His courses were fun and popular with the students, in part because Brennan was loath to give anyone a numerical grade below 88. According to campus folklore, Brennan would sometimes fling examination papers out of the window in his office and assign grades on the basis of the particular sector of grass where each paper had landed. Legend also had it that Brennan challenged 1949 Heisman Trophy winner Leon Hart to a bowling match to determine Hart's final grade in Brennan's philosophy course.

If Brennan's grading methods were unorthodox, there was a definite logic in the way he cultivated friendships. He interacted with everyone. He was never known to refuse a request for help. Football and basketball players were his friends, but so were the tuba players, the coaches, introverted students, and locals from the South Bend community. It would come as no surprise, then, that Brennan was a friend of Julius Tucker. Tucker had made a fortune in trucking. He was the owner of Tucker Freight Lines, based in South Bend. An avid Irish football fan, Tucker contributed time and money to the university, with a touch of intrigue thrown in.

Julius Tucker's passions were readily apparent. He was fascinated with Mack, Studebaker, and GMC Astro tractor trailers, and he loved Notre Dame sports. He was known in South Bend's more shadowy cultures as a "fixer." Not every problem merited his attention but if you were a Notre Dame athlete and had gotten into trouble, Julius Tucker was your best friend.

By the fall of 1962, Notre Dame student Tim Reardon had gained a reputation on campus as a tough, talented boxer and a good-hearted individual. In each of his first three years, Reardon had won the Bengal Bouts boxing tournament—a charity event held on campus each February to raise money for the missions of what is now Bangladesh. Advertisements for the event employed the theme "Strong Bodies Fight, So That Weak Bodies May Be Nourished." On a September evening in 1962, Reardon was drinking with Martin and others at Sweeney's Bar, a pub just off the Notre Dame campus. When the group left Sweeney's, Reardon attempted to take his beer with him. A policeman stationed outside the bar confronted Reardon, prompting Reardon to walk away. Other police officers grabbed Reardon. The boxer reacted by blocking the officers' arms, more an effort to defend himself than to resist arrest. The police quickly subdued him, placed him under arrest, and walked him to the police station. Martin followed behind.

Word of Reardon's arrest traveled quickly. South Bend police notified the university's student affairs office of the incident. Suddenly, Reardon's senior year was at risk; his pursuit of a fourth Bengal Bouts title was in jeopardy. Academic suspension seemed likely. Martin felt he had to do something. Though Martin was not particularly close to Reardon, he knew that Reardon was a good guy. Equally important in Martin's view, Reardon appeared to be getting a bad rap. Martin thought that the police, not Reardon, had been the aggressors.

Knowing "88 Brennan" only by reputation, Martin was nonetheless confident that the priest would help. Martin called Father Brennan and arranged a meeting to discuss Reardon's predicament. Brennan listened as Martin recounted the incident. Brennan then picked up his telephone receiver and dialed. "Julius, this is Father Brennan," he uttered into the phone. Brennan related the sequence of events. Julius Tucker listened. Brennan then hung up and said to Martin, "Meet him at Notre Dame Stadium at 10:00 a.m. on Saturday."

On the following Saturday, at 9:50 a.m., Martin walked to the stadium. As he passed through the stadium's iron gate, he could see a man sitting in the upper stands. He assumed it was Tucker. The gentleman wore a light gray fedora and a black overcoat. Walking forward, Martin glanced furtively around the stadium. It was eerily empty—just two individuals in a structure that accommodated 59,000. "This place is much too quiet," Martin thought to himself. It was, Martin imagined, much like a scene from a mystery movie. When he got within speaking range, Martin introduced himself. Tucker shook hands and got down to business. Martin explained Reardon's situation, Tucker nodded. "I'm going to try to stop this from getting into the papers," Tucker said, "but it may be too late." He then told Martin, "Same time, next Saturday." In an instant, Tucker was gone. Martin was both hopeful and mystified. Clearly Tucker was not one to waste time on either words or formalities.

Shortly thereafter, Martin came across an edition of the *South Bend Tribune*. A very conspicuous headline blared, "Irish Champ Takes On Cops." Martin didn't know what to think. Tucker's efforts to keep Reardon's name out of the papers had been futile. The following Saturday, Tucker and Martin again met. "Everything's greased," Tucker told Martin. Tucker did not elaborate, and Martin did not think it wise to press him for details. The two departed. Martin heard nothing more from either Brennan or Tucker, but Reardon served no jail time and was not suspended from school. He was, however, confined to the campus for a few weeks. The following February, Reardon won Bengal Bouts for a record fourth time.

The Reardon incident provided Martin with another favorable encounter with a member of the Notre Dame faculty, another encouraging episode to help eclipse the bad taste lingering from his experience with Father Hoffman three years earlier. In the intervening three years,

Martin's college career had been sprinkled with more successes than disappointments. He continued to flourish in the classroom. Freed from the obligation to spend time at wrestling practices and in traveling to matches, Martin found that he was able to achieve good grades. He finished the first semester of his senior year with a grade of 6.0 in marketing communication— the first time in his four years that he had "aced" a course. He received a 5.0 in his senior theology course, and solid 4.0 grades in social disorganization, fundamentals of sociology, and Professor Stritch's seminar class on mass media.

Martin spent many afternoons of his senior year working out in a makeshift weight room put together by a campus priest, Father Bernard Lange. Lange's résumé included a Ph.D. in biology, but he taught no classes and conducted no laboratory research. Stritch would write that "Lange taught not, neither did he lab" but simply "rolled into his natatorium building (to which he alone had the keys) and stayed on until the shades of evening fell."[33] Lange's full-time occupation was that of weightlifter; he claimed to being, at one time, the fourth strongest man in the world.[34]

Lange encouraged students to train with him. For the most proficient lifters, Lange would hand out medals to recognize their accomplishments. The medals were not easily won. One standard for winning a Lange medal was lifting one's own weight in a straight press, a feat of considerable difficulty. Martin achieved that goal, collecting his first medal. Another way to gain a medal was to extend one's arms straight up while lying prone on a lifter's bench and grasping 100-pound weights in each hand. In time, Martin passed that test as well.

Academically, Martin's success continued into the second semester of his senior year. He loaded up on courses in communication arts, with one class on TV production, one on oral interpretation, and the second segment of Stritch's mass media seminar. For each of his courses during the second semester of his senior year, his performance was sufficient to exempt him from the final exam. Ultimately, Martin would finish with a ranking in the top 25% of his class for all four years.

With time on his hands before graduation, Martin spent a good portion of his evenings in earnest discussions with lifelong friend and fellow senior Bud Vogel and other students. The discussions usually occurred over beers. On one such occasion, Martin was walking back to the campus with Vogel and another member of the football team, halfback Charlie O'Hara. The three walked along Notre Dame Avenue, passing the school's visitor center. Suddenly, Martin felt faint; he was incapable of exerting effort. With Martin struggling to breathe, O'Hara imagined the worst. It was, he thought, a prelude to death. The two football players carried Martin to the campus infirmary, where nurses administered oxygen and stabilized Martin's breathing. Subsequent tests revealed that Martin had asthma. The attending physician found that he was particularly sensitive to dust, mold and ragweed.

Martin's doctor prescribed a regimen of oral steroids, which proved successful in controlling the effects of the asthma. The scare passed, and Martin returned to his studies, resumed weightlifting, and continued with his occasional evenings at South Bend's beer haunts. Three weeks before commencement exercises, in a conversation that could only have taken place at Joers or Strats, Martin's preferred off-campus hangouts, someone offered Martin $10 if he could finagle his way onto the football field during the traditional Notre Dame Old-timers vs. Varsity spring football game.

Coach Knute Rockne had initiated the Old-timers game in 1929, scheduling the contest at the end of the varsity's spring practice each year. Rockne saw the game as a way to gauge the progress of his varsity teams. In the years since 1929, the game had become more spectacle than measuring stick. Many of the football alumni, especially those displaying a midriff bulge, would play only briefly. Alumni who had moved on to pro football would usually make only token appearances, for fear of injury. The alumni who chose to play would arrive on campus on the Thursday before the game, attend practice on Friday, and suit up for the game on Saturday. With only one day to work out before the game, the alumni did not have sufficient practice time to provide useful competition for the varsity; in the years from 1946 to 1962, the alumni had defeated the varsity in only four of the seventeen contests. In one particularly inept performance by the alumni, the varsity team routed the Old-timers by a score of 72-0.

The coach of the Old-timers was Bill Earley, a former assistant coach during Frank Leahy's years as the head coach of the Fighting

Irish. Earley left the coaching profession in the mid-1940s and took a job in the cardboard production industry. The move paid off. While still relatively young, Earley became a successful businessman. As a sideline, Earley began coaching the Old-timers' squad in 1946, a commitment that he would continue through the 1950s and 1960s. Though the alumni teams were hamstrung by a lack of practice time, Earley was forever hopeful of pulling off an upset. Toward that end, he always tried to entice the more recent Irish stars to play. If he learned that an alumnus of the caliber of fullback Nick Pietrosante, the 1959 NFL rookie of the year, was lurking around South Bend, he would crank up his network of contacts. "Oh, is Pietrosante in town?" he would say. "Tell him I'm looking for him, will you?"[35] In May 1963, as Earley attempted to track down Pietrosante, Nick Buoniconti, and other former Notre Dame stalwarts, the one certainty was that he was not looking for Martin. Martin, however, was undeterred. He knew his way around the Notre Dame athletic department; his relationship with long-time equipment manager Nick Walz was solid. On game day, May 18, 1963, Martin walked into the equipment room flaunting a smile born of mischief. Walz asked him what he wanted. Five feet, five inches full of bravado if not common sense, Martin replied, "a uniform for an old-timer."

"Who might the old-timer be?" Walz inquired. "Jim Martin," Dick responded, borrowing at once the name of both his older brother and that of 1950 Notre Dame All-American end and campus boxing champion, "Jungle Jim" Martin. Further discussion ensued. Walz insisted that the real Jim Martin might actually show up for the game. Martin persuaded Walz that what had started as a barroom challenge had evolved into an imperative. Walz found the smallest pads and pants that he could find and a jersey bearing the number 10. The uniform served as Martin's ticket onto the field.

Martin's presence in the alumni locker room prompted curious looks. To some of the old-timers, Martin had the appearance of a field goal kicker, albeit an unusually small one. Few questioned his credentials. Sitting beside Martin, former Heisman Trophy winner Johnny Lattner, alternately talking and puffing on a cigarette, asked Martin, "When did you play?" Martin confessed that he was an imposter. He told the story of the late-night dare, the product of a few beers. "That's neat," Lattner responded.

By the time Martin and his teammates took the field for pre-game warm-ups, there were nearly 20,000 spectators in the stands. Before the game and again during the half-time intermission, Martin caught passes from former quarterback Bob Williams. In the stands, fans were bewildered by the diminutive "alum." Some of Martin's friends, on-lookers to the action, fabricated stories to document Martin's place in Notre Dame lore. They circulated the story that he was the smallest quarterback in Notre Dame history.

To collect on the bet, Martin would not only have to be in full football gear but also participate in the game for at least one play from scrimmage. Throughout the first three quarters, Martin accumulated an abundance of stories that he would later pass along—amid laughter—during late nights at the pubs. He had not, however, accumulated even a second of playing time. Well into the fourth quarter, Martin remained firmly affixed to the bench. With time running out, Martin approached Earley and asked if he could go in for a play. Earley nodded. Martin ran onto the field and took a position in the defensive backfield. Martin picked out an alum positioned at defensive halfback and said, "I'm in for you." The player replied, "The hell you are." Martin found himself the twelfth man in an eleven-man game. Hoping to avoid drawing a penalty, he took a three-point stance ten yards back from the line of scrimmage.

The ball was snapped, a thundering herd of beefy Notre Dame linemen moved forward, with a running back tucked in behind. Some members of the varsity, having learned of the bet from banter in the dorms before the game, recognized Martin. "Martz, get the hell out of the way," the lead blocker yelled. Martin darted out of the action, surrendering dignity but preserving his body. The final gun sounded.

As Martin walked off the field in the company of some very big men, he was pursued by a trail of little kids. Each clamored for him to hand over his chin strap—a treasured souvenir from Notre Dame's "smallest quarterback." Martin gave away his chin strap, as he imagined Johnny Lujack, Angelo Bertelli, Paul Hornung and other Notre Dame stars doing over the years. Martin thought of his father, knowing his dad would have laughed at the tall tale of Notre Dame's smallest quarterback. Martin had not made it onto Notre Dame's football field in the way that his father had imagined, but that was of little concern to Martin. He had rubbed shoulders with Johnny Lattner and caught passes from Bob Williams. He had won the bet.

Between the Old-timers game and the graduation exercises scheduled for June 9, Martin filled the time by working with Bud Vogel and other classmates laying sod on the grounds of the university's new Memorial Library. The library was being prepared for opening on September 18, 1963. With a mural of the resurrected Jesus dominating the front of its structure, the building would soon become a popular addition to the Notre Dame mystique. The mural depicted Jesus with hands raised skyward, much like a football referee signaling a touchdown. Even after the facility was re-named the Theodore Hesburgh Library in 1987, Notre Dame partisans most often referred to the building simply as "Touchdown Jesus."

By day, Martin laid sod for "Touchdown Jesus." By night, he regaled his friends with the stories he had accumulated over the preceding four years—from Father Hoffman to Julius Tucker to the Old-timers game.

Even as Martin rejoiced in his successes at Notre Dame, he was painfully aware that his future was completely uncharted. The only certainty was that he would soon be bidding farewell to his college classmates and to his life at Notre Dame. In Martin's quiet moments, mild anxiety turned into distress. He had rejected Nancy and voluntarily given up his position on the wrestling team. He had developed asthma. The things he had previously counted on—the support of his steady girlfriend, the rewards of wrestling, his good health—were gone, or at least in question. After four years of the protective and insulated environment at Notre Dame, Martin was on his own. He had no idea of what he would do next. He lacked purpose. He lacked a plan.

---

[23] The Communist government of East Germany constructed the physical barrier known as the Berlin Wall in 1961 to prevent residents of Soviet-occupied East Berlin from fleeing to West Berlin, which was under the control of the Western Allies (United States, England, and France). In 1989, residents of East and West Berlin, reacting to the tide of a democratic movement, joined forces to knock down the wall using hammers and chisels. Between 1961 and 1989, an estimated

5,000 residents of East Berlin had attempted to cross the wall. The number of people who died during those attempts is estimated at between 100 and 200.

[24]"CILA: The Emerging and Awakening Layman," *Dome*, 1963, p. 152.

[25]*Dome* Yearbook, vol. 54 (Notre Dame, IN, 1963), 14.

[26]"Fourteen Days in October: The Cuban Missile Crisis," Oracle ThinkQuest Education Foundation, http://library.thinkquest.org/11046/days/index.html.

[27]*Ibid.*

[28]As with other prominent universities in the United States, the insular and relatively parochial nature of the Notre Dame campus would persist until the late 1960s, when the U.S. effort to expand the Vietnam War resulted in widespread protests by college students and faculty members throughout the United States. On November 18, 1969, a small group of Notre Dame students engaged in a peaceful sit-in in the corridors of the main campus building at Notre Dame to protest student recruiting interviews being conducted by the U.S. Central Intelligence Agency (CIA) and Dow Chemical Co. The protesters targeted Dow Chemical because it produced napalm, an incendiary gel then being used by U.S. forces in Vietnam as an anti-personnel weapon. Ten student protesters, who came to be called the "Notre Dame Ten," were suspended from school. Years later, Brian McInerney, one of the "Notre Dame Ten," commented, "We were a minor irritation at a very conservative school." In April 1970, after President Nixon announced plans to conduct bombing raids over Cambodia, more than half of Notre Dame's student body boycotted classes in protest. The student protests left their mark. One Notre Dame student, John Girardot, who was prevented from attending a scheduled interview with Dow Chemical by the 1969 protesters, said that the tumultuous times "probably opened my eyes for the long term." Girardot came to believe that "everything needs to be challenged." Margaret Fosmoe, "Former Students Reflect on 15-Minute Protest Rule," *South Bend Tribune*, 16 February 2009.

[29]Roy Terrell, "Hope Revives in South Bend," *Sports Illustrated*, 9 October 1961.

[30]As Note Dame's head coach from 1941 to 1943, Leahy compiled a sterling record of 24 wins, 3 losses and 3 ties. In 1944-45, he served on active military duty as a U.S. Navy lieutenant. With the end of World War II in 1945, Leahy returned to Notre Dame and resumed his coaching duties. He continued coaching the Fighting Irish until 1953. When he left the coaching ranks, his overall mark at Notre Dame was 87 wins, 11 losses and 9 ties.

[31]Frank Deford, "Sportswriter Is One Word," *John W. Gallivan Program in Journalism, Ethics & Democracy* (Notre Dame, Indiana, 2010), 9.

[32]Frank Deford, *Over Time: My Life as a Sportswriter* (New York: Atlantic Monthly Press, 2012), 78.

[33]Thomas Stritch, *My Notre Dame: Memories and Reflections of Sixty Years* (Notre Dame, IN: University of Notre Dame Press, 1991), 85. (The term "natatorium" was an oblique reference to the fact that the campus building which Lange had appropriated contained an indoor swimming pool.)

[34]Stritch would write in his autobiography that Father Lange was "billed as the fourth strongest man in the world," suggesting it was unlikely that the claim was ever documented. *Ibid.*

[35]John Underwood, "Some Old Grads Get A Hazing," *Sports Illustrated*, 15 May 1967.

Chapter 7
The Influence of a Revolutionary

St. Joseph's Lake sits at the northwest corner of the Notre Dame campus, a short distance removed from another lake named after St. Mary. St. Joe's was the more intriguing of the two lakes, if only because a small island with a locked gate rested mysteriously in the middle. On a warm spring afternoon in May 1963, Martin visited his department head, Tom Stritch, seeking guidance. The two walked along the path that encircled St. Joe's Lake. With graduation looming, Martin's thoughts would inevitably turn to the future. Faced with several potential areas of endeavor, Martin had no idea what he wanted to do. His chosen field of study, communication arts, opened up an exciting array of possibilities—and the breadth of those possibilities contributed to Martin's uncertainty. The island with the locked gate provided a convenient metaphor for the uncertainty and mystery surrounding Martin's future. It was at times like this that Martin most felt the absence of his father—and most missed Nancy's support.

The introductory pages in the 1963 *Dome*, the yearbook for Martin's graduating class, included the comment, "Alongside a dramatic decline in football victories, Notre Dame has undergone greater physical, academic, disciplinary, and 'spiritual' change than during any other four-year span in the University's history. More than previous classes, this Senior Class has been acutely aware of the tortuous evolution that Notre Dame is undergoing—Seniors have felt the strain of values past and present, the struggle between a Catholicism of yesterday and a University of today."[36] Notre Dame, the yearbook observed, has "a monumental internal problem. Simply stated: Notre Dame, a Catholic university, has to resolve the tension between what the two terms 'Catholic' and 'university' have come to mean."[37] In the view of the *Dome*'s editors, "the Catholic college was, and to some extent, still is, seen as an institution for the protection of morals instead of a place of preparation for independent thought."[38] The yearbook phrased the fundamental question as, "Is religious dogma incompatible with the spirit of free inquiry expected at a university?"[39]

The discussion presented in the pages of the *Dome* captured the essence of a movement that was then gaining traction at Notre Dame and at other Catholic universities.[40] For Martin, there was a degree of irony in the *Dome*'s words. There were two identity crises playing out before him—only one of which held any significance to him. The university's struggle was not Martin's struggle. His more immediate concern was his own future. He would have to resolve the uncertainty regarding his own path in life before he could worry about the fate of Notre Dame as a Catholic institution.

During his four years in South Bend, Martin participated in numerous conversations with Professor Tom Stritch, both individually and in the context of classroom discussions. None of the conversations with Stritch were as memorable to Martin as the last one. As Stritch and Martin circled St. Joe's Lake, Stritch told Martin that vocational indecision is a natural stage in life. Stritch's words conveyed a suspicion of individuals who were so self-assured as to know their way through life at an early age. Stritch and Martin walked around St. Joe's Lake for more than an hour. They talked about communication arts, journalism, television and radio. They discussed the implications of establishing personal goals and the consequences of career choices. They talked about life.

When he would later put his thoughts in writing, Stritch drew a distinction between two types of individuals, those who were self-assured and seemed to have their future path already laid out, and the "doubters," who were undecided as to what lay ahead. "The trouble with those self-assured physicians, clergymen, and others who seem to know their way through life," Stritch would write, "is that they become narrow, interested only in their professions."[41] In contrast, he believed that the doubters would become more tolerant adults, "more widely concerned with community, wiser."[42] The doubters held greater value for Stritch because, with experience, they learn that life is not so much a product of rational decision making but the result of "some prompting of the blood, some urgency in the heart."[43]

From his earliest days at Notre Dame, Martin fell within Stritch's group of "doubters." However, with the help of both Stritch and Professor Edward Fischer, Stritch's long-time sidekick, Martin had found his niche in the study of mass media and communications. Martin enjoyed a success he could never have anticipated a few years earlier. In his junior and senior years at Notre Dame, Martin took eight courses in the Communication Arts Department, some taught by Fischer, most taught by Stritch himself.

Fischer had written several books on cinematography and produced films himself. He taught his students how to relate makeup artistry to fine art and how to apply the techniques of journalism to writing of any kind. Stritch credited Fischer with helping to bring respectability to the serious study of film as art and documentary.

Stritch was equal parts revolutionary and iconoclast. He was a former sportscaster and an enthusiastic sports fan.[44] Nonetheless, he believed that the prominence of Notre Dame football distracted the university from more noble pursuits. He liked Knute Rockne, but disliked the inflated legend accorded the coach.[45] At a time when college journalism departments focused primarily on the tricks of producing a newspaper, Stritch sought to ensure that graduates of his journalism program were conversant in the great books and had mastered the fine points of writing with style.

In his role as professor, Stritch did not distinguish between his responsibilities as an educator and what he believed to be his obligation to respect the dignity of others. Some thirty years before Notre Dame appointed Stritch as a professor, the U.S. Supreme Court had issued its landmark decision in *Plessy v. Ferguson*. Using the language of the time, *Plessy v. Ferguson* declared that a Louisiana law which mandated separate public conveyances for the "white and colored races" was constitutional, as long as the facilities made available for colored individuals were substantially equal to the facilities used by whites.[46] The doctrine of "separate but equal"—and the rigid racial segregation on which it was based—became the law of the land. Stritch saw beyond the law. He believed that "separate but equal" was an affront to the dignity of all people.[47] From his earliest days as a professor, he worked to create an environment in which all students—African-Americans, whites, and those of other races—felt welcomed.

Stritch was especially skeptical of an educational system for Catholic clergy that emphasized minimal contact with women. In his view, "this resulted in an unreasonable fear of sex by far too many priests and religious men, and a frequently unwholesome brand of masculinity in schools and religious houses."[48] Some Catholic clergy, he suggested, "saw, apparently, something questionable in God's own creation of Eve."[49] He found it ironic that Christian churches would joyfully celebrate "the cult of Our Lady" and yet insist on perpetuating the dominant role of male leadership.[50] In his role as professor, Stritch made no effort to hide the fact that he considered women students to be more mature and more academically industrious than male students.[51] As early as the 1940s, Stritch actively lobbied the Notre Dame administration to admit women students. Stritch's enlightened views of the role of women in society and in the Catholic Church were not generally shared by his contemporaries at Notre Dame in the 1940s and 1950s. He would write, "I do not think coeducation immoral, as so many older priests and nuns did."[52] A genial man, Stritch rarely displayed anger. Invariably, however, he would become irritated when friends and relatives would ask him for tickets to Notre Dame football games. For Stritch, the minor sports on campus were infinitely more interesting than football. In particular, he loved the festive atmosphere that accompanied track meets, both indoor and outdoor. Stritch could often be seen at indoor track meets, sitting in the top row of bleacher seats in the Notre Dame field house. He had a special affinity for five-foot-five inch Greg "Little Dynamite" Rice, a superbly talented long distance runner for Notre Dame in the years before World War II. For Stritch, few spectacles were as exciting as watching Rice outrun much taller athletes in the two-mile.

In general, Stritch based much of his personal philosophy on the writings of Spanish philosopher José Ortega y Gasset, the intellectual leader of the Spanish Revolution. Ortega provided a voice for workers' rights in Spain in 1936. Ortega both feared and reviled "the self-satisfied age" and predicted the doom of any society that consisted of individuals who, in the face of problems, confined their thought to the ideas they had already developed. Ortega's philosophy seemed to have inspired Stritch's preference for "the doubters" over those who were more self-assured. When Stritch would speak of Ortega and his philosophical teachings, Martin was a willing listener.

From Stritch's perspective, if it took Martin some time to find his way after leaving South Bend, so much the better. Ortega valued the journey more than the destination, the mysterious gate rather than the well-worn path. Quoting the Spanish poet and novelist Miguel de Cervantes, author of *Don Quixote*, Ortega found great truth in the maxim, "the road is always better than the inn."[53] Ortega believed to his core that "authentic integrity, vital fullness, do not consist in self-satisfaction, in achievement, in final arrival."[54] For Ortega—and, by derivation, for Stritch—the reality of history lay in pure vitality, much like "the energy that agitates the sea, fecundates the beast, causes the tree to flower and the star to shine."[55] There is a value in insecurity, Ortega maintained, because it keeps man ever on the alert.

So, as Stritch and Martin talked during their walk around St. Joe's Lake, Stritch drew on Ortega for answers. For every concern that Martin expressed, Stritch found a corresponding benefit. Martin told Stritch that he was unsure about what he wanted to do in life. Stritch would counter that doubt was a useful source of motivation. Where Martin worried about leaving the protective environment at Notre Dame, Stritch found intrigue in the journey that lay ahead. Relying again on Ortega, Stritch would assert that "the impossibility of knowing what is ahead, the fact that our horizon is open to all possibilities, constitutes the fullness, the plenitude of life, of authentic life."[56] Where Martin saw insecurity, Stritch saw a productive vitality.

Martin was grateful for the wisdom that Stritch imparted during their walk around the lake and, especially, for his reassuring manner. Implicit in Stritch's message was the notion that indecision could be productive. Stritch himself had dabbled in journalism before landing at Notre Dame in 1930. In 1941, while teaching at Notre Dame, he became "fed up with what I was doing" and took a commission in the Navy.[57] He knew well, from his own experience, that vocational indecision would likely result in some false starts along the way—and perhaps occasionally the metaphorical locked gate. More importantly,

Stritch had observed Martin in class for the better part of two years. He had seen that Dick was an inquisitive and thoughtful student. He was confident that Martin was prepared for what lay ahead. In the end, Stritch offered reassurance more than advice. "Dick," he said, "you'll be successful at whatever you do."

Martin was 22 years old. Six years had passed since Mr. Lamprinakos, the wrestling coach at Mt. Lebanon High, had identified Martin as a natural. As with Lampy's high praise years earlier, Martin found encouragement and hope in Stritch's remarks. One way or another, Martin would soon be entering the workforce—an arena where nobody was a natural. Martin knew that in order to succeed, he would have to be both smart and industrious. He found reassurance in the fact that he had studied diligently during his four years at Notre Dame. He had succeeded academically when others expected him to fail. He had proven that the decision to admit him to Notre Dame was not a mistake. His most trusted professors had made it clear that they believed in Martin. As a result, his confidence soared.

---

[36]*Dome* Yearbook, Vol. 54 (Notre Dame, IN, 1963), 7.

[37]*Ibid.*, 4.

[38]*Ibid.*, 14.

[39]*Ibid.*

[40]Writing in 2001, Alan Wolfe, Boston College sociologist, Director of the Boisi Center for Religion and American Public Life at Boston College, and contributing editor of *The New Republic*, framed the essential issue as whether Catholic colleges and universities were obligated to reflect orthodox Catholic tenets. Wolfe stated, "As late as the 1960s and 1970s, Catholic colleges and universities tended to be insular institutions unwilling to compete in the academic marketplace. No longer. While insularity still characterizes many evangelical colleges and universities and at least one Jewish school, Notre Dame, Georgetown, and Boston College, all ranking in the top 40 of American research universities, have questioned the Vatican's recent efforts to reimpose orthodoxy on Catholic colleges and universities." Alan Wolfe, *Liberalism and Catholicism*, The American Prospect, December 19, 2001, http://prospect.org/article/ liberalism-and-catholicism.

[41]Stritch, Thomas. *My Notre Dame: Memories and Reflections of Sixty Years* (Notre Dame, Indiana: University of Notre Dame Press, 1991), 99.

[42]*Ibid.*, 99-100.

[43]*Ibid.*, 100.

[44]As a boy growing up in Tennessee, Stritch would delight in attending exhibition baseball games at Nashville's Sulphur Dell Stadium that featured major league stars such as Tris Speaker, George Sisler and Babe Ruth. Ruth was Stritch's favorite major leaguer, but not because of Ruth's prodigious home runs. Rather, Stritch favored the Babe because when his New York Yankees visited

Nashville, Ruth took the time to attend Mass at a local Catholic church on Sunday morning before his game.

[45]Stritch would refer to Rockne by his full name, Knute Kenneth Rockne. Stritch encountered Rockne in 1930 during a chance meeting at Notre Dame. Stritch was in his first year as a student at the university; Rockne was in what would be his last year as Notre Dame's coach. Stritch found Rockne to be "the right man for Notre Dame, shrewd but simple, confident yet unpretentious." At the same time, Stritch found it distasteful when Rockne fans would portray him as "St. Kenneth of the gridiron … the oracle as well as the orator of the locker room." Stritch, *My Notre Dame: Memories and Reflections of Sixty Years*, 135.

[46]The Supreme Court's decision dated back to 1896. The case originated when Homer Plessy, a 30-year-old resident of Louisiana attempted to take a seat in a railroad car reserved for whites. Plessy was of mixed descent, being "seven-eighths Caucasian and one-eighth African blood." Plessy was considered to be "colored" under the laws of Louisiana. The carrier had made available a comparable rail coach for "persons not of the white race," as it was required to do under Louisiana law. The U.S. Supreme Court ruled that so long as the coach that was available for "colored" citizens was equal, state law requiring separate facilities "did not destroy the legal equality of the two races." The Court's decision is located at page 1138 of Volume 16 of the *Supreme Court Reporter*.

[47]In 1954, the Supreme Court overturned the doctrine of "separate but equal" in *Brown v. Board of Education*. The Court ruled that "separate but equal" was contrary to the equal protection clause of the Fourteenth Amendment to the U.S. Constitution.

[48]Stritch, *My Notre Dame: Memories and Reflections of Sixty Years*, 78.

[49]*Ibid.*

[50]*Ibid.*

[51]*Ibid.* 194.

[52]*Ibid.*, 78.

[53]José Ortega y Gasset, *The Revolt of the Masses* (Notre Dame, Indiana: University of Notre Dame Press, 1985), 23.

[54]*Ibid.*

[55]*Ibid.*, 25.

[56]*Ibid.*

[57]Stritch, *My Notre Dame: Memories and Reflections of Sixty Years*, 181.

Chapter 8
Fighting the War on Poverty

Saturday, June 12, 1965, was a good day for Willie Mays. Facing the Pittsburgh Pirates in an afternoon contest at Forbes Field, Mays and his San Francisco Giants teammates shut out the Pirates, 4-0. Mays had gone two-for-four, including a first-inning home run, his twentieth of the season. At 7:00 o'clock that evening, Dick Martin drove to Pittsburgh's Carlton House Hotel. He was twenty-four years old and more nervous than usual. He asked the attendant at the front desk for Mays's room number. The attendant eyed Martin suspiciously. "Is Mr. Mays expecting you?" the attendant asked. Martin nodded. The attendant handed over the phone number for Mays's room and Martin dialed. He heard a soft but tired voice answer the phone. "Mr. Mays," Martin addressed the baseball legend, "this is Dick Martin. I believe that Mr. Nunn spoke to you about me and the program tonight?" "Yeah, man," Mays replied, "I'll be right down."

Martin and his classmates graduated from Notre Dame on Sunday, June 9, 1963. Shortly after, with diplomas in hand, Martin and Bud Vogel visited the Grotto on campus. Constructed in 1896, the Grotto consists of a cave built out of large stones and encompassing a statue of Mary, the mother of Jesus. The Grotto has long been a site for prayer and reflection by students facing the challenge of exams or needing a refuge from the complexities of life. Martin and Vogel said some prayers in thanksgiving for four good years and hopped into Vogel's Chevy convertible for the drive to Mt. Lebanon.

Thirteen miles east of Pittsburgh, Vogel took the Monroeville exit off the Pennsylvania Turnpike. Slowing for the tollbooth, Vogel asked Martin if he had any money. Martin had a pocketful of change but was well short of the $5 toll. Vogel was also short on change but loaded with gumption. He slowed as he approached the tollbooth and then stepped on the gas pedal with full force. "You're nuts, man!" Martin yelled. The next day, a Pennsylvania State Trooper showed up at Vogel's house with a summons for traffic court.

Vogel paid his fine and then he and Martin took off on a trip to Europe with a high school classmate, Dick Foster. Earlier that year, Martin's mother had asked him what he wanted for a graduation gift. Mrs. Martin was still living comfortably off the savings, investments, and insurance money left by Martin's father. Mrs. Martin proposed buying Martin a new car or paying for a summer in Europe. Martin chose the trip abroad, figuring that it might be his only opportunity to travel to the Continent and that he would be able to buy a car later.

Martin returned from Europe in late August. His immediate future was uncertain. During the four years at Notre Dame, Martin held a student deferment, which allowed him to complete his studies without being drafted into military service. The deferment had ended, and Martin was now subject to the draft.[58] He was not one to pay close attention to political developments in the world. However, it was becoming increasingly difficult to ignore the situation in Vietnam, where rebels were waging a jungle war against the South Vietnamese government. The January 25, 1963 issue of *Life* magazine, on sale at newsstands for 20 cents, featured a cover story titled, "The Vicious Fighting in Vietnam." Martin was wary.

By the middle of 1963, there were more than 10,000 U.S. troops stationed in Southeast Asia as advisors to South Vietnam. In Germany, there seemed to be no solution for the antagonism between the U.S. and the Soviets engendered by the Berlin Wall. The uneasy peace between the countries of North Korea and South Korea continued. Clearly, there were major trouble spots throughout the world that had the potential to erupt. Martin saw little purpose in attempting to find a job if he was likely to end up spending two years in military service.

Martin woke up early on Friday, November 22, 1963. It was a crisp Mt. Lebanon morning. Martin was scheduled to take an aptitude test for the Air Force. With some anxiety, he prepared for the drive to the Greater Pittsburgh Airport, the site of the test. It was a trip of roughly 30 minutes. Before leaving home, Martin quietly talked with his mother about his hopes for the future. He was not eager to serve in the military. If required to spend two years on active duty, however, the Air Force was his preferred branch of service. After conversing with his mother, Martin set out for the airport.

On that same morning, a thousand miles southwest of Pittsburgh, President John F. Kennedy was delivering an 8:45 a.m. speech to an enthusiastic crowd in a parking lot outside the Hotel Texas in Fort Worth. It was raining and chilly in Fort Worth, causing the president to remark to his audience, "There are no faint hearts in Fort Worth." The First Lady, Jacqueline Kennedy, was not present for her husband's speech. The president explained to the estimated crowd of 2,000, "Mrs. Kennedy is organizing herself. It takes longer." The crowd laughed. Kennedy then quipped, "But, of course, she looks better than we do when she does it."

The president addressed the issue of national defense. He told the Fort Worth crowd, "What we are trying to do around the world, I believe, is quite simple, and that is to build a military structure which will defend the vital interests of the United States." He then praised the role that the citizens of Fort Worth had played in producing bombers for World War II and extolled the benefits of the work that Fort Worth's General Dynamics Corporation would soon perform in developing the TFX tactical fighter plane.

Back in Pittsburgh, Martin was satisfied that he had done well on the Air Force test. By 1:45 p.m., he was back on the road to Mt. Lebanon, his car radio tuned to a pop music station. Shortly before 2:00 p.m., Martin listened in shock as an urgent news message came over his car radio. President Kennedy had been shot during a motorcade in Dallas, Texas. Martin was stunned. Nothing so earthshaking had ever happened in his lifetime. He pulled his car off to the side of the highway, unable to continue driving. He listened intently to the broadcast and tried to collect himself. Thirty minutes passed, then forty. Martin thought of his mother, all alone at home, probably listening to the same shocking news by herself. Martin slowly edged his car back onto the highway and began the painful trip home. Once back at the house, Martin sat glued to the television, awaiting further news. Shortly thereafter, he and his mother heard the TV newscasts confirm that the president had died.

Within weeks, Martin learned that Pittsburgh's Selective Service draft board had classified him as 1-Y. The asthma that had developed during Martin's senior year at Notre Dame proved to be chronic. A draft board physician determined that, upon exertion, Martin was at risk of experiencing severe difficulties in breathing. The risk was so extreme that Martin would be exempt from military service, barring a formal declaration of war or a national emergency.

The 1-Y classification allowed Martin to pursue permanent employment in the civilian sector. Through his sister, Dolly, Martin learned that the Greater Braddock Chamber of Commerce in Braddock, Pennsylvania was seeking to fill the position of executive director. Dolly put in a good word for Martin with one of her friends who served on the chamber's board of directors. At Dolly's request, the friend arranged for Martin to come in for an interview. Martin made a favorable impression and, in December 1963—two months shy of his twenty-third birthday—Martin began working for the Greater Braddock Chamber of Commerce.

Within months of taking the position with the chamber of commerce, however, Martin was ready to move on. He found that the position provided a decent paycheck but not a vocation. He was brimming with youthful energy and enthusiasm. He discovered that these attributes were not always appreciated at the chamber of commerce, a very traditional organization that was often not receptive to changes.

On January 8, 1964, President Lyndon B. Johnson, the successor to John F. Kennedy, delivered his State of the Union address. Johnson used the opportunity to outline his concept for a ground-breaking "War on Poverty." At the time, an estimated twenty percent of all Americans were living in poverty. Johnson found it disgraceful that poverty was so pervasive in a nation that served as the flag-bearer for democracy throughout the world. In August 1964, Johnson signed the first of his anti-poverty bills, which provided funding for job training and educational programs. Four months later, Bernie Powers, Martin's former teacher and coach at St. Bernard Grade School, called Martin with a lead on a position that was opening up as part of a federally funded tutorial, cultural, and recreational program for youths in the low-income areas of Pittsburgh's West End. The federal government was going to be contracting with the City of Pittsburgh to run educational programs for disadvantaged youths. The city would then subcontract with the Catholic Diocese of Pittsburgh to run the centers. St. James Center, situated at a Catholic elementary school of the same name, would be one of five educational centers in the Pittsburgh area under Bernie Powers's supervision. Martin listened intently, then told Powers to count on him. In December 1964, Martin was installed as the educational director for the St. James Center—a foot soldier in the War on Poverty.

The position came with little in the way of a job description or performance standards. Guidance was in short supply. There was no primer on how to structure tutorial programs and no book on what might attract and inspire inner city youths. Martin viewed the lack of an existing structure for the program as an advantage. Without a set of operating procedures to guide him, Martin was free to make his own rules. Left to his own devices, he flourished. In tandem with co-worker Dan Beyer, Martin composed and distributed advertisements touting the program. He went out into the community and recruited children to join the program. He met with the parents of young students and spoke of the unique opportunities for academic and cultural enrichment. He devised a curriculum for tutorial sessions and summer school classes, hired teachers, and designed schedules for classes. He also reserved time for the youths to play softball games and take part in other athletic events.

More than four hundred children participated in the program at the St. James Center. School schedules dictated that elementary school remedial reading classes would have to be held in the early afternoon. Tutoring for high school students, whose school classes extended until late afternoon, would begin at 6:00 p.m. and end at 9:00 p.m. Aside from those scheduling constraints, Martin enjoyed virtually complete discretion.

In the spring of 1965, Martin began planning for the inaugural St. James Center athletic awards ceremony. The ceremony was scheduled for the evening of Saturday, June 12. Martin wanted the awards ceremony to be memorable. Checking the Pittsburgh Pirates' schedule of home games, he found that the date of the ceremony coincided with a series of games that Willie Mays and his San Francisco Giants would be playing in Pittsburgh. The easy part was checking the schedule. The hard part, Martin knew, would be getting in touch with the great Mays. Beyer was skeptical. "You'll never get Mays," Beyer told Martin. "You never know until you try," Martin replied.

Martin pondered the situation. He decided to contact Bob Prince, the long-time radio voice of the Pittsburgh Pirates. After getting Prince on the telephone, Martin explained that he was hoping Mays might be able to attend the St. James Center awards ceremony. Prince suggested that Martin call Bill Nunn, the socially prominent sports editor of the *Pittsburgh Courier*.

In the 1940s, Nunn had been a prolific scorer for the West Virginia State basketball team. He possessed sufficient artistry with a basketball that he was offered tryouts with the New York Knicks and the Harlem Globetrotters. He passed on professional basketball, however, and instead began to carve out a career as a journalist and promoter of sporting events. Nunn was a friend and confidante of black entertainers and athletes. He socialized with boxer Joe Louis, track star Jesse Owens, and musicians Lionel Hampton, Count Basie, and Billy Eckstine. Up until the 1960s, Nunn had been instrumental in bringing the Negro League Indianapolis Clowns to Pittsburgh to play games at Forbes Field.[59] He befriended Pittsburgh Pirates stars Roberto Clemente and Willie Stargell and others in the Pirates' organization. Nunn was the ideal point man for putting Martin in touch with Willie Mays.

With some anxiety, Martin called the *Pittsburgh Courier*. He found Nunn eager to help. On Thursday, June 10, the Giants took on the New York Mets at Shea Stadium and came away with a 3-0 victory. Following the game, Willie Mays and his teammates boarded a plane for Pittsburgh. That same day, Martin spoke with Nunn on the phone. "How many kids will be there?" Nunn asked. "A couple hundred," Martin replied. "Willie will do it," Nunn said. Martin was nearly speechless. "Are you kidding?" he asked Nunn. "No, I'm not kidding, Mr. Martin," Nunn replied, "Willie just wanted to make sure the event was primarily for kids."

When June 12 came, Martin's colleague, Dan Beyer, was poised to chauffeur Mays to the awards ceremony. Martin told Beyer, "No way!" Martin was reserving that privilege for himself. There was a part of Martin that remained skeptical. "Why would Willie Mays do this?" he wondered. There was nothing in it for him, no money and no publicity.

If it turned out that Mays decided to cancel at the last minute, Martin would at least hear the news first-hand, rather than from Beyer.

Early on that Saturday evening, Martin drove his 1965 lavender Corvair to the Carlton House Hotel at the corner of 6th Avenue and Grant Street in downtown Pittsburgh. The Carlton House was a grand structure, a landmark in Pittsburgh at the time. It had opened in 1952, the first hotel to be built in Pittsburgh since the time of the Great Depression. The building was ahead of its time. Advertisements touted it as "the best hotel in the world," with air conditioning throughout all sixteen floors. Arriving at the hotel, Martin asked the desk attendant for Mays's telephone number. Martin called the room and then waited anxiously for Willie to answer. When Mays picked up the phone, Martin identified himself. Shortly thereafter, Mays appeared in the hotel lobby wearing a dazzling sharkskin suit.

As Martin and Mays walked out the front entrance of the Carlton House, the hotel doormen greeted them as if greeting royalty. Mays then settled into the cozy black bucket seats of Martin's Corvair, and the two headed to the St. James Center. Martin was well aware that two other contemporary center fielders who, like Mays, had spent their formative years playing in New York, Mickey Mantle of the Yankees and Duke Snider of the Dodgers, each had a reputation for being unapproachable. Martin could not easily picture either Mantle or Snider heading off with him in his Corvair, no matter how new or flashy the car. Martin marveled that Mays, in contrast, was quiet, unassuming, and immediately likeable. Martin would laugh about it later but, at the age of 24 and two years removed from his college days, he lacked the poise to be able to speak freely with an individual of Mays' stature. The Giants' star was only ten years older than Martin but, in Martin's mind, the gap in age and achievement was monumental. While driving Mays to the St. James Center, Martin could manage only some minor chatter with the renowned center fielder. "I hope you did well in the game," Martin heard himself say. Even before he had completed the sentence, Martin found himself wishing that he had taken the time to find out how the Giants had fared at the ballpark. Eager to impress, Martin didn't want to present the impression that he was anything less than an avid baseball fan.

Once Martin parked his car at the St. James Center, he and Mays climbed up a fire escape that led to the back of the auditorium. Martin still had some crucial coordination to do. Aside from Bernie Powers and Dan Beyer, Martin had not told anyone other than his immediate family that Mays was coming to the awards ceremony. Martin quickly conferred with the boy who would be serving as master of ceremonies for the evening. The conversation was brief, the instructions explicit. Martin informed the boy that Willie Mays would present the softball MVP awards and that the boy should acknowledge him as "possibly the greatest baseball player of all time." With Mays waiting off-stage, the master of ceremonies called the crowd to attention. His presentation was flawless. "And now," the emcee intoned, "to present the Most Valuable Junior and Senior Softball Awards, possibly the greatest baseball player of all time, Willie Mays."

When the curtain at the front of the stage opened, Mays walked out. At first, the audience of nearly three hundred students and parents sat in complete silence, as if stunned. Older individuals in the audience quickly recognized the perennial all-star center fielder and began to clap wildly. The younger children soon caught on. En masse, the audience rose to their feet, shouting, whistling, and clapping for minutes.

Mays walked to the microphone. When the crowd finally quieted, Mays began to speak. He told the assembled audience that it was an honor to join them. Speaking directly to the young ballplayers, he said, "Some people may think that winning a softball award in a neighborhood youth league is no big thing, but I'm telling you that when you win the most valuable award in anything, you're doing something." Mays then called out the names of the two winners of the most valuable player awards, brothers John and William Moran. The Morans ascended the stage and posed for a picture with Mays. When Mays completed his remarks, Martin led him out the exit and down the fire escape. Martin's sister, Mary Jane, met them at the bottom of the fire escape and snapped a picture of an exuberant Martin standing side-by-side with Mays. Martin then drove Mays back to the Carlton House.[60]

After the awards ceremony, Mays quickly returned to his regular off-field routine. A Sunday afternoon game against the Pirates loomed next on the schedule, with Pittsburgh right-hander Vernon Law facing San Francisco's Gaylord Perry. Mays was unable to repeat his Saturday heroics, going 0-for-4 as the Giants lost, 2-1. Willie and his teammates then boarded a plane to Los Angeles for a Tuesday game against the Dodgers. Even as the Giants were flying to Los Angeles, however, the euphoria surrounding Mays's appearance at the awards ceremony continued unabated in the Martin household. There were Willie Mays stories to be told and retold. There were photographs to be developed. There were notes of appreciation to be written.

Within three years, John Moran, winner of the St. James Center senior softball award, would be dead, a casualty of the war in Vietnam. Following high school, Moran joined the U.S. Army. In 1968, he served as a member of the 173rd Airborne Brigade, assigned to Vietnam's South Central Coast Region, near the city of Qui Nhon. Moran died on May 4, 1968, five days after the Viet Cong launched Phase II of the Tet Offensive.

As time passed, and particularly after learning of the death of John Moran, Martin would sometimes gaze at the picture that showed himself and Willie Mays standing outside the St. James Center. He would think back to the events of that day. Things had come together perfectly, almost as if preordained. Bob Prince and Bill Nunn were willing to help. By luck of the schedule, the Giants would be in town. Mays, with his unfailing soft spot for kids, was eager to oblige.

It was easy to think, too, of the bigger picture. At a time when the futures of many young men were clouded by the prospect of being drafted, Martin's future was more settled because chronic asthma exempted him from military duty. The same fortunes that had been kind to Martin would prove, later, to be unsparing to John Moran. However, for one magical day in 1965, the lives of Martin, John Moran and William Moran had intersected in a way that would create enduring memories for all three. Photographs from that day show Mays and the Moran brothers on stage, with broad smiles etched on the faces of the teenagers—smiles made possible because of Martin's tenacity in arranging the surprise visit of "possibly the greatest baseball player of all time."

---

[58]At the time, all U.S. male citizens who were 18½ years of age or older were subject to the military draft. The draft laws and Executive Orders provided numerous bases for exemption from

conscription, the most prominent of which were deferments for high school and college students (1-S or 2-S), teachers (2-A), men with families (3-A), and deferments for disqualifying or limiting physical conditions or illnesses (4-F or 1-Y). During the time that he was in college, Martin was classified as 2-S. Upon graduation, his 2-S status expired.

[59]The Indianapolis Clowns baseball team began playing in Indianapolis in 1946. Previously, the team had played in Cincinnati. The team was a member of the Negro American League. When competing against other Negro American League teams, the Clowns played serious baseball. The Clowns also had a barnstorming team that specialized in antics similar to those of basketball's Harlem Globetrotters. For a time, baseball Hall-of-Famer Henry Aaron played second base for the Clowns. As with other Negro league teams, the Clowns had difficulty attracting top African-American players once baseball's major leagues became fully integrated. The Negro American League formally disbanded in 1960. Even after the League disbanded, however, the Clowns continued to play as a barnstorming team until 1962. The term "barnstorming" harkened back to the days of vaudeville, when theatrical shows traveled around the United States and staged performances for paying customers who would assemble in makeshift venues, even in farmers' barns.

[60]The story of Mays's visit to the St. James Center is reported in a biography of the Hall-of-Famer, *Willie Mays: The Life, The Legend* (New York: Scribner, 2010), by James S. Hirsch, 385.

OF MICE AND MIRACLES

A portrait of the Martin family in Mt. Lebanon, circa 1944. SITTING: Dick, sister Mary Jane, and brother Bill. STANDING: Brother Jimmy, mother Mary Elizabeth, father Dr. James Martin, and sister Dolly.

The 1954 "Thoroughbreds" of St. Bernard Catholic Grade School, Mt. Lebanon. FIRST ROW (from left): Harold "Bud" Vogel, Mike Geis, Howard "Butch" Breinig, Ray Blockinger, Weslie Kerlin, Paul Black, Bill Sterner. SECOND ROW (from left): Asst. Coach Raymond "Red" Pulaski, Head Coach Bernie Powers, Lee Wells, Jackie Smith, Denny Phillips, Ned Doran, Gene Breen, Francis Audia, Dick Martin.

The 1958 Mt. Lebanon High School varsity wrestling team. Martin is in the front row, third from left.

The 1960 University of Notre Dame varsity wrestling team. Martin (front row, second from left), a sophomore, opened the season with six consecutive victories in dual matches.

Dick Martin at his graduation from the University of Notre Dame, June 9, 1963.

Dick Martin and his mother, Mary Elizabeth, at home shortly after Martin graduated from college.

Martin with baseball Hall-of-Famer Willie Mays on June 12, 1965. Mays, then with the San Francisco Giants, had just spoken to an audience of disadvantaged youths enrolled in the federally funded tutorial and recreational program at Pittsburgh's St. James Educational Center.

Martin with his high school wrestling coach, George "Lampy" Lamprinakos, on the occasion of Martin's induction into the Bishop Denis J. O'Connell High School Athletic Hall of Fame in 1993.

Martin with his three daughters, (from left) Kim, Kerry, and Kelly.

Martin with Rev. Edward A. "Monk" Malloy, C.S.C., former president of the University of Notre Dame. As assistant principal at O'Connell High School, Martin arranged for Father Malloy to deliver the commencement address to O'Connell's graduating seniors.

Picture taken at a Martin family reunion. From left, granddaughter Emma, daughter Kelly, son-in-law Mike, son-in-law Corbett, granddaughter Grace, daughter Kerry, daughter Kim, son-in-law Nate.

Martin shown climbing the twenty-eight steps at the entrance to the Basilica of Sainte Anne-de-Beaupré in Quebec, Canada. Martin was repeating the climb his father had made in 1945 while praying for a cure for the nephrosis that afflicted Martin in childhood.

Martin pictured with the "Play Like A Champion Today" inscription that has inspired generations of athletes at the University of Notre Dame.

Chapter 9
Expunging the Bureaucrat

On a pleasant autumn evening in 1965, Dick Martin and a couple of his friends found themselves at a Young Republicans social event at the Mt. Lebanon Castle Shannon Fire Hall. Politics held little attraction for Martin. He would, however, feign interest when there was the promise of a fun evening. On this particular night, the Young Republicans event was the best that Martin could do. His pals led the way; Martin followed. As Martin approached the entrance to the Hall, a young woman at the admission table raised a leg and stretched it across the doorway, blocking Martin's path. Martin was perplexed, intrigued, and momentarily trapped.

Mary Christine Smith, 21 years old, was playful, bright, and pretty. Known as "Chris" to her friends, Smith was the product of a devoutly Catholic family. She had briefly been a postulant with the Sisters of Charity in Pittsburgh.

Several weeks after his first encounter with Chris Smith, Martin was working at the St. James Center one night when the phone rang. It was 8:00 p.m. Smith was on the other end.

"What are you doing?" Martin asked her.

"Selling encyclopedias," came the reply.

"You're out this late selling encyclopedias?" Martin inquired.

Smith confirmed that she was indeed selling encyclopedias, going house to house. The two chatted briefly and then hung up.

A half-hour later, Smith popped into the doorway of Martin's office. Martin was, at once, attracted and puzzled. He enjoyed her sense of humor but thought her behavior strange. Smith might well have reached a similar conclusion about Martin. His car was in the parking lot. Inexplicably, he allowed Smith to leave the St. James Center on a city bus. Brian Foley, a colleague at the St. James Center, lit into Martin. "Man, you ought to call her," Foley said, "she's definitely interested in you."

There was a link between Smith and Martin that could have been interpreted as a destiny of sorts. In 1944, when Martin himself was three years old and had yet to be afflicted with nephrosis, Martin's father was the physician who delivered Smith at St. Joseph Hospital. Whether it was destiny or simply a commonality of interests, there was an undeniable affinity between Smith and Martin. They dated for six months. It became apparent to both that they would be getting married, sooner rather than later. Smith's father managed to slow the process down, if only for forty days. He made it clear to the couple that he would not permit his daughter to get married during the forty days of Lent. Easter Sunday of 1967 fell on March 26, marking the end of Lent. Once Lent was over, Smith and Martin wasted no time, marrying on the next Saturday, April 1. The marriage was held at St. Bernard Church, with Father John Rebel officiating. After the wedding was over, Smith and Martin left Pittsburgh for the island of Aruba. Located twenty miles north of Venezuela, Aruba was rustic in nature. The married couple found the island remarkably free of tourist attractions and very appealing.

When the honeymoon ended, Martin and Chris took time out to assess where, and how, they were going to live. Martin had given up his position at the St. James Center in December 1966. He was a man in need of a challenge. The work at the St. James Center had become both routine and somewhat tedious, leading Martin to take a position as a part-time English teacher and assistant wrestling coach at Pittsburgh's South Hills Catholic High School.

Martin and Chris took up residence temporarily in Pittsburgh while Martin finished out the school year at South Hills Catholic. Once the academic year ended, they relocated to Provincetown, off Massachusetts' Cape Cod Bay. For the duration of the summer of 1967, Martin's challenge lay in scraping barnacles off boats. Martin had no prior experience in scraping boats; he found it to be work that required a tolerance for tedious effort but little in the way of skill. If the work was mundane, it at least allowed him to live in a desirable setting. The two settled in easily in Cape Cod, with Martin refinishing boats and Smith working as a waitress.

When the summer ended, Martin and Chris again relocated, this time to Washington, D.C. The lure was an interview that Martin's sister, Dolly, had arranged for Martin with a gentleman named Milton Fogelman. Fogelman headed up the East Coast office of the Jobs Corps, an agency under the U.S. Department of Labor. Fogelman was impressed with Martin's work at the St. James Center and, in particular, with the commendations that Martin had received in that job from Sargent Shriver, director of Lyndon Johnson's Office of Economic Opportunity. Martin's interview went favorably. Days later, Martin reported to work as Fogelman's executive assistant. Fogelman also found a job for Chris Martin at the nearby Volt Technical Corporation.

With Martin's annual salary approaching $10,000, he and Chris lived in relative splendor. The pay was intoxicating, the work less than enticing. Martin's job was to manage the desk, monitor the flow of documents into his in-box, and then distribute the papers to others. Two-and-a-half months into the job, Martin knew that he was miscast as a bureaucrat. Day in and day out, the most interesting part of his work routine was joining Chris at Washington's Dupont Circle for a brown bag lunch.

"I've got to get out of here," Martin told Chris one day over lunch.

"What do you want to do?" she asked.

Martin did not have a precise answer. "I don't know," he replied, "I've always wanted to coach."

Smith immediately pointed out the practical matter that Martin seemed to be overlooking. "We won't get a lot of money doing that," she observed.

Martin could only respond, "I know, but I'm miserable."

Martin learned that Bishop Denis J. O'Connell High School in Arlington, Virginia was looking to hire a wrestling coach. At the time, O'Connell had segregated classes, with the boys' classrooms on one side of the school and the girls' classrooms on the other. Martin interviewed with Brother Theodore, a religious in the Order of Christian

Brothers, who served as the boys' principal. In addition to serving as principal, Brother Theodore was the wrestling coach and drama teacher. The competing responsibilities were proving to be too much. Impressed with Martin's degree from Notre Dame and his three years as a collegiate wrestler, Brother Theodore hired Martin as wrestling coach.

The job was exactly what Martin wanted, although the pay was almost negligible. Martin was to receive $500 per year for coaching, more an allowance than a salary. To Martin's dismay, O'Connell did not have a teaching position that it could offer him. However, Brother Theodore dangled a proposal that was palatable. "There's a physical education teacher position open at St. Thomas More Cathedral School," he told Martin. Brother Theodore arranged for Martin to interview with Mother Mary Ivo, the principal of the cathedral school, an elementary school consisting of classes from kindergarten to eighth grade. Encouraged by Brother Theodore's enthusiastic recommendation, the nun hired Martin as a physical education teacher.

The arrangement fulfilled Martin's desire to coach. He experienced lingering doubts, however, as to whether he had chosen wisely, especially in view of the financial sacrifice involved. Martin reached out to a Jesuit priest, Father Angelo D'Agostino, a medical doctor and psychotherapist who maintained a counseling practice near Georgetown University. D'Agostino, known as "Father D'Ag," encouraged Martin to follow his dreams but wanted to make sure that Chris was comfortable with the tradeoffs involved. D'Agostino met with Martin and Chris jointly to discuss the couple's long-term goals and the corresponding economic realities. Father D'Ag became satisfied that the two shared the same long-term objectives and so encouraged Martin to devote his full energy to teaching and coaching.

For a period of eight months, from November 1967 to June 1968, Martin taught physical education classes to grade school students at St. Thomas More from 8:00 a.m. to 3:00 p.m. each weekday. Then, at 3:00 p.m., he would drive to O'Connell and coach the high school wrestling team. The following year, an opening developed for an English teacher at O'Connell. Brother Theodore hired Martin for the position, enabling Martin to quit the physical education position at Thomas More. Beginning in September 1968, Martin taught five English composition classes at O'Connell. The focus on writing was intense. Every two weeks, he would have a stack of 150 compositions to grade. Then, after school each day, he donned his coaching gear to work with the wrestling team. It was a routine that he maintained for nine years, until he was appointed as O'Connell's assistant principal for student life at the start of the 1977-78 academic year.

Martin's appointment to the teaching position at O'Connell brought a sense of stability at a critical time, for Martin and wife Chris were intent on starting a family. A year-and-a-half after Martin and Chris married, Chris gave birth to a daughter, Kelly, born September 4, 1968. Two years later, Chris gave birth to a second daughter, Kim, born December 21, 1970. A third daughter, Kerry, arrived October 30, 1976.

Over time, Father D'Agostino and Martin became close friends. Father D'Ag took a liking to the Martin family, stopping by at least once a year, usually at Christmas, to bring presents for Martin's daughters. D'Agostino occupied a position of power in Washington. He was the first Catholic priest to practice in the field of psychoanalysis. People from all walks of life benefited from his unique perspectives in regard to spirituality and emotional growth.

For a time, D'Agostino led the good life. He was a frequent guest at D.C.'s most acclaimed restaurants. He maintained a comfortable residence in the upscale Georgetown area, and he partied with politicians. Nonetheless, he found something lacking. In the mid-1980s, he left Washington and moved to East Africa, where he became the director of a retreat house and served on the board of governors of a Kenyan orphanage.

During the course of his work for the orphanage, Father D'Ag found himself deeply affected by the plight of abandoned children in Kenya. D'Agostino was distressed to learn that the orphanage refused to accept children who had tested positive for HIV. He proposed that the orphanage establish a special facility to house HIV-positive orphans. When his fellow board members voted against the proposal, D'Agostino pursued the idea on his own. He initiated a vigorous campaign to raise money for a home to accommodate HIV-infected children.

By 1992, D'Agostino had the funds he needed. On September 8, 1992, he opened the Nyumbani Children's Home in Nairobi. Even after opening the children's home, Father D'Ag continued to fight on behalf of children with HIV. He filed a lawsuit seeking to force Kenyan public schools to admit children infected with HIV. When the case was heard in 2004, D'Agostino brought a busload of Nyumbani children to the courtroom so the judge could better appreciate what was at stake. The tactic worked; D'Agostino prevailed.

Father D'Agostino died suddenly on November 20, 2006 after having undergone surgery for diverticulitis. He had spent the final 21 years of his life working in Kenya on behalf of orphaned children, returning to Washington only once each year to raise funds for his charities. During one of D'Agostino's fund-raising trips, Martin asked the priest to speak to the O'Connell community at the school's annual communion breakfast. D'Agostino happily agreed, devoting an entire morning to a discussion of the problems in Kenya and the urgent need to develop sources of clean water for the residents.

Martin was awed by Father D'Ag. He once asked his friend why he had given up life in the United States in favor of living in Kenya. Father D'Ag responded, "Life was too easy for me here. I had it made. It was too nice." D'Agostino found Kenya to be a better fit for his time, talents, and spiritual needs. At his death, the entire country of Kenya showed its appreciation for his efforts on behalf of children. Thousands of mourners, including the president of Kenya, attended the funeral service held for Father D'Ag in Nairobi.

"Follow your dreams," Father D'Ag had told the 26-year-old Martin. As Martin was considering the choice that he faced between working in the Federal government or coaching wrestling, it dawned on him that he had entered the real world. Many of the decisions that he had previously faced in life seemed like child's play. His choice of Notre Dame rather than the University of Michigan had been influenced by his father's preference. The choice he faced when graduating from Notre Dame, whether to buy a new car or spend the summer in Europe, carried no lasting consequences. Now, four years out of college, the choice confronting Martin would help to determine his life's direction. Bolstered by Father D'Ag's advice, Martin chose to coach wrestling. He was reassured to know that, even in the adult world, dreams still mattered.

Chapter 10
Touchdown Twins

On the morning of June 16, 1968, a Sunday, Martin attended early morning Mass at Mt. Lebanon's St. Bernard Church, the same church he had attended in his youth. At the age of 27, he had just completed his first year as wrestling coach at Bishop O'Connell High School and was enjoying a summer visit with his mother. Martin's wife, Chris, was pregnant with their first child. The future looked bright. During the Mass, the lector requested prayers for deceased parishioner Harold Raymond Vogel. Martin was stunned.

Air Force Captain Harold "Bud" Vogel died on June 14, 1968, fifty-seven days into his year-long assignment as a pilot in Vietnam. His Cessna Bird Dog had struck a radio tower and crashed during a reconnaissance mission over the Mekong Delta. Back home, he had a wife and two young children.

Martin and Vogel shared common ground. Like Martin's father, Bud Vogel's dad had been a physician. As had been the case with Martin, Bud Vogel lost his father to an early death before Vogel reached college age. Classmates since the third grade, Martin and Vogel had hooked up on more passes on the playground than either could remember, Martin as the diminutive but strong-armed passer, Vogel as the end with excellent hands. The passes diminished once Martin and Vogel reached Mt. Lebanon High. Martin never experienced the growth spurt necessary to quarterback a high school team; Vogel sprouted to six-feet-two inches and developed into a formidable tight end. An aggressive athlete and fearsome blocker, Vogel gained the nickname "Thor," after the Norse god of thunder. Following high school, both Vogel and Martin attended Notre Dame, Martin as a wrestler and Vogel as a football player. As seniors, the two roomed together and spent a good portion of their spare time conversing over beers at South Bend's popular hangouts.

Like Martin, Vogel was passionate about football. Though Vogel saw little playing time for the Fighting Irish, he yearned to be part of a winning tradition. One day during the fall of 1962, Martin found Vogel in a particularly foul mood when Bud returned to the dorm after football practice. The team had won its season opener against the University of Oklahoma, but then self-destructed, losing four games in a row. Vogel was tired of losing. He knew that lack of talent was not the problem; the team possessed an abundance of outstanding athletes. Vogel had grown weary of head coach Joe Kuharich's conservative game plans and, particularly, his distaste for playing sophomores. Upon seeing Martin in the dorm room they shared, Vogel complained, loudly, about Kuharich. "He's got John Huarte and Jack Snow on the bench," Vogel told Martin. "Those guys are great players, and he's not playing them. He's driving us crazy."[61]

Notre Dame finished Vogel's senior season with five wins and five losses. He would have relished going out as a winner, but his aspirations were much bigger than anything he could have accomplished on a football field. He dreamed of being an astronaut. In joining the Air Force and pursuing flight school, Vogel hoped to accumulate credentials that would later qualify him for the space program. In Vietnam, he was a member of the proud fraternity of forward air controllers who piloted small Cessna airplanes. Flying at low altitudes, the forward air controllers located enemy targets and maintained visual contact in order to direct U.S. artillery. They flirted with danger on each flight. The FACs, as they were known, would each adopt a distinctive call sign, a *nom de guerre* that would often provide insight into a pilot's personality. The call signs added glamor as well as mystique. In Vogel's 22nd Tactical Air Support Squadron, there were FACs known as "Sidewinder" and "Viper," and still others who went by "Helix" and "Hound Dog."

Vogel strayed from convention. He eschewed a colorful, more commonplace call sign in favor of the more enigmatic "Sa Dec," the name of the riverport city in Vietnam where his unit did much of its flying. Located ninety miles from Saigon, Sa Dec was a city of lush vegetation, beautiful flowers, and aging but picturesque villas. Perched nearby Vietnam's Mekong River, Sa Dec provided a vantage point from which U.S. troops could monitor the flow of vessels on the river and launch interdicting fire.

For Martin, the immediate shock of Bud Vogel's death was followed by a profound sadness. He wanted to reach out to his friend's family but didn't know how. Martin had lost touch with Vogel after Bud joined the Air Force. Information was scarce. Martin knew that Vogel had married a student at Notre Dame's "sister school," St. Mary's College, but he had never met Bud's wife. In high school and into college, Vogel and his mother and sister had lived on Sumner Place, not too far from Mt. Lebanon. Later, Bud, his mother, and sister moved to Longridge Drive, also near Mt. Lebanon, but Vogel hadn't lived there since the time of his marriage. Through former classmates, Martin heard that Vogel's wife and children were living in Kentucky when Bud died. However, none of Martin's friends knew the address or even the city. Unable to attend Vogel's funeral service or send condolences to Vogel's wife, Martin contented himself with offering prayers for the man who had been his tight end, teammate, roommate, and friend.

Vogel was the first childhood friend that Martin would lose to death. Denny Phillips would be the second. Phillips succumbed to cancer in 1981 at the age of 40. Though not as sudden as Bud Vogel's passing, the death of Denny Phillips was equally traumatic for Martin. Phillips was an outstanding student, a versatile athlete, and a friend to all. Honors came easily, both in academics and athletics. At six feet and 186 pounds, he was big, strong, and fast. In his senior year at Mt. Lebanon High, he was selected for the Ed Sullivan All-American High School Football Team. Few of his high school classmates could ever remember Phillips doing anything wrong. He was universally regarded as sensitive, kind, and caring.

Phillips had been a three-year starter for the Mt. Lebanon Blue Devils football squad. In his sophomore and junior seasons, he played defensive back. As a senior, Phillips took over as the starting fullback for the Blue Devils and led the team to an undefeated season. He piled up 1,112 yards as a ball carrier and receiver and scored sixteen touchdowns. His accomplishments were even more remarkable in light of the fact that Mt. Lebanon's head coach, Ralph Fife, was a disciple of Ohio State's Woody Hayes. Like Hayes, Fife disdained the forward pass, preferring to pound the ball into the line and run occasional sweeps around the ends. Mt. Lebanon's opponents did not have to do much in terms of advance scouting. It was well-known that Fife was going to run the ball—and that Phillips would get the bulk of the carries. For teams playing Mt. Lebanon, the defensive game plan invariably focused on stopping Phillips.

In addition to being named to the Ed Sullivan All-American Team, Phillips was selected for the *Sporting News* All-American High School Football Team and was a member of the Associated Press Big 33 All-State Team. Several prominent collegiate programs came calling with offers of scholarships, Notre Dame among them. Phillips was drawn to Notre Dame from the start. He would be one of a group of seven students from the St. Bernard Grade School graduating class of 1955 who attended Mt. Lebanon High and then moved on to the University of Notre Dame.

For the 1960 football season, Notre Dame's faithful looked for Phillips, then a sophomore, to team up with junior Angelo Dabiero in the backfield. Before the season got underway, however, Phillips suffered a debilitating knee injury that sidelined him for the entire year. He would come back the following season and see considerable playing time as a defensive back for head coach Joe Kuharich. Even after the knee injury, he still possessed the explosive speed that had earned him accolades in high school. However, he no longer had the ability to cut sharply, a trait that had previously allowed him to slip through minute creases in the defensive line.

Though Phillips never regained the form he had shown before his injury, he was a valuable performer for the Irish at defensive back and in limited duty as a halfback. His best year on offense for Notre Dame came in 1962 when he carried the ball 18 times for 38 yards and had two pass receptions. That same year, he also returned three punts and two kickoffs, for a total of 47 yards. Indicative of his status on the team, the photograph of the Notre Dame football team that appeared in the 1961-62 school yearbook shows Phillips sitting in the third row, flanked by team leaders Ed Rutkowski and halfback Charlie O'Hara on the left and Daryle Lamonica and fullback Mike Lind on the right.

After Martin left Notre Dame, he had few chances to speak with

Denny Phillips. Each Saturday during the fall of 1963, however, Martin saw Phillips on television. Denny had graduated with Martin's class in June 1963. Because of his knee injury, however, Phillips had missed the entire football season in his sophomore year. Even though he had already graduated, Phillips was eligible to play one more season of football. For that reason, Phillips remained at Notre Dame during the 1963-64 academic year and took post-graduate courses. Playing primarily as a defensive back that season, Phillips was credited with breaking up 10 passes.[62]

Phillips left Notre Dame in 1964, hoping to play professional football. He reported to the Pittsburgh Steelers' training camp in the summer of that year, auditioning as a defensive back. He remained with the team for the entire camp and was one of the last casualties when the Steelers made their final cuts. He then took a job with Gulf Oil Company in Pittsburgh and, on weekends, often worked as a referee at college football games.

Martin regarded Phillips as a genuine friend and an enthusiastic supporter, as well as the best athlete and one of the finest gentlemen he had ever known. The memory book compiled after Phillips died gives further evidence of the esteem with which others regarded him. To high school classmate Victoria Anderson, Phillips was "this wonderful person." To Bunni Segall, he was "truly a kind-hearted young man." When given the opportunity to speak of Phillips, another classmate, Dan McCown, utters similar words of praise. One of McCown's most distasteful memories of high school had arisen during an otherwise routine lunch period when he dug his fork into a garden salad and discovered a dissected frog leg buried beneath the lettuce. McCown and Phillips had just come from fourth-period biology class. There was no proof, but all signs pointed to Phillips as the culprit. "Kind and gentle," McCown wrote in the memory book. He refrained from adding "mischievous."

Phillips's wife, Pattie Ann, had attended St. Bernard School with Phillips and Martin. She and Phillips had six children together. A devoted and loving wife, Pattie Ann possessed unique insight into the personality lurking behind the heroic facade. She knew that Phillips was devious enough that he might well have planted the frog leg in

Dan McCown's salad. She knew that, at times, Phillips's halo could be ever so slightly tarnished. "You know," she would say to Martin in mock praise, "Denny was the perfect person," suggesting that her husband may have had a few character flaws after all.

When Phillips died, Martin was living in Virginia. Upon receiving the news that Denny had passed away, Martin packed a suitcase and drove to Pittsburgh for the funeral. The priest officiating at the funeral Mass was Charlie O'Hara, Phillips's former teammate at Notre Dame. O'Hara had joined the seminary after graduating from Notre Dame and was later ordained. At the Mass, the organist played the Notre Dame victory march during the distribution of Holy Communion. When the funeral service was over, Martin had an opportunity to talk with O'Hara. The halfback-turned-priest told Martin that Phillips had found a small, seemingly innocuous growth on his stomach. Phillips apparently regarded the growth as insignificant and did not have it checked by a physician until it was too late. The growth proved to be malignant. Death came quickly.

Vivid memories are all that Martin has left from his friendships with Bud Vogel and Denny Phillips. A photograph of the 1953 St. Bernard Grade School football team, co-champions of the South Hills Catholic Grade School League, lies in Martin's desk drawer. The same photograph also occupies a prominent spot on a wall at the Atria's Restaurant & Tavern in Mt. Lebanon, the only picture of a grade school team displayed among an assemblage of high school, college, and professional team pictures. Deeper down in Martin's desk drawer is a picture of Denny Phillips that appeared in the *Washington Post* on Sunday, November 4, 1962. The picture shows Phillips carrying the football for Notre Dame against Navy in a game played in South Bend on the previous day. Notre Dame emerged victorious over Navy and its All-American quarterback, Roger Staubach, 20-12, with Phillips scoring the winning touchdown on a 45-yard pass reception.

With the pictures come a flood of memories. It was Vogel who was on the receiving end of Martin's only touchdown pass for St. Bernard's during the 1953 season. It was Phillips who couldn't contain his excitement after Martin beat a Purdue wrestler to capture his first victory as a member of the Notre Dame wrestling team.

Denny Phillips was a gentle man who sprinted through life sporting a friendly smile and offering a kind word to everyone. Bud Vogel was sometimes shy and sometimes outgoing, but always a caring man with big aspirations—a man who lived life on the edge. To Martin, both Phillips and Vogel were treasured friends. Each had known success on the football field, but neither had allowed football to define them. Nor did they permit the disappointments they had experienced to overshadow their enthusiasm for life.

The deaths of Bud Vogel and Denny Phillips reinforced what Martin already knew—life is both fragile and precious and, regardless of the dimensions of one's dreams, there is a true heroism in responding to the challenges of each day, in extending a kind word to others, and in sharing a smile.

---

[61] The future would validate Vogel's assessment. In 1964, incoming coach Ara Parseghian named Huarte as his starting quarterback. Huarte responded to the challenge, leading the Irish to a 9-1 record and earning the Heisman Trophy. That same season, Snow shed 15 pounds and moved from flankerback to split end. Snow was on the receiving end of many of Huarte's passes and finished fifth in the Heisman voting. Both Huarte and Snow were named consensus All-Americans.

[62] Fifty years after his playing days, Phillips is still ranked sixth on Notre Dame's all-time list for passes broken up during a single season.

Chapter 11
The Imposing Figure of Father McMurtrie

Dick Martin counted himself among the lucky ones. In his years as Bishop O'Connell's wrestling coach, he developed a close friendship with Father James McMurtrie, principal of the school from 1972 to 1977. Not everyone enjoyed that privilege. McMurtrie was a shy man. Some would mistake his shyness for arrogance. Martin himself thought McMurtrie to possess a touch of arrogance, right up until the day in 1974 when Martin buried his mother in Mt. Lebanon, Pennsylvania. As Martin and his family entered St. Bernard Catholic Church on the morning of his mother's funeral, Martin glanced up at the altar and was stunned to see McMurtrie's imposing figure. If there was arrogance, there was also caring.

Martin knew from experience that it was difficult to predict how an individual would react when a friend or acquaintance was in need of solace. Martin sometimes found that individuals whom he expected to be a source of strength had difficulty in offering genuine support and empathy. As the friendship between Martin and Father McMurtrie developed, Martin came to see that McMurtrie was steadfast during times of difficulty or sadness, when others might tend to remain distant. Consistently, the priest would often go far out of his way to comfort those who were experiencing sorrow. McMurtrie seemed to believe that if others were going to allow him the privilege of sharing in their moments of joy, then he was going to share in their sadness as well. He was present for the funerals as well as the baptisms and weddings.

Father McMurtrie died on October 20, 2003. Two months before his passing, Bishop O'Connell High School erected a plaque in McMurtrie's honor at the entrance to the school's football field. The plaque extolled McMurtrie's "extraordinary leadership and commitment to the community of Bishop O'Connell High School."

In the years that followed, Martin often walked past the plaque, occasionally pausing to focus on the reference to McMurtrie's leadership. In times past, Martin had worked under administrators whose leadership skills were deficient, perhaps even non-existent. McMurtrie was not like that. Martin had come to view him as an exceptional leader, a man who inspired others to pursue their dreams with determination. McMurtrie would tell churchgoers on Sunday, "With God, you are everything. Without God, you are nothing." In Martin's view, McMurtrie possessed a unique style of leadership, a style that reflected his complete faith and unwavering trust in God.

There were occasions when McMurtrie exhibited his leadership in a grand manner, such as his well-publicized efforts to refurbish the school's image and lead the school to a firm financial footing. McMurtrie was first assigned to Bishop O'Connell in 1970 as the assistant principal. The school had experienced several years of declining enrollment. By the time McMurtrie was named principal of the school in 1972, enrollment had fallen to 1,100—some 400 students below capacity. Absent a significant increase in the student population, the school was in danger of closing.

Once named principal, McMurtrie embarked on an unprecedented campaign to revitalize O'Connell. He spoke with civic groups to tout the school's academic and sports programs. He made presentations to groups of grade school parents to encourage them to enroll their children at O'Connell. Mostly, however, McMurtrie's efforts were directed at elementary school children themselves. He visited almost every parochial grade school in the counties of Arlington and Fairfax to speak to seventh and eighth graders. He shared his vision for the future with the students. He would tell the children about O'Connell's stellar academic record. He also let it be known that, under his administration, O'Connell intended to develop an athletic program that was second to none.

McMurtrie proved to be an effective salesman. By the second year of McMurtrie's term as principal, enrollment was on the rise. Over time, the school emerged as an athletic power. In the latter years of McMurtrie's tenure at Bishop O'Connell, *The Washington Post* rated O'Connell as the second best school in the Washington, D.C. metropolitan area for athletic achievement, trailing only Winston Churchill High School of Potomac, Maryland. Success on the playing fields led to continued surges in enrollment. By 1977, O'Connell was flourishing. Enrollment had increased to more than 1,600 students. In the span of five years, McMurtrie had almost singlehandedly put O'Connell back on stable financial footing.

Martin believed that one of the keys to McMurtrie's success lay in his willingness to allow others to use their talents effectively. McMurtrie encouraged everyone at O'Connell, teachers and staff as well as students, to take the lead on activities. He was happy to spread the credit for successes and share the limelight. In 1976, a student-led committee was formed to plan the inaugural O'Connell "Superdance," a fund-raising effort to benefit cystic fibrosis research. The driving force of the effort was senior Maura O'Donnell. O'Donnell, who suffered from cystic fibrosis herself, was an honor student and an accomplished athlete. Despite the congestion and breathing difficulty that resulted from her cystic fibrosis, O'Donnell inspired others with her courage and perseverance. During her four years of high school, O'Donnell earned nine varsity letters in field hockey, softball, basketball, and diving. She was a Virginia Independent School state diving champion as a senior.

Funding for cystic fibrosis research was an issue that weighed heavily on O'Donnell. In 1975, the median age of survival for children afflicted with cystic fibrosis was sixteen years. The genetic disease had killed her sister, Brenda, at age 16. It also took the lives of Maura's younger siblings, Catherine and Sean. Maura O'Donnell knew that it was only a matter of time before the disease would likely take her life as well.

McMurtrie had high hopes for the Superdance. He saw the event as equal parts therapy and fundraiser. He knew that O'Donnell was too energetic to stand idle while cystic fibrosis ravaged the lives of children and young adults. The Superdance was a way for O'Donnell to fight back. When planning the initial Superdance, O'Donnell and her classmates relied heavily on McMurtrie for guidance. If McMurtrie was engaged in a late afternoon staff meeting, O'Donnell would have difficulty getting to see him. On those occasions when her patience was wearing especially thin, O'Donnell would stand on the ground outside McMurtrie's second story office and throw pebbles at his window. No matter how busy, McMurtrie would respond in good humor to the pebbles, always making at least a few minutes available for O'Donnell's questions.

With McMurtrie's full and active support, the first Superdance raised $16,000. The result thrilled Martin, though he had long before learned never to underestimate what Maura O'Donnell was capable of achieving. As a former athlete and competitor, Martin could only cheer O'Donnell's endeavors. Martin knew the effort that it took to excel in sports, even without the physical limitations of cystic fibrosis. Moreover, as a survivor of nephrosis, he could identify with O'Donnell's fight against a potentially deadly affliction. When Martin saw O'Donnell competing and winning, whether off a diving board, on the basketball court, or against a killer disease, he could see reminders of his own struggles in athletics and in other venues.

In the years since 1976, the O'Connell Superdance has developed into the single largest school-supported fundraiser for cystic fibrosis research in the United States. It has been held each year since its inception and over the years has raised approximately $3.5 million to combat cystic fibrosis. Maura O'Donnell did not survive to see the full benefits of her work; she died in 1978 at the age of twenty. Nonetheless, the effort begun by McMurtrie and O'Donnell has yielded dramatic results. It has spawned similar fundraising events throughout the U.S. As a result of the medical research that the Superdance and other fundraisers have made possible, the life span for individuals afflicted with cystic fibrosis has increased dramatically. Thirty-five years after the advent of the Superdance, individuals with cystic fibrosis routinely live to be nearly 40 years of age.

Martin deeply admired McMurtrie's efforts to promote financial stability at O'Connell and to raise money for charitable causes. Nonetheless, Martin placed equal value on the leadership that McMurtrie displayed in smaller ways. For Martin, it was the abundant gestures of kindness and concern that distinguished McMurtrie as a leader. During Martin's tenure as O'Connell's wrestling coach, McMurtrie attended each wrestling match that took place in O'Connell's gym. In both substance and style, McMurtrie was supportive of the wrestling program, even to the point of bringing cough drops to the matches. He would give Martin a cough drop at the beginning of each match, knowing that Martin's throat would later be worn sore by the frantic instructions he yelled to his wrestlers.

When Martin gave thought to the attributes that made McMurtrie an effective leader, he invariably came to the conclusion that McMurtrie's most endearing characteristic was the care he showed for others, through the cough drops that he dispensed, the pebbles to which he responded, and the funerals he attended. McMurtrie was available to students and faculty alike, extending encouragement and, when necessary, a dose of discipline.

McMurtrie mixed caring and kindness with a decisiveness that Martin found appealing. When an O'Connell student refused to recite the pledge of allegiance before morning classes, McMurtrie responded by calling the student into his office. Confident in the wisdom of his position, the student told McMurtrie, "I have my rights." McMurtrie responded, "Aren't you on the baseball team?" The student answered—with a touch of smugness—that he did play on the baseball team. McMurtrie told the student, "Not any more. I have a right to take you off the team. That's my right." His voice hardening in a way that suggested there was no alternative, McMurtrie asked the student, "Do you want to re-think the pledge of allegiance?" In a test of his leadership skills, McMurtrie won handily. With his spot on the baseball roster suddenly in jeopardy, the student agreed to recite the pledge of allegiance along with his classmates.

Both before and after his time as O'Connell's principal, McMurtrie worked as a parish priest in the Diocese of Arlington. He once introduced a Sunday homily by telling the congregation, "The best part of my job is that I don't have to drive to work." In McMurtrie's view, the primary benefit of living at the church where he worked was that he did not have to contend each day with the oppressive, sometimes obnoxious, rush-hour traffic throughout the Washington, D.C. region. Without a commute, McMurtrie explained, it was easier to refrain from anger and thereby adhere more faithfully to the tenets of the fifth commandment.[63] On those occasions when McMurtrie did hop into his bright red Jeep Cherokee and drive off, it was most often for one of three reasons—to help out a friend or former student, administer the sacraments, or attend a sports event.

McMurtrie had season tickets for Washington Redskins games. On Sundays when the Redskins were playing at home, McMurtrie routinely braved the afternoon traffic jams near Robert F. Kennedy Stadium to watch Sonny Jurgensen and later, Joe Theismann, quarterback the 'Skins. McMurtrie also had an uncharacteristic tolerance for driving when it came to Notre Dame basketball games. His two brothers, Bill and Alex, had attended Notre Dame. McMurtrie would tell anyone who would listen that, when he was growing up, attending Notre Dame was his fallback in case Plan A, enrolling in the seminary, did not work out.

On March 4, 1977, McMurtrie and Martin had a special reason for driving the 600 miles from Northern Virginia to South Bend, Indiana. The Notre Dame men's basketball team was set to play the University of San Francisco in a much-ballyhooed game on Saturday, March 5. The mood at Notre Dame was upbeat. It had been a harsh winter; the northern portion of Indiana had experienced record cold spells and more than 50 inches of snow during January and February. In stark contrast, the temperatures during the first week of March often reached the 60s and, on some days, soared into the 70s, giving rise to an early spring euphoria.

The University of San Francisco basketball team, nicknamed the "Dons," arrived in South Bend on the Thursday preceding the game, enjoying a hot streak of its own. San Francisco and its towering center, All-American Bill Cartwright, had won all twenty-nine of their games up to that point in the season. The contest was one of the most highly anticipated college games in years. On game day, Notre Dame's Athletic and Convocation Center was rocking well before tipoff. The chant "Twenty-nine and one!" reverberated throughout the arena.

At a campus pep rally the day before the game, Notre Dame coach Digger Phelps had made an impassioned plea for support from the students. "Here is the cheer for tomorrow," he told the crowd, "Twenty-nine and one! . . . Twenty-nine and one!" There was more. "I want all of you here at 12 noon, Saturday," Phelps told the assembly of more than a thousand. "San Francisco will be getting dressed. Start yelling it then and they're bound to hear it."

Phelps had recruited a superb cast of players for the 1976-77 season, good enough to be ranked 14th in the nation in pre-season polls. Leading scorer Donald "Duck" Williams could put up points in a hurry. Forwards Dave Batton and Toby Knight, centers Bruce Flowers and Bill Laimbeer, and guard Rich Branning formed a talented supporting cast. USF featured its own quintet of stars. In addition to Cartwright, the team's starting lineup included six-foot-eight James Hardy and the Redmond brothers, Marlon and Marion, each six-foot-six.

The oddsmakers had installed Notre Dame as a six-point favorite. The consensus was that San Francisco had built its unblemished record on a schedule that was considerably weaker than the competition faced by the Fighting Irish. There was also the fact that Notre Dame had a well-deserved reputation for toppling teams that were riding winning streaks. Most importantly, however, the oddsmakers knew that opposing teams had great difficulty maintaining their composure when they encountered 11,000 screaming Notre Dame fans inside the Athletic and Convocation Center.

Not wanting to leave anything to chance, Phelps had conveniently arranged to take San Francisco's coach, Bob Gaillard, out for drinks on both the Thursday and Friday nights before the game. Gaillard suspected there was a hidden motive underlying Phelps's hospitality. He remarked to a reporter, "Digger has missed curfew two nights in a row now. He waited until he saw himself on all four channels before he kicked me out of his place last night." It was as if Phelps was testing Gaillard's endurance.

McMurtrie and Martin watched the game from seats that were right behind the Notre Dame bench, close enough that when the six-foot-eleven Laimbeer stood up, Martin's vision was blocked. McMurtrie and Martin erupted in applause when Branning, Notre Dame's precocious freshman, scored a basket with 12:18 left in the second half to give the Irish a 61-58 lead. From that point on, Duck Williams took over for Notre Dame. He drove the lane and scored to give Notre Dame a five-point lead, then scored again on a fast break pass from Branning to increase the lead to seven. With 3:44 left in the game, the Irish led by ten. The lead proved insurmountable. Notre Dame cruised to a 93-82 victory.

The atmosphere in the arena was electric. For the last eight minutes of the game, McMurtrie, Martin, and most everyone else in the building had remained on their feet. When the final buzzer sounded, the Notre Dame faithful stormed the court. Almost an hour after the game, the court remained flooded with fans. Later that evening, McMurtrie and Martin, still ecstatic, walked to a post-game party at Digger Phelps's home. The coach was heard to say over and over, "It was a gas, man!"

McMurtrie lived for such times. He lived to see his favorite teams compete and win. He lived to take part in the victory celebrations. He lived to hear a jubilant coach bellow, "It was a gas, man!"

When it came to O'Connell's athletic teams, McMurtrie employed tricks that would have made Digger Phelps proud. A year or so before Notre Dame took on the undefeated University of San Francisco basketball team, O'Connell's basketball team was slated to play local rival Bishop Ireton High School in a semifinal game at the Virginia State Catholic High School Championship in Richmond, Virginia. McMurtrie and Martin had traveled to Richmond to take in the game. The two spent the night before the game sampling the Richmond night life, returning to their hotel at 2:00 a.m. McMurtrie was not yet ready to settle down. He said to Martin, "Dick, let's have some fun." McMurtrie then proceeded to knock on the hotel room occupied by Ireton's basketball coaches. One of the coaches opened the door, at which point McMurtrie said, "Hey, boys, let's have a few drinks." For the next two hours, McMurtrie entertained the Ireton coaches with stories and friendly chatter and, in the process, wreaked havoc on the coaches' sleeping cycle. Perhaps not coincidentally, when O'Connell and Ireton squared off at the Richmond Coliseum the next evening, O'Connell came away with a convincing win.

Away from sporting arenas, McMurtrie had two primary interests: tending to his priestly obligations and helping others. He approached both of those activities, and everything else that he did, with a well-defined sense of humor. When obligated to attend an uninspiring convention of the National Catholic Education Association in New Orleans, he would say to Al Burch—then O'Connell's assistant principal—and Martin, "Stick with me, we'll do this thing in ten minutes." Almost exactly eleven minutes later, McMurtrie, Burch, and Martin would be off to explore the sights of the French Quarter. With or without his priestly collar, McMurtrie cut a fine figure and, in his younger years, could run at a brisk pace. He would sometimes use his foot speed to play pranks on friends. When walking with others, McMurtrie would, on occasion, spontaneously break into a near jog, leaving his companions no choice but to run and catch up or miss out on the fun that McMurtrie was so adept at finding.

To Martin's amusement, women seemed to pay special attention to McMurtrie, particularly when the two were visiting New Orleans. On one occasion, while walking with Martin on Bourbon Street and wearing casual clothes, the priest was approached by a streetwalker. The woman asked McMurtrie if he was looking for a date. Always ready with a snappy response, McMurtrie answered, "Sorry, babe, I'm taken." The streetwalker quickly moved on.

McMurtrie seemed to be constantly constructing things. He was equally adept at building a sense of community in a school or a parish, or building a physical structure. In addition to transforming O'Connell into a prominent and financially successful school, he oversaw the formation of a new parish community, St. Theresa Catholic Church, in Ashburn, Virginia. Bishop John R. Keating, then head of the Diocese of Arlington, appointed McMurtrie as founding pastor of the new parish in 1991. With Keating's consent, McMurtrie named the parish after "The Little Flower," Saint Theresa of Lisieux. McMurtrie chose the name as a way of honoring his mother, Mary Theresa McMurtrie. Father McMurtrie would remain at St. Theresa's for eleven years, transforming the congregation into a vibrant community.

McMurtrie took on a new role after Bishop Keating passed away unexpectedly on March 22, 1998. Four days after Keating's death, the priests in the Arlington Diocese elected McMurtrie to serve as the administrator until Pope John Paul II appointed a new bishop. For a period of nearly a year, McMurtrie functioned as both the pastor of St. Theresa Church and as diocesan administrator, responsibilities which required him to commute each workday from St. Theresa Church to the diocesan offices. In 2002, McMurtrie assumed the position of pastor at St. Agnes Church in Arlington. He took over St. Agnes Church at a time when the parish buildings, especially the rectory, were in need of repair. McMurtrie tackled the renovations with enthusiasm, transforming the living quarters for clergy and the rectory into more hospitable facilities.

In his 41 years as a cleric, McMurtrie worked as a teacher, principal, parish priest, pastor, and substitute bishop. In total, he spent seven years at O'Connell High School, from 1970 until he was reassigned in 1977. He also served as Chairman of the O'Connell Board of Governors from 1986 to 2002. Though McMurtrie never said so directly, acquaintances and friends suspected that his natural exuberance suffered a bit when his tenure at O'Connell ended in 1977.

In the end, however, McMurtrie would surely have been inclined to say, as did Digger Phelps before him, "It was a gas, man!"

On the morning of October 20, 2003, nine days short of his 67th birthday, McMurtrie passed away. He had been hospitalized for a week, as physicians tested for colon cancer. His death was unexpected, the result of infection from septicemia. From the time McMurtrie was admitted to the hospital, his sister, Elizabeth Capetola, served as his primary caretaker. In the latter stages of hospitalization, McMurtrie slipped into a coma. When it became apparent that he was not likely to survive, family members summoned Martin to the hospital. Along with Elizabeth and her brother Bill McMurtrie, Martin maintained a vigil at the hospital. Martin marveled at Elizabeth's deep affection for her brother.

The experience of witnessing Father McMurtrie's final days created a common bond between Martin and McMurtrie's siblings, especially Elizabeth. In Elizabeth, Martin found many of the qualities that had endeared him to Father McMurtrie, most notably the sense of caring and compassion, the easy laughter, and a mischievous sense of humor. Martin found also the loyalty and resolve that Father McMurtrie had shown on so many occasions. As with her brother, Elizabeth's commitment to friends and family was enduring. Like her brother, Elizabeth possessed a talent for cultivating deeply personal relationships.

Martin's 30-year friendship with McMurtrie provided Martin with a unique opportunity to learn from a man who could find joy in the smallest details of daily life. Even the sound of a pebble gently striking his office window could prompt McMurtrie to break out in laughter. More than most, McMurtrie seemed to possess the ability to place his worries squarely in the hands of God. For Martin and many others, McMurtrie's faith provided a template for embracing the uncertainties of life in a more patient and accepting manner.

[63] Taken literally, the fifth commandment instructs observers to refrain from killing others.

Chapter 12
"Will Anybody Stop O'Connell?"

On the evening of December 30, 1998, twenty years after Dick Martin had coached his last high school wrestling match, Martin watched with interest as Bishop O'Connell's wrestlers took on the most potent wrestling teams in Northern Virginia at the annual St. Stephen's and St. Agnes School Holiday Classic Tournament. O'Connell's team was led by coach Bill Carpenter, captain of Martin's 1975-76 team. That evening, it was obvious that Martin's influence extended far beyond Bill Carpenter. Martin looked over at the team from Oakton High School and saw its coach, Harry Van Trees, a member of Martin's 1976-77 O'Connell team. Harry Murphy, captain of Martin's last team, was coaching the host team from St. Stephen's and St. Agnes. The head official at the tournament was Mike Ingrao, O'Connell class of 1972. Martin thought to himself, "This is what coaching is all about." As a teacher and former coach, Martin could not imagine a more fitting testament to the influence that educators have on the lives of their students.

Carpenter, Van Trees, Murphy, and Ingrao were determined, dedicated, and talented scholastic wrestlers. Measured against the many accomplished athletes whom Martin coached during his eleven years as head of the wrestling team, however, the four were not unique. Martin had the good fortune to have many enthusiastic, if raw, wrestlers join his program. Just as Martin had flourished during his high school years under the coaching of "Mr. Lamp" at Mt. Lebanon High, each year a number of accomplished athletes took to the mats and flourished under Martin's tutelage. In terms of work ethic and the desire to excel, Carpenter, Van Trees, Murphy, and Ingrao had plenty of company at O'Connell over the years.

As far back as Martin's first year as O'Connell's coach, 1967-68, the wrestling team possessed considerable talent. O'Connell won eleven matches, lost four, and tied one that season. Mike Pappas (112 pounds), Kevin Kerrigan (157 pounds), and senior Jay Kimmit (180 pounds) won all their matches at the prestigious St. Albans Invitational Tournament that year. Competing against sixteen schools, O'Connell took first place. At season's end, Kimmit was selected as a high school All-American.

In the 1971-72 season, Martin led O'Connell to a 13-3-1 record. Competing at 185 pounds, Bob Carpenter went undefeated in dual matches for the entire season, registering pins against all but two of his opponents. Carpenter had a lot of help. Mike Garcia in the 138-pound class, Ted Breiner (145 pounds), Pat Donohoe (155 pounds), and heavyweight Mike Ingrao were stalwarts throughout the season. Midway through the season, Martin's intensity got the best of him, nearly causing Mike Garcia to quit the team. On a Friday night, O'Connell hosted the wrestling team from Stonewall Jackson High. Martin thought his team should have dominated the match. When the contest ended, however, O'Connell was on the losing end of a 36-15 rout.

After the Stonewall Jackson match, Martin sat the entire team down in the locker room and addressed each individual in sequence. "You quit!" he said to the first wrestler. To the second, he said the same, "You quit!" Proceeding down the length of the entire bench, he uttered the identical words to each wrestler. When Martin reached Garcia, the senior took issue. Garcia stood up, nose to nose with Martin. "I didn't quit," he told Martin emphatically.

Garcia's response infuriated Martin. Incensed, Martin pushed Garcia over a bench and held him down. The skirmish prompted athletic director Floyd Foley to rush in. Foley pulled Martin off of Garcia. Knowing that words would only make the situation worse, Martin said little. He left the building, a dejected man. He had engaged in conduct unbecoming a coach—conduct that his coaching idol, George Lamprinakos, would find unthinkable. Martin went home and explained what had happened to his wife, Chris. He was unsure how he would explain his conduct to others.

Late that same evening, the telephone rang at the Martin home. Garcia's father, who came to all the wrestling matches and knew Dick well, was on the line. He was both angry and perplexed. "Dick, what in the hell did you just do?" Mr. Garcia asked. "I was just an idiot," Martin told him, "There's no excuse. It was totally my fault. I lost my temper." Garcia's father told Martin that his son wanted to quit wrestling. Martin responded, "I hope he doesn't. We have practice tomorrow morning at 9:00 a.m. I will be there at 8:00 a.m. I'd like to talk with Mike. If you would ask him to come, I would appreciate it."

Mike Garcia came in the next morning, but he was seething. Martin could see that Garcia's face was blanched, his anger visible. Martin told Garcia, "I just want to apologize. I was totally wrong. I did think that you had quit, but nothing justifies what I did. I'd like you to stay on the team. I apologize to you and later I will apologize to the team."

When Martin went to practice at 9:00 a.m., Garcia was there. Martin acknowledged that he had let the emotion of the moment get the best of him. As he had promised Garcia, he apologized in front of the entire team. Garcia continued wrestling and, over time, he and Martin were able to patch up their relationship. For a much longer time, Martin remained puzzled as to how he could have allowed his anger to run rampant. For the first time since the day he angrily kicked girlfriend Nancy Rhoades out of his car, he had completely lost control of his emotions. For one of the few times in his life, he was unable to explain or find justification for his actions. He was deeply embarrassed. The incident caused Martin to take stock. He was 30 years old and married with two children. It had been his long-time dream to coach wrestling. He was living out that dream and now, as the result of one intemperate display, he had given the school reason to question his fitness for the job. Upon reflection, Martin knew that, when challenging Garcia, he was reacting with the unbridled instincts of a frustrated competitor, not as a responsible husband and parent whose first obligation was to his family. He also knew that in order to provide for the emotional and financial needs of his family, it was imperative that he exercise restraint in his work and set a positive example in his conduct.

Around the school, Mike Garcia was recognized both for his courage in standing up for himself and for his decision to remain on the team. For Martin, the chatter at school was less approving. It was, Martin knew, a situation that only time could heal. True to form, time did heal the situation, more quickly than Martin could have hoped for. Almost from the morning of Martin's Saturday apology, the team began to flourish. Garcia would go on to have his best season ever. At the finals of the Virginia State Independent School Tournament, Garcia, Breiner, Donohoe, and Ingrao came in first in their weight classes, leading O'Connell to its first-ever state title. With that title, the school cemented its reputation as a powerhouse in the Virginia-District of Columbia-Maryland region. At the St. Alban's Invitational Tournament, held shortly after the Virginia State Independent School Tournament, Garcia was the champion of the 138-pound weight class. At season's end, Garcia's teammates voted him as the team's most valuable wrestler.

Martin resisted the urge to speculate as to whether his mid-season outburst had provided motivation for the team in its march to the state championship. Clearly, the incident had cemented Mike Garcia's position as a team leader, the one wrestler who was not afraid to challenge the coach. Martin supposed that, if anything, the incident may have unified the team behind Garcia, with Garcia's defiance serving as motivation for the entire squad. Mostly, Martin was content not to delve too deeply into the reasons for the team's success, but simply to celebrate that success. For whatever reason, the team had done well. His wrestlers had learned what it took to win.

The 1972-73 squad returned veterans Bob Carpenter, Dennis Caffi, and Steve Strickland. Though Carpenter was sidelined for the first four matches of the season with a leg injury, O'Connell did not miss a beat. Martin led the team to a stellar 13-1-1 record in dual matches, with the only loss coming at the hands of Bishop Ireton in the final match of the season. With Carpenter fully recovered, Martin and his team again competed in the Virginia State Independent School Tournament. This time, however, the team finished third, three points behind Blue Ridge School, a private prep school that had the advantage of being able to recruit the more stellar athletes from other high schools.

Entering the 1973-74 season, Martin held high hopes. He considered incoming freshman Pat McAteer to be a diamond in the rough. McAteer was a different breed—talented but sometimes inclined to be lackadaisical. He came from athletic royalty. His father, a native of

Merseyside, England, had been the middleweight boxing champion of the British Empire in the 1950s. Known affectionately as "Patmac," the elder McAteer had once won 40 consecutive bouts. He finished his professional career with a record of 49 wins, 6 losses, and 2 draws. He had held the British Empire middleweight crown for three years before losing to Nigerian great Dick Tiger in a March 1958 fight decided by knockout.

As a 98-pound freshman, the younger McAteer possessed the potential to be a superb wrestler. However, several other wrestlers on O'Connell's 1973-74 team had the ability to be dominant as well. Junior Joe Morrissey, wrestling at 105 pounds, looked to be one of the top wrestlers in the tri-state area. Behind McAteer and Morrissey, there was a strong supporting cast consisting of Mike Strickland, Tom Breiner, Alex Perwich, Bill Carpenter, Jim Garcia, Andy Mould, and two brothers, Tom and Bill Lawler. The squad lived up to Martin's expectations, finishing the season with 13 wins. The only blemish on its record came in a hotly contested dual meet loss to Blue Ridge. O'Connell and Blue Ridge would meet again in February at the Virginia State Independent School Tournament. In the tournament, Blue Ridge registered $92^{1}/_{2}$ points. O'Connell finished second with 80 points.

Almost from the start of the 1974-75 season, Martin noticed a difference in Pat McAteer. He suspected that McAteer's early success had caused a change in his attitude. The precocious freshman had become, as a sophomore, an unwelcome distraction. His practice habits were sloppy; he lacked the focus that Martin expected. Nonetheless, O'Connell's dominance continued. Martin's 1974-75 team put together a string of ten consecutive wins in dual matches to end the season. Impressive as it was, the winning streak was only the beginning. From mid-December of 1974 to early January of 1978, the O'Connell varsity never lost a dual meet—a streak of 42 meets.

By early in the 1975-76 season, Martin tired of McAteer's attitude and suspended him from the team. "He was loafing," Martin told *The Washington Star*. Even without McAteer, Martin's 1975-76 squad was experienced, deep, and talented. Led by captain Bill Carpenter, and a corps of seven other seniors, O'Connell raced through the season without any serious challenge, winning 15 dual meets in all. In the process, Martin recorded the 100th victory of his coaching career, a 25-19 win over Yorktown High School. Following in the footsteps of his brother Bob, Bill Carpenter wrestled at 185 pounds and proved to be nearly invincible. The team closed out the 1975-76 season by claiming the inaugural Tri-State Catholic Invitational Wrestling Tournament, recording 121.5 points to win the eight-team meet. Bill Carpenter lost his Tri-State Invitational matchup against John Casey of McNamara High, the only defeat that Carpenter would suffer the entire season. Senior Kevin Holley, wrestling in the 98-pound division, helped to compensate for Carpenter's loss with a victory in the Invitational, his twenty-first win of the season.

The following year, McAteer met with Martin before the season began and asked to rejoin the squad. McAteer promised to show greater commitment to the sport and to the team. As the season progressed, it was clear that McAteer was determined to fulfill his promise. In the 1977 Tri-State Catholic Invitational Wrestling Tournament, he defeated all of his rivals to claim a berth in the 126-pound championship match. Along the way, he suffered a painful pinched nerve in his neck. In the tournament final, he was up against a cagey and powerful opponent, Bishop Ireton veteran Pat Richter. Throughout the match, McAteer was in agony, the pinched nerve clearly hampering his efforts. At two different stages, Martin pleaded with the official to stop the match. Despite Martin's pleas, McAteer was determined to finish the match. Each time that Martin attempted to intercede, McAteer told the official he wanted to continue. And each time the action resumed, the crowd roared its approval.

Five minutes and fifty seconds into the match, McAteer pinned Richter for the title. To no one's surprise, McAteer was named the tournament's Most Outstanding Wrestler. It had been a rocky, four-year road to the trophy table for McAteer. In the end, he was able to overcome not only persistent pain and a formidable opponent, but his once rebellious attitude as well.

McAteer was one of the undisputed leaders of the 1976-77 squad, but there were plenty of other key contributors. Harry Murphy, Fred Ball, Joe McGuire, Scott Carpenter, Phil Baltazar, and Bob Kurtzke were stalwarts throughout the season. The team won all 13 of its dual meets; at season's end, the winning streak stood at 38 meets. As the streak progressed, the press began taking regular note of O'Connell's success. Virtually every newspaper article on high school wrestling made mention, in one way or another, of the streak. Bill Newlin, writing in *The Washington Star*, led off an article with the headline, "Everybody's Cry: Beat O'Connell's Wrestling Team." Similarly, Skip Major of the *Arlington Journal* authored an article that appeared under the headline, "Will Anybody Stop O'Connell?" The same question was on the minds of many in Virginia who followed the sport.

As the victories continued, Martin maintained a quiet confidence, proud of the streak but aware that it could end abruptly if the injury bug struck or if the team ran into a more highly motivated opponent. During the streak, there had been several key injuries and illnesses that could have led to defeat. Louis Mack struggled with mononucleosis in 1976. Harry Murphy suffered a dislocated elbow in 1977. McAteer had to contend with his pinched nerve. Other starters sustained injuries that, though more minor in nature, could have left O'Connell vulnerable.

Martin refused to speculate as to how long the streak might continue. His comment at the end of the 1976-77 season was characteristic. "We will have five starters back and there are some good young wrestlers in the program," Martin told the *Arlington Journal*, "but I will have to wait and see what happens." It was difficult to ignore the obvious benefits flowing from the streak. The publicity brought a well-deserved prominence to O'Connell's wrestlers and the school. The significance of the wrestling team's streak was not lost on Father McMurtrie, Martin's boss, mentor, and friend. McMurtrie was impressed with Martin's usually cool, well-practiced demeanor under pressure and his knack for pumping up his wrestlers at precisely the right moment. McMurtrie liked to think that he—or at least his cough drops—also played a role in the team's success. As the winning streak mounted with each successive meet, McMurtrie's presentation of a cough drop to Martin before each match took on the aura of a superstitious ritual, an essential prelude to victory. Even after McMurtrie's tenure as O'Connell's principal ended in June 1977, McMurtrie still made an effort to attend O'Connell's wrestling matches, always with cough drops in hand.

On a wintry December evening in 1977, as the O'Connell wrestlers prepared to take on Langley High School in a home contest, Father McMurtrie handed Martin the traditional cough drop. For the better part of four years, the cough drops had been magical. The winning streak stood at 42. The chatter in the school hallways and in the press focused on the significance of win number 43. Martin's wrestlers knew that, in addition to competing against Langley, they were also competing against history. The wrestling team's 42 consecutive victories had tied the school's all-time winning streak set by O'Connell's baseball team during the 1963-65 seasons. In the years since 1965, the baseball teams that had set the record were spoken of in almost reverential tones. Baseball players Bart Steib, class of 1963, and Pat Laing, class of 1965, were entrenched as local heroes.[64] When talk turned to "the streak," there was no need for elaboration; everyone at O'Connell knew the reference was to 1963-65. In addition to McMurtrie, O'Connell's new principal, Al Burch, and the former athletic director, Floyd Foley, were on hand to witness the wrestling team's potentially historic match against Langley. The presence of Burch carried heightened significance; it was Burch who had been the baseball coach during the 1963-65 seasons. The 42 consecutive wins was a record of which Burch was rightfully proud.

Langley came out aggressively. In the opening match of 98-pounders, Langley's David Cascio pinned Tony Fontana of O'Connell. Next, Langley sent James "Nabi" Michaels up against Freddie Ball in the 105-pound class. As Martin commented later, Ball "just never got started against their kid." Two matches into the meet, Langley looked strong. At that point, Langley proceeded to forfeit matches at 112 and 119 pounds, putting O'Connell ahead 12-10. However, Langley's Steve Ouellette defeated O'Connell's John Washko on points, putting Langley back in front. Langley followed with three straight pins, and the rout was on. In the final match of the evening, O'Connell's John Schmidt pinned Stuart Morrison of Langley, but it was too little, too late. The final tally stood Langley 39, O'Connell 22.

It was a crushing defeat for Martin and his team. Afterwards, in the O'Connell locker room, there was visible frustration and more than a few tears. When he spoke to his wrestlers, Martin took responsibility for the loss. Martin had focused on the significance of the winning streak in his pre-match comments. He had bought into the hype, portraying the contest as more than a routine dual match, more like a match to make history. In comments to newspaper reporters, Martin speculated that the specter of victory number 43 may have been too overwhelming for his wrestlers. "Everybody in the school was very aware of that record and the fact that a win would have broken the old record," Martin told the *Arlington Journal*. "I think the kids were too psyched," he said. Martin speculated that perhaps he had not done enough to shield his team from the pressure of establishing the new mark.

Martin also thought back to his role as the architect of O'Connell's wrestling schedule. When lining up opponents, he had briefly considered arranging the schedule so that the attempt to win number 43 would come against a less formidable opponent. In the end, however, he had chosen to play it straight. He purposely composed the schedule so that his team would have to take down Langley in order to set the school record. Martin was conscious of the risk involved. He had seen the Langley team in action; he knew his wrestlers might not match up well.

Martin determined that the next time, if there were to be a next time, he would make a better effort to keep his wrestlers grounded and to avoid pre-match comments that hinted of an expected celebration. Of more pressing concern, Martin had to find a way to quickly restore the team's focus. Langley was history. In a few days, O'Connell would take on the Bishop McNamara High team. Martin knew that his wrestlers possessed the talent to beat McNamara handily. He also knew that if his wrestlers were still lamenting the loss to Langley, they could be easy prey for McNamara. The thought provided ample motivation. Before the match, Martin reminded his wrestlers that a loss to McNamara would further tarnish the team's season. In the end, Martin's concerns were unfounded. From the outset, his team wrestled with uncommon determination, as if to show that the loss to Langley was a fluke. O'Connell cruised to a 51-2 win. The headline in O'Connell's student newspaper read, "Wrestlers Beat McNamara, 51-2, To Start New Streak."

For Martin, there would be no new streak of any significance.

Having been appointed as assistant principal for student life in September 1977, Martin was ready to devote all of his attention to the challenges of that office. The 1977-78 season would be his last as coach of the wrestling team. He finished his coaching career by leading O'Connell to victory over fifteen other schools in the St. Albans Invitational, with a slim half-point margin over the second-place school. The championship was O'Connell's fourth St. Albans Tournament victory in Martin's eleven years as coach. His teams had also claimed one Independent School Virginia State Championship, three Tri-State Championships, and three Northern Virginia Christmas Tournament Championships. Overall, Martin's teams won 132 dual matches during his tenure as coach, lost thirty-one, and tied three.

Martin's angry reaction to the loss to Stonewall Jackson High during the 1971-72 season proved to be an isolated incident, never to be repeated. On those occasions when Martin would speak to his wrestlers about the privilege of competing for O'Connell, the incident was never far from his thoughts. Martin would remind his wrestlers that there was honor in competing well. He suggested that, long after finishing high school, they would remember the losses with greater clarity than their victories. Martin spoke from experience. When he thought back to his own high school wrestling career, one of his most prominent memories was his loss in the semi-finals of the 1959 Western Pennsylvania Interscholastic Athletic League regionals. Decades after that loss, it still pained him to think that he had wasted a commanding 4-0 lead over his opponent, the muscular Dugan boy.

Years after Martin's last season as O'Connell's wrestling coach, one of his former wrestlers, Harry Van Trees, introduced his son to Martin. Van Trees said to his son, "This is the man who taught me everything that I know about wrestling." Van Trees and others often spoke of Martin's observations about life and the world outside O'Connell High School. When Richard Nixon resigned as President in 1974—a casualty of his attempt to cover up White House involvement in the 1972 break-in at the Watergate headquarters of the Democratic National Committee—Martin would impress on his wrestlers and students in his English classes, the need to take responsibility for one's mistakes. When Martin would receive a report that a wrestler's academic grades were slipping, he would use the occasion to repeat the lesson he had heard so many years earlier from his own high school wrestling coach, George Lamprinakos. Echoing Lampy, Martin would tell his wrestlers that if they worked at their studies, they could find the same exhilaration in the classroom that they experienced after winning a wrestling match.

With the passage of years, the coach grew, as did his wrestlers. Martin emphasized that his wrestlers should not dwell on the losses so much as on the lessons learned from those losses. Martin shared a few of those lessons in his comments when he was inducted into the O'Connell Athletic Hall of Fame in 1993. Martin's first wrestling coach, George Lamprinakos, and Lamprinakos's wife, Bea, had traveled from Pittsburgh for the induction ceremony. With Coach Lamp in attendance, Martin told the story of his first conversation with the coach nearly 40 years earlier. Martin would chuckle as he told listeners, "This is the man who said basketball wasn't my sport." Lamprinakos took delight in listening to Martin recount the story, marveling at how a few well-timed words had made all the difference in the life of his former protégé.

Over the years, Martin has seen ten members of his wrestling teams inducted into the O'Connell Hall of Fame. The most recent—and most gratifying—occurred in June 2013, when Mike Garcia, O'Connell class of 1972, was inducted. Upon learning that Garcia had been selected for the Hall, Martin called Garcia to offer congratulations. During the course of their telephone conversation, Garcia asked Martin to serve as his presenter at the ceremony. Before responding to Garcia's request, Martin felt the need to make sure that there were no hard feelings left over from their locker room encounter years earlier. With that incident clearly in mind, Martin said to Garcia, "We've had our differences, Mike." Garcia replied, "No big deal, Coach." Martin then told Garcia that he would be delighted to present him at the induction ceremony. The two talked for a few more minutes before saying goodbye.

For Martin, there was profound satisfaction in hearing Garcia's words, "No big deal, Coach." He marveled at how painful moments can be transformed into opportunities for growth. There was no question that Garcia had grown. So had Martin.

Martin is proud of the 42 straight wins. He remembers the cough drops from McMurtrie and the victory celebrations. However, what he remembers most of all is his encounter with Mike Garcia after O'Connell's disappointing loss to Stonewall Jackson. The incident forced Martin to look at himself and take stock. He wanted to be a coach who molded his wrestlers, a man who engendered respect, not fear. Martin resolved always to remember that he was coaching teenagers, not seasoned professionals. He resolved to find a better way to release his emotions when frustration began to mount.

---

[64]Steib was named the most valuable player on the 1963 baseball team. He went on to play baseball and basketball for the College of William and Mary and, in 1972, returned to O'Connell as a teacher and coach. Laing was a pitcher for O'Connell's baseball team continuously from 1963, when the streak began, until 1965, when the streak ended. During his three years on the team, Laing won 16 games and lost only one. During his senior season, 1965, Laing pitched a perfect game for O'Connell. He later played for the University of South Carolina.

Chapter 13
Four Glasses of Bourbon

Martin vividly remembers the spring day in March 1977 that his friend and mentor, Father McMurtrie, drove away from O'Connell for a meeting with McMurtrie's boss, Bishop Thomas J. Welsh, head of the Diocese of Arlington. Over the previous four years, Martin had grown ever closer to McMurtrie. The two could talk about most anything. McMurtrie placed great trust in Martin and pushed him to expand his résumé. In 1976, when the position of athletic director at O'Connell came open, McMurtrie appointed Martin to the post, knowing that Martin would be able to successfully balance the duties of athletic director with his existing responsibilities as wrestling coach. McMurtrie saw the summons to report to Welsh's office as an ominous sign. Naively, Martin expected that McMurtrie's meeting with Bishop Welsh was simply routine. McMurtrie knew better. Forty-five minutes after McMurtrie drove off from O'Connell, he was back at the school. Upon returning, McMurtrie called Martin and assistant principals Al Burch and Sister Maria Virginia into his office. He opened a cabinet and pulled out a bottle of Virginia Gentleman bourbon and four glasses. With tears running down his face, he filled the four glasses.

For a short interlude, the room was quiet. Then McMurtrie spoke. "I'm being transferred," he said to those assembled.

Hours before McMurtrie poured the Virginia Gentleman, hours before his meeting with Welsh, McMurtrie had called Martin on the telephone. "Dick, I want to take a walk with you," McMurtrie told Martin. Martin hung up and grabbed his sport jacket off the hook in the cramped office that he occupied as athletic director. He was anxious, knowing that McMurtrie was not accustomed to taking walks during the school day. The two met at the front of the school. They went up Little Falls Road, and took a right onto Trinidad, a right onto 26th

Street, and then a final right onto Underwood, circling the school that McMurtrie loved.

"I think I'm being transferred," McMurtrie told Martin as the two walked. Martin was shocked. McMurtrie was a fixture at O'Connell. He had done so much for the school. McMurtrie continued, "I'm going to tell you something. I want you to go to school and get your master's degree. I think you would make a great administrator."

Within two months, McMurtrie was gone. He relocated to the neighboring city of Alexandria, Virginia as the newly appointed pastor of St. Louis Catholic Church. Burch assumed the position of principal. At McMurtrie's urging, Burch appointed Martin as his deputy, with the formal title of assistant principal for student life. With his appointment as assistant principal, Martin relinquished his duties as athletic director. However, for that one year, 1977-78, he continued as the school's wrestling coach, his final year of coaching. As a condition of his promotion, Martin would have to obtain a post-graduate degree. Almost immediately, he applied for admission to the master's program in school administration at George Mason University in Fairfax, Virginia. On the verge of turning 37, Martin found himself back in school.

Adjusting to the routine of attending classes, reading homework assignments, and writing papers was more difficult than Martin could have imagined. The carefree days of attending classes at Notre Dame were long gone. There were three fun-loving children in the Martin home, Kelly, age 9, who was in fourth grade; Kimberley, age 7, who was in second grade; and one-year-old Kerry. Each demanded the time and attention of their equally fun-loving daddy. When enrolling in the master's program, Martin had little idea of the emphasis that would be placed on researching and writing papers. In one span of three months in 1979, he had to write seventeen papers. The task of typing the papers fell to Chris. Chris's mornings were occupied with preparing breakfast for Kelly, Kim, and Kerry. Then, armed with a bountiful supply of typing paper, typewriter ribbons, correcting tape, and erasers, Chris would spend her days typing Martin's school papers, while also caring for infant Kerry. It was a life that Chris enjoyed. When she needed a diversion, Chris would take time out to indulge her artistic flair, often painting colorful cartoon characters on the walls and ceilings of the children's bedrooms.

Martin would put in a full day at O'Connell, first in his capacity as assistant principal and then as wrestling coach, before heading to George Mason for night classes. The drive to George Mason University was tedious, requiring Martin to navigate rush-hour traffic along Braddock Road for ten miles. When O'Connell closed for the summer months, Martin worked the day shift as a salesman at a local Duron Paint store to supplement the family's income. There were days when Martin's eyes seemed to shut as soon as he had plopped himself down in his chair in the George Mason classroom. On some days, the only glimpses he would have of Kelly, Kim, and Kerry came when he was eating dinner with the family before his night class and, then again, upon his arrival home as the children were preparing for bed. It was a particularly frenetic stage in Martin's life, one that he was glad to leave behind in 1979 when he received his master's degree. When Martin would take the time to reflect on the additional career options that the degree opened up for him, however, he was especially grateful to Father McMurtrie for having pushed him to undertake graduate studies.

Once Martin settled in as O'Connell's assistant principal, he found the work to be both challenging and enjoyable. For a period of seven years, from September 1977 to June 1984, Martin and principal Al Burch were a formidable duo. O'Connell students referred to the pair as "Batman and Robin," with the taller, stouter Burch playing the role of Batman and the shorter Martin cast as Robin. Both former jocks, they were known as no-nonsense administrators but with a sense of humor.

Over time, the relationship between the two frayed a bit, most noticeably in the early 1980s when reports surfaced that one of O'Connell's varsity coaches and an assistant had permitted members of their team to consume beer and watch adult movies during an extended trip to compete against schools in the southern part of Virginia. Martin believed the coaches should be relieved of their duties. Burch, the coach of the powerful O'Connell baseball teams of the 1960s, preferred lesser sanctions. In the end, Father Bill Davis, the diocesan superintendent of schools decided to terminate both the baseball coach and the assistant.

In spite of the conflict over the coaching situation and other occasional disagreements, the partnership between Burch and Martin endured, even flourished. For students and faculty alike, the two created an atmosphere that proved to be both productive and largely enjoyable. Their methods often defied convention.

Burch was particularly unorthodox in the way he sorted through candidates for teaching positions. When a gentleman once applied to teach physical education, Burch cut to the chase quickly. He asked the candidate, "Can you teach wrestling to P.E. classes?" The applicant responded that he could. Not convinced, Burch asked the man if he knew the wrestling hold called "the pretzel." "What's the pretzel?" the man responded. Martin jumped in, "You know, the guillotine." The applicant said, "Yeah, I know the guillotine." Burch asked, "Do you think you can get out of the pretzel?" The applicant said, "Yeah, man, I can get out of the pretzel." Burch then glanced at Martin. "Dick, put him in the pretzel," Burch directed. Martin hadn't seen it coming. "What?" he exclaimed. "Yeah, go ahead!" the candidate said. Martin turned to the applicant and said, "Take your coat off and get down on all fours."

The candidate seemed to welcome the direction the interview had taken; in business attire, the five-foot-five Martin could be mistaken for a pushover. The gentleman took off his suit coat and got down on all four limbs on the office floor, allowing Martin to apply the guillotine. Not so long removed from his wrestling days, Martin applied a sturdy hold around the candidate's neck and leg, locking the man in place. The gentleman struggled mightily but could not break Martin's hold. When it became clear that the man's efforts were futile, Martin released his grip. The applicant got up off the floor and put his coat back on. After taking his seat in the chair, the applicant saw Burch shaking his head. "Can't hire you," Burch told him. "Why not?" the man asked. "You didn't get out of the pretzel," Burch responded.

The candidate's inability to break out of the pretzel was not, in itself, a fatal flaw. There were other deficiencies that detracted from the gentleman's résumé. However, Burch and Martin were each left with the sense that, in his eagerness for the job, the man had overstated his knowledge of wrestling.

Martin favored action. Burch tended to deliberate more over events and possible outcomes. Most often, their differing temperaments complemented one another, as when it came to evaluating teaching candidates whose qualifications were suspect or determining how to deal with disruptive students. The two functioned as a team. Together, they proved capable of handling any crisis. They effectively responded to situations where coaches had turned a blind eye to the conduct of their players. Burch tended to view the code of student conduct as a flexible standard. Martin was more inclined to enforce the school's rules as written. In the case of student misconduct that might warrant dismissal, Burch would lean toward giving the student a second chance; Martin was less tolerant of aberrant behavior and less willing to extend second chances. To reconcile the two conflicting approaches, Martin developed the framework for what became known as the "Strict Disciplinary Probation Program." The essence of the program was that a student found to have engaged in conduct that warranted dismissal would have the opportunity, during a probationary period, to demonstrate his or her commitment to complying with school rules. Students who satisfied the terms of the probationary period would be restored to non-probationary status.

Over time, Burch and Martin became intimately familiar with each other's inclinations. Martin found that it did not take long to grow into the position of assistant principal. He felt fortunate that Father McMurtrie had prodded him to pursue a career in school administration. For the most part, Martin enjoyed playing "Robin" to Burch's "Batman." The two made the system work. They developed the willingness to make concessions and the ability to reconcile any conflicting views that might arise. In lighter moments, the two would find amusement in telling the story of how Burch had instructed Martin to put a prospective P.E. teacher in the "pretzel," Burch's own term for the classic wrestling move known as the guillotine. They never tried that approach again, a tacit admission by both that there were better methods for evaluating the competency of candidates.

Chapter 14
Professor of Love

*I*n *June 1982, Mother Teresa of Calcutta traveled across the United States, from the East Coast to the West Coast, to tell her story and spread the gospel of love. On June 1, Mother Teresa spoke to the students and faculty at Bishop O'Connell High School, followed by commencement addresses at Thomas Aquinas College in Santa Paula, California on June 5 and at Harvard University on June 9. In her speeches, Mother Teresa told of meeting a family in Venezuela that had donated a plot of land for use by her Missionaries of Charity. One of the children in the family was a small disabled boy with beautiful shining eyes. Mother Teresa told her audiences that she had never seen anyone so handicapped. Upon meeting the child's mother, Mother Teresa asked the child's name. The mother responded, "We call him the 'professor of love' because he keeps on teaching us how to love."*

By the early 1980s, Dick Martin thought he had seen it all. He had survived his encounter with nephrosis, shared a beach with Grace Kelly, buried his father, mother, and older brother. He had met Heisman Trophy winner Leon Hart, traveled throughout Europe, and met Hall-of-Fame baseball player Willie Mays. Martin had married a woman whom his physician-father had delivered at Pittsburgh's Saint Joseph Hospital. He had seen the birth of three beautiful daughters. He had guided the Bishop O'Connell wrestling team to a record-tying, forty-two consecutive victories in dual matches. Nothing he had experienced, however, prepared him for Mother Teresa's visit to O'Connell.

Mother Teresa often expressed her distaste for overseas travel. She would have preferred to remain at home in Calcutta with her fellow nuns and continue her work among the impoverished segments of India's population. Nonetheless, Mother Teresa frequently traveled outside India to tell the world about the work of her Missionaries of Charity and to raise funds to support their efforts. From 1981 until Mother Teresa's death in 1997, a woman named Sandy Andreas McMurtrie was Mother Teresa's friend and traveling companion. As a relatively young woman, Sandy Andreas McMurtrie was married to Bill McMurtrie, one of Father McMurtrie's two brothers.

Sandy McMurtrie came from money. Her father, Dwayne Orville Andreas, became chief executive officer of the Archer Daniels Midland company in 1971. He served in that capacity for twenty-five years, transforming Archer Daniels Midland into the largest processor of farm commodities in the United States, a company with annual revenues exceeding $12 billion. Along the way, Andreas cultivated the acquaintance of government leaders, influential politicians, and individuals from all sectors of society. Among the individuals whom Andreas counted as friends were Pope John Paul II, former president Richard M. Nixon, long-time Speaker of the House Thomas "Tip" O'Neill, and Hubert H. Humphrey, the vice president of the United States from 1965 to 1969. O'Neill and Dwayne Andreas were regular golfing partners. O'Neill once said of his friend, "He's a real gentleman, although he's not much of a golfer." Thomas Dewey, the former Republican governor of New York who lost the 1948 presidential election to Harry Truman in a stunning upset, was one of Andreas's closest friends. Dewey served as a lawyer for Archer Daniels Midland for many years after he left political life.

When Dwayne Andreas was once confronted with an unexpected speaker's vacancy for a high-level seminar on foreign trade that he was organizing in New York City, he placed a hurried call to Richard Nixon at the former president's residence in San Clemente, California. Within hours, Nixon made arrangements to attend the seminar as a guest speaker, asking only that Andreas keep his attendance a secret until the seminar was held. It is said that Hubert Humphrey took Dwayne Andreas along with him on nearly every overseas trip that he made during his time as vice president. Sandy McMurtrie herself once served as Humphrey's appointments secretary when he represented the State of Minnesota in the U.S. Senate.

Dwayne Andreas and his wife, Inez, and daughter Sandy, were particularly fond of Mother Teresa and were extremely supportive of her efforts on behalf of the poor. In return, Mother Teresa went out of her way to accommodate the Andreas family when circumstances permitted. With the enduring ties between the Andreas family and Mother Teresa, coupled with the affinity of Sandy and Bill McMurtrie for O'Connell High School, Mother Teresa did not have to be coaxed into making time for a visit to O'Connell.

Roughly two hours before Mother Teresa was to address the O'Connell students, Martin received a telephone call from the Arlington County police. "You have Mother Teresa coming over there?" the officer asked. "Yes," Martin responded. "Well, there is a threat on her life," the officer said. "Oh God, you've got to be kidding me!" Martin replied.

For Martin, the message from the police presented a new and frightening experience. The school had an emergency evacuation plan for responding to catastrophic events, but there was no emergency plan for dealing with death threats. Burch and Martin had to do some quick thinking. There was a lot to consider. Time was running short. There were only two viable options, either cancel Mother Teresa's speech or proceed as planned and hope for the best. Mother Teresa was no stranger to death threats. When she had first established her home for the dying in an abandoned building in Calcutta, angry mobs staged protests and issued death threats against her. The mobs accused Mother Teresa of launching a secretive campaign to convert Hindus to Catholicism. Mother Teresa's response to the death threats in Calcutta was to ignore the threats, persist in her work, and seek opportunities to extend the love of Christ to the individuals who had made the threats.

Burch and Martin knew that a death threat would mean little to Mother Teresa. Her entire history suggested that she was not one to cower. Rather, she found a fearlessness in her faith, often quoting chapter 43 of the book of *Isaiah* to her audiences, as she did in her visit to Harvard University. "I have called you by your name," she would recite to her audiences. "You are mine. Water will not drown you. Fire will not burn you." Burch and Martin had to consider other factors aside from the immediate consequences for Mother Teresa. To proceed with the speech could place O'Connell's students at risk. On the other hand, canceling the event would deprive the students of one of the most memorable experiences they would ever have. Whatever their decision, Burch and Martin knew the impact on the students would be significant.

Police had no way of gauging whether the threat was a hoax. The caller had provided no clues as to his identity or location. If the threat was more than a hoax, everyone at the school could be at risk. After consulting with the police, Burch and Martin decided to proceed with the event. They also determined not to burden Mother Teresa by telling her of the threat. To avert the possibility of panic, Burch and Martin informed only the members of the school's administrative staff. News of the threat was not communicated to either faculty members or students.

Mother Teresa spent the hour before she was to address O'Connell's students resting in the convent that adjoined the school. Martin met her in a convent waiting room. One of the O'Connell nuns introduced Martin to Mother Teresa. "Good morning, Mother Teresa," he said, "I'm Dick Martin, assistant principal for student life." Mother Teresa stood up, took a few steps toward Martin and said, "It's an honor to meet you." "No," Martin responded, "the honor is all mine." The legendary nun was much smaller than Martin had anticipated and distinctly frail in appearance. The two talked for a few minutes, then Martin left to make final arrangements in the school auditorium. Foremost in his mind, Martin prepared for what he would do if the death threat proved to be more than a hoax.

When it came time for Mother Teresa to address the students, she ascended to the auditorium stage along with Bishop Welsh, Martin, Burch, the school chaplain, Father Mark Pilon, and the assistant principal for academics, Sister Margaret Mary. Martin and Burch sat in an alert mode on the stage, each scanning the auditorium for any sign of a shooter. An Arlington County detective dressed in plain clothes stood to the side of the stage, out of sight. On the auditorium floor, another plain-clothed officer kept watch over the audience, while administrative staff members maintained a vigilant lookout for anyone who did not appear to be either a student or teacher.

Mother Teresa addressed the O'Connell students for twenty minutes. Speaking largely without notes, she told of the unbounded love that she had seen in others. She told the story of a newly married young couple in Calcutta who had once presented her with a large amount of money. "Where did you get this money?" Mother Teresa asked. The response surprised Mother Teresa. "We decided not to buy wedding clothes, not to have a wedding feast, but to give you the money to feed the poor," they told her. To appreciate the significance of that act, Mother Teresa told her audience, it must be remembered that it is scandalous in India not to have a wedding feast and not to purchase wedding clothes. Still curious, Mother Teresa asked the couple why they chose not to have a wedding feast. They responded, "We loved each other so tenderly, we wanted to give each other something special, and that special something was that big sacrifice."

Another gift, considerably smaller in size but motivated by an equal amount of love, came from a four-year old Calcutta boy. The boy had learned that Mother Teresa's nuns had exhausted their supply of sugar. The boy told his parents, "I will not eat sugar for three days. I will give my sugar to Mother Teresa." Three days later, the boy and his family came to Mother Teresa's residence carrying the boy's gift of a small bottle of sugar. Mother Teresa also told of the time that a man had come to see her with an urgent request. "There is a family with eight children who have not eaten for a long time," the man said. "Do something for them." Mother Teresa quickly took some rice and brought it to the mother of the children. Mother Teresa could see big black lines under the eyes of the children, an unmistakable sign of malnutrition. Upon receiving the rice, the mother took it and left the room, only to return a few minutes later. Upon her return, Mother Teresa asked, "Where did you go?" The mother explained that she had gone to the home of a neighbor to share some of the rice. "They are hungry, also," the mother said. The most amazing aspect of the mother's act of sharing, Mother Teresa commented, was not that she was willing to share the rice but, rather, that she had noticed that the family next door was also suffering. "In a suffering like that," Mother Teresa observed, "very often we have no time to think of others."

Anecdote by anecdote, Mother Teresa illustrated the depth of love that she had found in a city swarming with individuals in desperate need. At the conclusion of her speech, Mother Teresa walked off the

O'Connell stage to a thunderous applause. The would-be assassin was nowhere to be found.

On that remarkable June day in 1982, Martin found that his thoughts flowed in quick, random succession. He was alternately apprehensive, awestruck, alert, and, in the end, fatigued. Even as Martin was shaking Mother Teresa's hand during their early morning meeting at the convent, he was fretting about the death threat. Nonetheless, he sensed a calming presence, as if Mother Teresa possessed an unshakable sense that she was exactly where God wanted her to be. Martin drew inspiration from Mother Teresa's uncompromising commitment to the unique mission that, in her view, God had carved out for her. For Martin, more than thirty years later, the thought of Mother Teresa's visit to O'Connell continues to conjure up a wide range of diverse emotions—terror, amazement, serenity and, ultimately, relief.

In an era when school security was minimal and when an individual intent on inflicting harm would have had little difficulty entering O'Connell's facilities, so much could have gone wrong. Instead, everything about Mother Teresa's visit unfolded perfectly. From beginning to end, the saintly nun offered a crash course in sharing the love of God with others. Mother Teresa's visit served as a tangible demonstration of the joy that she derived from caring for "her poor."

For Martin and the entire O'Connell community, June 1, 1982 provided an unparalleled opportunity to learn from the one person in the world who could most authentically lay claim to the title, "professor of love."

Chapter 15
Yes, There Really Is A Kalamazoo

Martin had a bad feeling about the conversation almost from the beginning. The caller was a dentist, the father of a senior at Monsignor John R. Hackett High School. "Hey, Dick, my son is ineligible for tennis," the parent said. Martin replied, "I am sorry to hear that." The dentist continued, "He's a good kid, just slips up here and there, but he's a good kid, and he's got a chance to win a scholarship. He's got a couple of big matches coming up. It would be great if he could play." Knowing what seemed certain to follow, Martin agreed that it would be great if the boy could play, but quickly added, "You're not asking me to change any grades here, are you?" "Well ...," replied the dentist, his voice trailing off.

By 1984, after seven years as assistant principal at O'Connell, Martin was eager to try his hand at running a school on his own. Al Burch was entrenched at O'Connell and would not be retiring any time soon. Martin's preference was to remain in Northern Virginia. Early on, he had ruled out working at a public school, a decision that significantly narrowed the available opportunities. At the time, the Diocese of Arlington had just completed the purchase of a facility in Fairfax, Virginia that had previously served as the campus for George Mason University. Bishop Welsh had already announced plans to use the site to establish a new high school named in honor of Pope Paul VI.

Martin called Welsh to let the bishop know of his interest in being considered for the position of principal at Paul VI High School. The two met. Welsh informed Martin that, if he were to select a lay person as principal, Martin would be in the top tier of candidates. However, the bishop also stated that, for financial reasons and to reinforce the school's identity as a Catholic institution, he hoped to appoint a member of a religious order as principal.

Martin crossed Paul VI off his list and broadened his search. He interviewed for the position of principal at Benedictine High School in Richmond, Virginia and was offered the position. However, Benedictine was a military school. Martin was leery of the rigid environment. It also concerned him that Benedictine was not co-educational; the Martin girls would likely have had to attend an all-girls school. The arrangement did not appeal to any of Martin's daughters, so Martin declined the offer. Martin was also offered the position of principal at Linton Hall School in Bristow, Virginia, but the proposed salary fell below his compensation as assistant principal at O'Connell.

In the spring of 1984, Martin applied for the position of principal at Monsignor John R. Hackett Catholic Central High School in Kalamazoo, Michigan. During the introductory interviews, Martin met individually with three members of the Hackett board of directors. Each interview lasted an hour. After Martin returned home to Virginia, he received a call from the school informing him that the board of directors wanted him to come back for another round of interviews.

Martin was intrigued and returned to Kalamazoo for what would be the second phase in the interview process. Upon walking into the school library, the site of the interviews, Martin was stunned. There were 50 people crammed into the library, all apparently poised to interview him. The group included members of the school board, teachers, parents of students, and members of the Kalamazoo community. Martin took a seat in front of the crowd. After extending a brief welcome to Martin and others in attendance, the chairman of the school's board of directors invited the crowd to write questions for Martin on sheets of paper. The papers were passed to the chairman, who read the questions aloud and waited for Martin to respond. It was an experience unlike any other in Martin's professional career. At the conclusion of the session, Martin was equal parts flabbergasted and irate. He kept his thoughts to himself, but felt the board of directors had violated common courtesy by staging what amounted to a town hall meeting.

The experience notwithstanding, Martin was eager to land the job. He wanted the experience of being a principal. He planned to accept the position if it were offered. Within days after the "interview" in the library, the chairman of the board extended an offer. Martin discussed the offer with his wife, Chris, and she helped him to assess the advantages and disadvantages. When Chris proved receptive to the move, Martin met with Father D'Ag to seek advice. D'Agostino was encouraging. "Take a shot," he urged. Martin decided to accept the offer. First, however, he had to resolve the issue of salary. The pay that Hackett initially proposed was less than Martin's assistant principal's salary at O'Connell. Martin held out for more money. The school then increased the pay to a more attractive level, and Martin accepted.

On the day that Martin was to sign his contract with Hackett, he and his family stayed at the home of Martin's brother, Bill, in Ann Arbor, Michigan, a three-hour drive from Kalamazoo. Martin made the trip to Kalamazoo, met with members of the school board, signed the contract, and returned to Ann Arbor. Upon walking into his brother's home, Martin received a telephone call from one of the Hackett directors. "We've just discovered a bill for yearbooks for $12,000 that was due a year ago," the director stated. "Do we have your permission to pay it?" he asked.

Martin was perplexed. For the second time in two months, he was thrown into what he felt was a very unfair situation. First, it was the interview conducted by a random assortment of 50 individuals. Now, barely three hours into the job, he was being asked to spend money to cover a sizeable debt that arose on someone else's watch. Martin wondered what other surprises might be waiting.

In July 1984, with the start of the new academic year less than two months away, Martin relocated to Kalamazoo with daughters Kelly and Kim, both of whom would be enrolling at Hackett, Kelly as a junior and Kim as a freshman. Chris stayed behind in Virginia with Kerry to oversee the process of selling the family's home. Upon arriving in Kalamazoo, Martin lived for a time in an otherwise unoccupied dormitory at Kalamazoo's Nazareth College. He later moved into the rectory at a local parish. In the weeks before the start of school, Kelly and Kim stayed at a convent until Martin was able to find a house to purchase.

Early on, Martin learned that there was an abundance of conspicuous wealth among the Hackett families. The presence of wealthy families did not come as a shock. The real surprise came when Martin discovered that the school was $365,000 in debt. Once again, he could not help feeling that he had been misled. During the interview process that led to his hiring, school officials had informed him that the school was in debt but suggested that the debt was in the neighborhood of $50,000. After several meetings with the school's bookkeeper and members of the board of directors, Martin learned the truth: Money was going out at a much faster clip than it was coming in.

As Martin surveyed the school's budget, he knew that there would have to be severe cuts in both the school's programs and in the faculty. He knew, as well, that it would be essential to persuade wealthy families to increase their donations. Some parents gave freely. Others expected favors in return. When the father of the Hackett tennis player appealed to Martin for help in keeping his son eligible for the team, the parent said to Martin, "I have been a supporter of Monsignor Hackett for years. This is only your first or second year here. You're a new guy."

New guy or not, Martin was not willing to play along. Martin told the dentist, "I am the principal of this school. If any principal would do this, they ought to fire him."

Other Hackett parents were blunt as well. One parent asked Martin to fire the school's baseball coach. "Why?" Martin asked. The parent said, "Look at the won-lost record." Martin responded, "There's got to be more to it than that." The parent said, "Dick, I think you should remember who signs your contract." Martin replied, "I know who signs my contract. You see that door behind you? I want you to leave right now." The parent left, but not before attempting to clarify his stance. He said to Martin, "You can forget about any more ..." Martin did not let him finish the thought. "Fine," he told the parent, "Get out of here."

Weighed down by the budgetary crisis, Martin would look back on the factors that had led him to Kalamazoo. He had come a long way from his job scraping boats in Cape Cod. From his earliest days of wrestling for Coach Lamprinakos at Mt. Lebanon High, Martin thought it might be rewarding to work as a wrestling coach. Then, after his tenure as coach, teacher, and athletic director at Bishop O'Connell, he decided to become assistant principal—with a push from Father McMurtrie. That decision led to his occupying the post of Assistant Principal for Student Life at O'Connell from 1977 to 1984. When it came time to pursue a principal's position, Martin evaluated the available opportunities and concluded that Hackett represented his best option for advancement.

Initially, Martin had great hopes for his tenure at Hackett. Even after the realization that the school was seriously in debt, Martin remained optimistic. He liked the fact that the school was Catholic. He knew there were segments of the Hackett community that he could call on for financial and moral support. Before he had completed his first year in Kalamazoo, however, Martin would begin to question whether he had been too hasty in taking the position. To his mind, Hackett was in the midst of an identity crisis. Martin found constant tension between a sector of the community that wanted to make the school an elite private—but not necessarily Catholic—institution and those who wanted the school to be more overtly Catholic. In his first few days at Hackett, it had dawned on Martin that none of the school's classrooms had crucifixes. One of his first actions upon taking over was to have a crucifix installed on the front wall of each classroom. With that small act, he signaled his intention to honor the core Catholic beliefs upon which the school had been founded. The significance was not lost on those who would have preferred that Martin downplay the school's affiliation with the Catholic Church.

Martin's next step was to focus on the budget. He had the good fortune to come in contact with a woman named Lynn Tecca. Tecca had been employed with a bank in West Virginia and had moved to Michigan with her husband when he changed jobs. Her credentials were impeccable, her references enthusiastic. Martin liked the fact that a former supervisor had described her as "mentally tough." It was helpful, also, that Tecca had received high marks in positions where she had to deal with budgetary problems. Martin persuaded Tecca to join his staff as Hackett's business manager. The hiring paid dividends almost immediately. Tecca was meticulous and thorough, and she possessed an extraordinary grasp of the intricacies of budgets. On the nights before board meetings, Tecca and Martin would stay at the school until midnight to make sure that Martin was fully prepared on the issues that might arise. Invariably, when the hands of the clock closed in on midnight, Tecca would stand up, pat Martin on the back, and say, "Now go ahead and look brilliant."

In the environment that Martin inherited, the effort to "look brilliant" was a constant struggle. Inexplicably, the Hackett bookstore had lost $50,000 in the year before Martin's arrival. As best as Martin could determine, the loss was due to loose management or sloppy accounting. The bookstore was not the only school activity that was hemorrhaging money, only the most conspicuous. The financial statements painted a picture of an organization whose coffers were riddled with gaping holes in virtually every major category of the budget.

Once Martin fully understood the dire budgetary crisis, he realized that there would have to be significant cuts in programs and personnel. In his first year alone, Martin found it necessary to slice eight positions from the payroll, including the full-time athletic director, other staff members and various teachers, some full-time and some part-time. He cut programs such as classes in fine arts, some foreign language classes, a few minor sports, and some extraneous electives. He also imposed a freeze on his salary as well as the salaries of all teachers and other staff. The moves sent ripples throughout the Kalamazoo area.

To Martin, the changes that he had instituted were drastic but imperative. Perhaps later, if the financial outlook improved, he could restore the programs that were cut. For the present, however, Martin saw no other option. Nonetheless, the budget cuts drew the ire of many, including some of the teachers, a wide cross-section of parents, and some members of the school's board of directors. With each cost-cutting measure, the reaction was swift. Opponents of the reductions were vocal and caustic. To Martin's chagrin, however, no one offered a more realistic approach for dealing with the debt.

Martin understood that there would be opposition to his budget cuts. He failed to realize, however, the intensity of the opposition. His oldest daughter, Kelly, who spent her last two years of high school at Hackett, was in a better position to appreciate the antagonism that had developed. Ever the protective child, Kelly would later tell Martin that there were times when she feared that opponents of the budget cuts might threaten him with physical harm in order to hasten his departure from Hackett.

The difficult times at Hackett caused Martin to recall the experiences of Father McMurtrie at O'Connell. When McMurtrie started as principal at O'Connell in August 1972, the school was in trouble. Revenue from tuition was falling. Student enrollment had dropped precipitously. From 1972 to 1977, Martin had watched as Father McMurtrie instituted bold, aggressive changes to combat the falling enrollment. Martin assumed a similarly aggressive attitude in his efforts to lead Hackett toward financial stability. He quickly realized, however, that his constituency in Kalamazoo was vastly different than the population with which McMurtrie had to work. The Bishop O'Connell community was dispersed over the Washington, D.C. metropolitan area and represented a wide range of ethnic, social and economic backgrounds. In contrast, a significant percentage of the students at Hackett were the children of professionals employed by the prominent Kalamazoo pharmaceutical manufacturer, the Upjohn Company. There was a perception in the Kalamazoo community that the city's public schools offered an inferior brand of education. As a consequence, many Upjohn employees and other Kalamazoo families were hesitant to trust the public schools with the education of their children. For those parents who were seeking to send their children to a private high school, Hackett was one of the few options available in Kalamazoo.

A long time before Martin and his family migrated to Kalamazoo, Upjohn had pioneered and patented a unique process that made possible the large-scale production of cortisone. In subsequent years, a group of Upjohn chemists perfected a process for preparing cortisone from a soybean steroid. In 1974, Upjohn introduced the anti-inflammatory agent, Motrin, to the United States. Within ten years, Motrin accounted for 40% of Upjohn's earnings. Bolstered by its successes with cortisone and Motrin, Upjohn and its workforce exerted a large influence over the city of Kalamazoo.

For Martin, Upjohn's presence meant that the changes he implemented at Monsignor Hackett were invariably scrutinized by an organized, vocal and affluent sector of the Kalamazoo population. In that environment, the risk of offending potentially important allies was far greater than the risk that Father McMurtrie had faced at O'Connell. The relationship between Martin and the members of Hackett's board of directors, several of whom were Upjohn employees, became testy at times. There were occasions, also, when Martin's relative inexperience in school administration exacerbated the tensions—occasions when a more diplomatic, less confrontational approach might have soothed personalities and resolved disputes.

Martin found, also, that individual members of the faculty were less mature than one would expect. One evening late in the spring semester, Martin arrived at the school's administrative offices near midnight, hoping to get some work done in preparation for the next day's activities. As he walked down the school's main corridor, he saw a light on in one of the classrooms. Intending to turn the light off, he entered the classroom and noticed a small paper bag lying on the teacher's desk. At the far end of the classroom, there were two adults kneeling, attempting to hide. When Martin asked the intruders what they were doing, the two stood up. Martin recognized them as members of the school faculty, one a religion teacher, the other the band director. The two bolted out the classroom door without responding and fled from the school.

Finding pursuit to be futile, Martin remained in the classroom and examined the paper bag. It contained a single item—a condom. The apparent intent of the two faculty members was to embarrass a fellow teacher who conducted classes in the room, the expectation being that the teacher would remove the contents of the bag while students were seated in his class. Outraged at the incident, Martin advised the diocesan superintendent the next day that he planned to discharge the two faculty members. The superintendent concurred with Martin's decision.

After speaking with the superintendent, Martin called the two teachers into his office and demanded an explanation. They told him that they were making a joke. Martin told the two that he failed to see any humor in the situation. He then advised them that their employment contracts were being terminated. The band director asked Martin, "How are you going to have a band for the graduation ceremony?" Martin responded, "That's not your problem." Martin then placed a call to nearby Western Michigan University and arranged for members of the University band to provide musical accompaniment for the graduation exercises.

Martin spent three years at Monsignor Hackett, 1984 to 1987. When looking back at his time in Kalamazoo, he found the experience beneficial. He learned valuable lessons about managing school politics. With Lynn Tecca's capable guidance, he succeeded in balancing the budget. He was proud of putting the school on a solid financial footing. Martin took pride, also, in reestablishing the school's Catholic identity and streamlining the curriculum. He also witnessed the success of Hackett's athletic teams, most notably the football squad.

Led by head coach Dick Soisson and his sidekick, assistant coach "Big John" Rapacz, the Hackett football team had long been a powerhouse in southwest Michigan. Rapacz, a product of Kalamazoo High School, played an especially important role in Hackett's gridiron success. Standing six-foot-four and weighing 252 pounds, Rapacz was a throwback to the days of "three yards and a cloud of dust." Big John was born in 1924 and had come of age while World War II was raging. In 1945, at the age of 21, Rapacz served on active duty with the U.S. military. After his discharge, he played football for the University of Oklahoma, where he developed into a consensus All-American at center and linebacker. Upon graduation, Rapacz signed to play professionally with the Chicago Rockets of the All-American Football Conference. From 1950 to 1954, he played for the New York Giants. When not playing football, Rapacz earned a living as a professional wrestler. He often competed against the 424-pound Frenchman, André René Roussimoff, known professionally as André the Giant.

Rapacz was 60 years old when Martin took the job at Hackett. The first thing that Martin noticed, aside from the man's intimidating size, was that one of his eyes looked glassy, seemingly not moving in concert with his other eye. The next thing that Martin noticed was his rather uncomfortable gait. Big John attributed the "rogue eye" to being poked during a wrestling match. The awkward walk, he would explain, was a result of the constant pounding that came from his lifelong participation in football and wrestling. If Rapacz's knees produced the creaking sound expected of an aging athlete, his heart was sprightly and expansive. His experiences had left him with an abundance of stories—and he could tell a story with the best of them. He talked of André the Giant. He talked of growing up in Kalamazoo during the Great Depression. He talked of competing against Otto Graham and other football stars of his generation.

Rapacz was fond of his beer and told stories that, if true, would have ranked him among the most prodigious beer drinkers in the state of Michigan. One story had him in Detroit wrestling André the Giant. After the match, Big John made the three-hour trip back to Kalamazoo in the car of an acquaintance. A thirsty man under normal circumstances, Rapacz was especially thirsty after having battled the man whom wrestling insiders called "the Eighth Wonder of the World." Rapacz claimed to have consumed fifty-two bottles of beer during the trip. Upon arrival in Kalamazoo, Rapacz emerged from the car steady and upright and with another story to tell.

It was not the "rogue eye" or the creaky knees or even the spirited stories that Martin found most fascinating about Rapacz, however. Rather, Martin was drawn by the inherent contradictions between appearance and reality. Rapacz's size would lead listeners to expect a gruffness in his speech, but his voice was mellow, if not soft. His background would lead one to expect a rough, perhaps hardened outlook on life, but Rapacz exuded kindness and caring. His stature as a former big-time athlete might cause onlookers to expect an individual with an ego; instead, Rapacz was humble to his core. His physical stature suggested an individual who might exhibit little interest in understanding the ways of the heart, but Rapacz took the time to get to know people. He possessed uncanny insight into human nature, a quality that served as a healing agent during the times that Martin would find himself in need of counsel and understanding. In those times when the conflicts at Hackett seemed so monumental and the rewards so slim, Martin was grateful for the friendship and support of Big John Rapacz.

After three years as the principal at Monsignor Hackett, Martin was ready to move on. His efforts to balance the budget had taken a toll. Martin found the internal politics at the school to be disturbing. There was a segment of teachers at the school who were supportive of Martin's efforts. Just as many teachers, however, resisted Martin's initiatives to cut costs. There was one dispute with teachers that spilled outside the school walls, leading the superintendent of schools for the Kalamazoo diocese to schedule a mediation session. During the course of the mediation, Martin became particularly incensed at some of the inflammatory comments made by the teachers' representatives. "If this keeps up," Martin was heard to say, "heads will roll." In a matter of days, Martin's statement appeared in an article in Kalamazoo's daily newspaper, the *Kalamazoo Gazette*. Publication of the quote further exacerbated the tension between Martin and a portion of the teachers at Hackett.

Martin left Monsignor Hackett in the summer of 1987. At his departure, the *Kalamazoo Gazette* had nothing but kind words for Martin. An editorial that appeared in the June 12, 1987 edition of the newspaper stated,

> We've been tremendously impressed with the work Dick Martin has done as principal at Hackett Catholic Central High School. So has the rest of the community. All of Dick's friends in the community—and he's made a wealth of them—are invited to give him the kind of a sendoff appropriate for a man who has done so much for young people.[65]

Despite the words of praise, Martin was eager to put his experiences at Hackett behind him. He found it difficult to shake the feeling that school officials had misled him from the start. He faulted the Hackett board of directors for their lack of candor concerning the school's finances. Martin had surmised that when he was hired, Hackett was compelled to consider candidates from outside Michigan because the school's troubles had scared off prospective candidates from within the state. Martin himself would never have accepted the position at Hackett in 1984, especially for his first job as principal, if he had been aware of the staggering debt facing the school.

In his final days in Kalamazoo, Martin met with a local lawyer to ask whether he might have grounds for a lawsuit against Hackett for misrepresentation. The lawyer concluded that Martin likely had ample grounds for suing the board members who had misrepresented the budget situation. Ultimately, Martin decided against taking legal action, primarily because it would have required him to make frequent trips back to Kalamazoo for depositions and court appearances.

With his tenure at Hackett over, Martin moved his family back to Virginia. He took the position of principal at Holy Cross Regional School in Lynchburg. For Martin, it was a difficult transition, a transition made more challenging by the fact that he was the first lay person ever to serve as principal at the school. Teachers, administrators, and students had to adjust to the notion of a lay principal at the same time that Martin was adjusting to a new institution in an unfamiliar locale. To complicate matters, Martin had to contend with increasing tensions at home. During their three years in Michigan, Martin and his wife, Chris, had begun to experience difficulties in their relationship. The difficulties continued in Lynchburg. At various points, Martin and Chris participated in marriage counseling sessions. In 1988, Father McMurtrie, then pastor of Holy Spirit Church in Annandale, Virginia, had traveled to Lynchburg to meet with Martin and Chris. He spent time talking with them, both individually and jointly, but his efforts were of little help. The couple also consulted with a marriage counselor in Roanoke, Virginia, but their differences continued.

Martin's three daughters were his first priority. With Chris and Martin in the same household, the girls had prospered. Martin hoped to keep the marriage intact. Chris, however, did not. She had made it clear that she no longer had any desire to be married. From her perspective, the marriage was finished. With reconciliation out of the question, Martin and Chris separated in 1989. At the time, the couple's two older daughters, Kelly and Kim, had already left home for college, with Kelly enrolled at Martin's *alma mater*, Notre Dame, and Kim at the University of Virginia. Twelve-year-old Kerry was still living at home.

Chris moved out of the family home and took a separate residence in Lynchburg. By agreement, Kerry moved with her mother. Martin agonized over Kerry's situation; it pained him to see her leave. For a brief period, Martin considered petitioning the court for shared physical custody. After mulling over the situation, however, Martin concluded that Kerry would have a more stable life if she were to live with her mother full-time, instead of rotating between the homes of Martin and Chris. Martin settled for bi-weekly visitation with Kerry, spending every other weekend with her until she turned 18.

In the weeks following the separation, Martin experienced the loneliest period of his life. Up to that point, he had shared a residence with family or friends at every stage of life since his birth. Suddenly, he was living by himself in the family's large house in Lynchburg, a city that even under the best of circumstances held little attraction for Martin. In those days of living alone, he had never known his house—any house—to be so quiet. The emptiness magnified the sound of every creak in the floor and every trickle of water in the overhead plumbing. To make matters worse, in the weeks after Chris and Kerry moved out of the house, a prolonged rainfall left several inches of water and mud in the basement. No longer having the luxury of calling on his family for assistance, Martin summoned a man named Rick, the head of maintenance at Holy Cross. After several hours with an industrial vacuum, Rick and Martin removed the muddy water and debris. Neither could do anything, however, to repair Martin's sense of detachment from the area; any fondness that Martin felt for Lynchburg was irreparably ruptured the day the basement flooded.

A year after Chris and Martin separated, Chris filed for divorce. By early 1990, the 23-year marriage was over. The couple's separation agreement cited "irreconcilable differences." It could have said so much more. Chris and the family had followed Martin to Kalamazoo. When Martin's employment situation in Kalamazoo proved less than desirable, Chris packed the family up again and moved to Lynchburg. In Lynchburg, the marriage crumbled. Chris began to assert her independence. For twenty years, Chris had been the supportive wife. She was behind the scenes when Martin coached his O'Connell wrestlers to 42 consecutive wins and when Martin earned his Master's degree. She was behind the scenes when Martin was named principal at Monsignor Hackett High. Chris was talented and smart, the salutatorian of her high school class. She yearned to show that she could succeed on her own.

By 1996, youngest daughter Kerry was in college and living on her own. With no children left at home and no particular attachment to Virginia, Chris relocated to the island town of Ocracoke, North Carolina, located in Carolina's Outer Banks. The sunsets over Ocracoke's Silver Lake Harbor are unparalleled in their beauty, but there was a price to be paid for that beauty. The town numbered fewer than a thousand residents. The prospects for making new friends were limited. Nonetheless, Ocracoke served as Chris's home from 1997 until her death in 2010. During Martin's infrequent conversations with Chris, she never explained her reasons for the move. For reasons unknown, Chris seemed to feel at home in the isolation of Ocracoke.

There was a time when Martin and Chris were genuinely in love.

Martin once had occasion to show some older family photographs to his three daughters. He produced three aging photo albums containing pictures of Martin and Chris in their younger days together. There were pictures of summer vacations and pictures of Chris hosting end-of-season parties for the O'Connell wrestling teams. More often than not, the pictures captured joyful looks on the faces of Martin and Chris. The photos revealed a closeness between the two that was undeniable. Upon seeing one picture in particular, daughter Kerry was moved to say to her father, "You know, Dad, it's kind of fun to see that you two guys really liked each other." Martin replied, "We loved each other." "What happened?" Kerry asked. Martin turned cryptic. His failed marriage was a complicated issue that he was uncomfortable sharing with anyone, even his daughters.

In the aftermath of the separation, Martin felt, more than ever, a need for a familiar support system. He could picture Father McCarren, years earlier, placing his five fingers on the table and saying, "Dick, you need structure." Martin's closest friend in Lynchburg was lawyer Greg Britto, the gentleman whom Martin had relied upon for legal advice regarding his separation from Chris. After the separation, Martin and Britto would get together periodically for beers. Aside from Britto, Martin did not have any close ties to individuals in Lynchburg. He needed friends with whom he could share experiences. Martin called Al Burch at O'Connell and inquired about returning to the school. The timing was right on both ends. Burch wanted Martin back as an assistant principal; Martin was seeking a way out of Lynchburg. The two agreed that Martin would come back to O'Connell for the 1989-90 school year as assistant principal for student life, with primary responsibility for oversight of disciplinary matters involving freshmen and sophomores.

Once back in Northern Virginia, Martin renewed old friendships. He moved into the bottom floor of the home of his friends, Patrice and Joe Connolly, both of whom were teachers at O'Connell. Patrice taught religion classes; Joe taught calculus. Later, when Patrice gave birth to son Tim, Martin served as the boy's godfather. Years earlier, Joe Connolly had been Martin's assistant wrestling coach. In the period from 1972 to 1980, Connolly had coached the boys' tennis team at O'Connell, guiding the Knights to several State Catholic Championships. Connolly was also instrumental in starting a girls' tennis team at O'Connell.

Martin renewed his friendship with Steve Johnson, a man who both humored and comforted Martin in times of uncertainty. Initially, Johnson, like Martin, had been a teacher in O'Connell's English department. Later, Johnson became a member of O'Connell's security staff. In all, he spent 35 years at the school. He was the self-proclaimed king of O'Connell recycling, a title that brought no tangible rewards, only tedious work. After every school day, Johnson would walk to all of the trash bins in the school and gather up the aluminum soda cans that students and staff had tossed away. Periodically, he hauled the cans to a local recycling center, receiving cash in exchange for the cans. He would then donate the money he gained to the school to support student projects.

Martin's relocation to Northern Virginia was not without difficulty. He sought out the help of Sister Glenna Smith, a Catholic nun and psychotherapist who worked with Benedictine Counseling Services in the town of Bristow, Virginia. Martin came to Sister Glenna with specific objectives in mind. He wanted to gain a better understanding of his own personality and inner self. He hoped to use the knowledge and insights that he gained to become a more open and giving person and a better parent to his children. Initially, he visited with Sister Glenna once a week for a period of a couple of months, then two times each month. Martin found that one of the great benefits of talking with Sister Glenna was her insistence on complete honesty. She declined to make judgments and never told Martin how to think. Over time, she simply asked an abundance of relevant questions that required Martin to look candidly at the direction that his life was taking. After asking her questions, Sister Glenna would let Martin draw his own conclusions. With Sister Glenna's help, Martin learned to be more gentle with both himself and others.

The exposure to Sister Glenna helped to produce another beneficial change. With Sister Glenna's encouragement, Martin became more willing to critically examine long-entrenched behavioral patterns. In the past, Martin had shown a tendency to go easy on himself when it came to conduct that society judged as tolerable. He could be fiery with his wrestling team as long as the final product was a victory. His behavior with family members could tend to be domineering at times. He could enjoy alcoholic beverages on weekends as long as he continued to function productively. Especially when it came to his drinking, Martin had shown a tendency to avoid the hard questions. He had become adept at identifying solutions that did not require him to examine the inner layers of his personality. Along the way to self-awareness, Martin took up the habit of reciting the *Serenity Prayer* each day. Widely attributed to an American theologian and Lutheran minister, Karl Paul Reinhold Niebuhr, the *Serenity Prayer* asks three things of God: the gift of serenity, to accept the things that cannot be changed; the gift of courage, to change the things that can be changed; the gift of wisdom, to distinguish between the two.[66]

Martin did not have to look very deeply to identify what could be changed. Well into Martin's adult years, his colleagues considered him to be the life of the party when he was having a few drinks. It was a reputation in which Martin found little satisfaction. He recognized that, dating back to his youth, the times when he found himself in trouble were times that usually involved alcoholic beverages. Sister Glenna had purposely refrained from broaching the topic of Martin's drinking, recognizing that if Martin were truly honest with himself he would question his reliance on alcohol.

Martin reached that point shortly after his return to O'Connell in 1989. Now by himself and without the presence of Chris and the children, Martin knew he was vulnerable. More significantly, he was haunted by the difficulties experienced by his oldest brother, Jimmy, who had waged a losing battle with alcohol addiction for much of his adult life. Jimmy had fathered eight children. His addiction deprived him of the ability to enjoy the significant events in the lives of his children. Addiction also robbed Jimmy of the capacity to help his children through their own difficulties. More than anything else, Martin wanted to be present for his children during times of need. He saw his social drinking as, potentially, an impediment to a vibrant and rewarding relationship with his children. It was a situation he resolved to fix. Over time, he stopped drinking completely.

For Martin, the years from 1984 to 1989 were, to a large degree, unsettling. On a personal level, the rupture in his relationship with Chris proved heartbreaking. On a professional level, Martin encountered one stressful situation after another in his time at Monsignor Hackett. However, the years in Kalamazoo were a beneficial stage in Martin's professional development. He had solved the school's budgetary crisis. He had left the school in much better circumstances than it was when he had taken the job. And if the *Kalamazoo Gazette* had exaggerated somewhat when it reported that Martin had made a wealth of friends in Kalamazoo, it is true that he departed Michigan with more friends than adversaries.

---

[65] "A Leader Moves On," *Kalamazoo Gazette*, 12 June 1987.

[66] Most historians attribute the following stanzas of the *Serenity Prayer* to Niebuhr:

> God, grant me the serenity
> to accept the things I cannot change;
> courage to change the things I can;
> and wisdom to know the difference.
>
> Living one day at a time;
> enjoying one moment at a time;
> accepting hardship as the pathway to peace;
> taking, as He did, this sinful world
> as it is, not as I would have it;
> trusting that He will make all things right
> if I surrender to His Will;
> that I may be reasonably happy in this life
> and supremely happy with Him
> forever in the next.
>
> Amen.

Chapter 16
Mice, Mischief, and Miracles

Steve McGraw is a Catholic priest serving as the parochial administrator of St. Anthony of Padua Church in Falls Church, Virginia.[67] He relies on Aristotle to explain the sequence of events during the spring of 1984. McGraw notes that Aristotle had famously proclaimed, "Knowledge is not virtue." Thus Father McGraw reconciles the Serra Award for Excellence in Religious Study that was bestowed on him at O'Connell's graduation ceremonies with behavior that, at times, looked to be decidedly non-virtuous. Indeed, after McGraw was presented with the Serra Award at graduation, his fellow seniors howled—a recognition that while his excellence in the classroom was constant, his grasp on virtue was more tenuous. Though never rebellious in the classic sense of the term, Father McGraw had his moments. There was a scuffle with a fellow student early in his senior year in which McGraw directed a wild haymaker at his classmate. Then there were the mice.

Al Burch retired as principal of Bishop O'Connell at the end of the 2003-2004 academic year. Burch's retirement paved the way for Martin to become principal. He was named the first principal under a newly established president-principal model for the start of the 2004-2005 academic year.[68] In addition to his duties as principal, Martin's workload included teaching one section of his literature course, *The American Dream Revisited*.

Martin's prior experiences had prepared him well for the responsibilities of principal. He doubted there could be any more disturbing situation than the death threat against Mother Teresa or any more surprising situation than the sudden influx of mice in the school's hallways, courtesy of Steve McGraw.

McGraw's mice had caught everyone by surprise. At first, someone noticed a lone mouse, then multiple mice. In quick succession, a

Spanish teacher reported being bitten by a mouse, then came word of another mouse bite. In the middle of third period, Principal Al Burch took to the school's public address system to announce that there were 84 mice at loose in the school. Burch had assumed the worst. Logic dictated that if the intent was to honor the class of '84, nothing less than 84 mice would do.

Shortly after Burch's announcement, Steve McGraw began to notice the suspicious looks of his classmates. He sensed that it was only a matter of time before either "Batman" or "Robin" would catch up to him. Demonstrating a clarity that had been lacking hours earlier, McGraw decided it would be better to find Martin before Martin found him. Thus the two, assistant principal and student, met in Martin's office.

"Did you put a mouse in my office?" Martin asked.

"I put two of them in your office, sir," the student replied sheepishly. McGraw saw no point in mentioning the other 19 mice that he had unleashed at random throughout the building.

With compelling logic, McGraw assured Martin that the early report of 84 mice was greatly exaggerated. Eighty-four mice would certainly have required a crew of accomplices. McGraw had acted alone—unless one counted his friend, junior Karen Frye. More accessory than accomplice, Frye had brokered the deal that brought the repentant McGraw to the meeting with Martin.

After grilling McGraw, Martin called in the school's long-time science teacher, Sandra O'Shea, to look into the question of whether McGraw's mice would produce babies. O'Shea was a bit of a renegade, her loyalties difficult to predict. Once, beset by unwanted piles of pigeon droppings outside the rooms occupied by the religion department, Al Burch had directed the school's maintenance staff to place poison at the spot where the pigeons congregated. Outraged at the prospect of wanton killing, O'Shea protested the use of poison. She encouraged her students to do the same. O'Shea generated petitions in support of the pigeons, collecting the signatures of sympathetic students. Her petitions were not universally welcome. Countervailing signs soon sprouted in the school cafeteria encouraging Burch to "Kill the Pigeons." The controversy soon died out, as did the pigeons.

When it came to McGraw's mice, O'Shea tried to be helpful, possibly out of concern that the mice, like the pigeons, were at risk. She contacted the pet store where McGraw had purchased the mice and confirmed that McGraw had bought only twenty-one mice. More importantly, she learned that all of the mice were male. This revelation eliminated the concern that McGraw's mice might give birth to even more mice.

Dealing with one crisis after another, Martin would sometimes engage in morbid humor. "What next?" he would ask rhetorically. Even somewhat insignificant decisions could raise thorny issues. On one occasion, the chair of the school's science department instructed a male student who came to school with pierced ears and temporary studs to report to Martin's office. The student was in violation of O'Connell's dress code, which prohibited males from wearing earrings while in school. The student asked Martin for an exception to the rules because removing the studs prematurely would cause the piercings to close up. Martin's solution was to have the student cover up the studs with small strips of adhesive bandage while the student was on school grounds. The decision did not sit well with the science department head. As Martin thought about the situation, he knew that, in the years when he was a teacher and before becoming an administrator, he would likely have taken the same view as the department chair. As a school administrator, however, Martin felt more compulsion to attempt to balance both the underlying purpose of the rule and the student's situation. Though not favoring earrings on male students, Martin also knew that it would cost the student another $50 if he had to have his ears pierced again. He was not willing to impose that cost on the student.

Often, the disciplinary situations that Martin encountered were clouded by vague details and conflicting testimony. On many occasions, Martin was compelled to assume the role of sleuth to determine the responsible parties. One of the first crises Martin encountered as a teacher at O'Connell followed almost immediately upon what should have been a triumph. At Christmas time, the school's practice was to encourage the students to decorate their home rooms with a festive holiday display. The school awarded a $50 prize to the home room that was judged to have the best decorations. As the assigned teacher for freshman home room 111, Martin challenged his students to win the contest. The students went all out; their enthusiasm pleased Martin. The effort was especially gratifying because, at the conclusion of the contest, home room 111 was declared the winner. After the end of the contest, however, Martin learned that many of the decorations that the students brought to the classroom had been stolen from local stores. Martin ordered the students to return the $50 prize. Then he brought them out to the football field in their ties and sport coats and instructed them to run wind sprints until they had reached the point of exhaustion.

In a situation that arose after Martin became principal, the existence of videotape helped Martin to assess responsibility. On Friday night, November 3, 2006, O'Connell's football team traveled to Fairfax, Virginia to play Pope Paul VI High School in what would be the last game of the season for each team. Located approximately ten miles from O'Connell, Paul VI draws students from the same elementary schools as does O'Connell, leading to a natural rivalry. The football season had been disastrous for O'Connell. Entering the game against Paul VI, O'Connell's record stood at 1-8. A victory over Paul VI, however, would restore some of the luster. For the Paul VI Panthers, a win would give them a winning record for the season and a fitting conclusion to the school's "Senior Day."

Late in the game, with O'Connell trailing 23-19, the Knights' sophomore wide receiver Doug Howard caught a touchdown pass to put O'Connell ahead by two points. The point after attempt failed, leaving O'Connell with a 25-23 lead. With the game clock winding down, Paul VI had the ball on O'Connell's ten-yard line and was threatening to score. Before Paul VI could put the ball in play, however, time expired. O'Connell's team walked off the field with an emotional victory.

En route to their locker room, some O'Connell players and other students ran over to the Paul VI bench and exchanged words with their opponents. A fight broke out. Few, if any, punches were thrown, but there was considerable pushing and shoving. The skirmish lasted for less than a minute before the players were restrained. Afterward, Paul VI coach Pat McGroarty approached Martin and said, "Dick, that was deplorable." It was Martin's first inkling that there had been a scuffle. Darrell Snyder, O'Connell's athletic director, told Martin about the fight and indicated that O'Connell's players were responsible. Martin immediately went to the Paul VI locker room to apologize but was denied entry. A guard standing outside the locker room told Martin, "You're not welcome here."

The reactions of McGroarty and Snyder left Martin with a sense of what had happened. However, he was at a loss to understand how the scuffle had developed. The next day, Martin sat down to watch the video of the game that had been taken by the O'Connell staff. He was embarrassed by what he saw. He reached two inescapable conclusions—*first*, that the incident was serious and, *second*, that a couple of O'Connell's players and a few other O'Connell students had precipitated the fight. The following Monday, he gathered the athletic director, the head football coach, the president and vice president of the student council, and the captains of the football team and told them they would have to go to Fairfax to apologize to the Paul VI football captains, the student council, and the school's administrators.

Soon thereafter, Martin addressed the entire O'Connell football team. He told them that as long as he was principal, O'Connell's students were not going to engage in what he viewed as reprehensible conduct. To ensure that there would not be any repercussions, Martin also arranged a meeting with the top administrators and student council presidents for both schools.

Martin's concern was heightened because the two schools were scheduled to play each other again that same year in basketball. Days before the scheduled basketball game, Martin called each class of O'Connell's students together in the auditorium. He told them that there would be severe consequences if there were any incidents between students from the two schools. "If this happens at a basketball game," he told the students, "and I find out who is responsible, you're leaving the game and never coming to another sports event this year, and if it gets too hot, I will forfeit the game."

Martin's meetings helped to smooth the relationship between the two schools. They did little, however, to appease the parents of Paul VI's students. For the better part of three weeks, Martin received a constant flow of e-mail messages from adults with ties to Paul VI. Virtually all of the messages castigated Martin for being unable to raise good

Catholic youths and unable to control his students. One parent of a student who had been pushed to the ground threatened to sue both Martin and the school, though no lawsuits were ever filed.

In the wake of the O'Connell-Paul VI football game, Martin endured weeks of sleepless nights. Well aware that a repeat of the incident would bring harsh consequences, Martin hired O'Connell teachers to provide security at each home game in which O'Connell was playing a long-time rival. The teachers wore yellow "Staff" jackets—a visible warning to O'Connell's players and students alike that violence would not be tolerated.

A year later, another incident involving an O'Connell team caused Martin to take even more drastic action. In the aftermath of a varsity hockey game between O'Connell and Bullis High School, an independent school from Potomac, Maryland, Martin received an e-mail from the assistant athletic director at Bullis. "Your hockey team has to be the most undisciplined team I have ever seen," the message read. Other messages followed. The head official at the game labeled the O'Connell squad "the most undisciplined hockey team I have seen in 20 years of officiating."

Martin soon understood the reason for the scathing messages. There had been 25 penalties assessed to O'Connell's team during the game, with three of the Knights disqualified from the game for misconduct. Even worse from Martin's perspective, there were allegations that O'Connell's players had yelled racial slurs at members of the Bullis team.

Martin conferred with Darrell Snyder, who had watched the game from the stands. Snyder confirmed that the conduct of O'Connell's team had been crude, if not brutish. "I'm inclined to cancel the season," Martin told Snyder. Snyder concurred. "Call the team in," Martin said.

Martin was in a somber mood when he spoke to the hockey players. "Gentlemen, this is real bad," he said. "I have been in athletics all my life. I understand tough sports. I was a wrestler for a good part of my life. I understand that things get out of hand, but are you telling me that 25 penalties in one game and three misconducts is anything near normal? Here's what's going to happen," Martin continued, "the season is over." A collective gasp went up from the players; to a man, they were stunned. The players struggled to raise arguments in opposition.

"We got DeMatha coming up," a player said. "We win that, we're going to the playoffs." Martin could not be dissuaded. "That's too bad," he replied. "You're going to have to learn something here. You made the school look real bad."

For the players, their families, and the school, the cancellation of the remaining hockey games carried severe consequences. With one more victory, the team would have captured a spot in the Northern Virginia Scholastic Hockey League (NVSHL) playoffs. It would have been the first time in the history of O'Connell hockey that the team had made the playoffs. The prospect was particularly exciting because the playoff games were scheduled to be played at the state-of-the-art Kettler Capitals Iceplex in Arlington, the same facility that the National Hockey League's Washington Capitals used for team practices.

A few days later, the hockey team was a primary topic of conversation at a meeting of the school's Board of Governors. A couple of board members applauded Martin's action. "Hell of a decision," one director said. "We support you on that."

When dealing with the challenge of handling disciplinary problems, Martin often wished that there were instructional materials available to provide guidance. In a field where pre-packaged lesson plans abound, however, school administrators are left largely to their own devices in dealing with disciplinary issues. Martin himself had helped to compose the disciplinary code for the Bishop O'Connell Student Handbook, an effort that taxed his ability to forecast patterns of student behavior into the future. Martin knew well that neither the student handbook nor any primer on disciplinary issues could ever anticipate all of the scenarios that might arise—not a pack of mice in the school hallways and certainly not a student traipsing through the school hallways in a gorilla suit.

If Martin was surprised by Steve McGraw's mice, he was caught completely off guard one day when he received a frantic telephone call warning that an individual dressed in a gorilla suit was causing a commotion in the classroom corridors. Martin summoned his colleague, John Gutter, and quickly related the essence of the phone call. The two then spread out through the school in an effort to corner the culprit. The "gorilla" had appeared in various locations on different floors.

Martin surmised that the culprit would abandon the gorilla outfit in the school after classes and then attempt to leave the building, most likely through a back door near the religion department. Acting on intuition, Martin hopped into his car and drove to the religion wing. At the 3:00 p.m. dismissal, Martin spied a male student leaving the religion wing wearing a T-shirt, without the customary school uniform. He had his man.

Martin asked the student where he had put the gorilla suit. Feigning innocence, the student asked, "What do you mean?" "Don't lie," Martin warned him, "or it will get worse." The student confessed to having placed the costume in a bathroom near the athletic director's office. On the spot, Martin suspended the student from school for a day. In imposing the punishment, he tried to get the student to appreciate the danger in what he had done. "You are scaring some of these older people in the school," he said. He then asked, "What happens if you give some of these older teachers a heart attack?" The student apologized. "I didn't think about that," he told Martin.

Another student provoked even greater alarm when he brought a handgun to school one day. Martin was in the cafeteria when a student approached and said, "Mr. Martin, there's a kid here who has a gun, a real live gun." The student pointed out the individual to Martin. Martin caught up with the student and said, "Son, I need to talk to you upstairs about something." The student followed Martin to his office. Martin asked, "Do you have something in that backpack that you shouldn't have?" The student pulled out a pack of cigarettes and said, "Oh, you mean the cigarettes?" Martin said, "Well, you're not supposed to have those but, no, something else." The student stood up, reached in his belt and pulled out the gun. Visibly frightened, Martin grabbed the student's wrist, slammed it down on the desk, and said, "If you move, I will deck you." Martin twisted the boy's arm and took the gun. "What in the hell are you doing with this gun?" he asked. The student responded, "I just wanted to show it to some friends of mine." At that point, the Arlington police were notified. The police came and took the student to the police station for questioning. At the station, the police examined the gun; there was no round in the chamber. Nonetheless, the offense carried severe consequences. Martin made it clear that the student was no longer welcome at O'Connell. In response, the student withdrew from school.

On one occasion, Martin was called to escort a disruptive student out of class. The student was reciting passages from the Bible in a trance-like state, clenching a pencil and a chalkboard eraser. Periodically, the student would utter, "six, six, six." The student stood 6' 3", towering over Martin. The two walked to Al Burch's office, with the student still clutching the pencil and eraser. Martin feared the student might turn violent; he plotted what he would do if the student turned on him. Upon reaching Burch's office, Martin told the student to sit. Burch motioned for his secretary to call the emergency squad. In short order, three emergency medical technicians arrived. One grabbed the student from behind and applied a choke hold around his throat. The second jumped onto the student's lap. The third pinned the student's arms, forcing him to release the pencil and eraser. The student resisted mightily; the EMTs subdued him and applied a straitjacket. They then strapped him onto a stretcher and took him to the hospital. Later reports from the hospital indicated that the student was under the influence of the drug phencyclidine (PCP). The student never returned to O'Connell.

As Martin reflected on the events of that day, he concluded that the rage induced by PCP was the scariest situation he had ever experienced at school. A student packing a gun was one thing. At least Martin was able to reason with the gun-bearing student. In contrast, Martin found that it was impossible to have a coherent conversation with a person on PCP, let alone reason with the individual.

Not all of the crises that Martin faced resulted from the misconduct of students. Some resulted from students pushing themselves too hard, whether academically or physically. In 1978, Bobby Martel was a 15-year-old sophomore at O'Connell. A good athlete and a five handicap golfer, Martel was known to have a heart condition. However, his physicians had cleared him to take part in exercise as long as he did not overexert himself.

One day, Martel collapsed on the outdoor track while participating in the mile-run during physical education class. One of the PE teachers, Gayle Connor, quickly performed CPR while another summoned the local emergency medical squad. When the EMTs arrived, Martel had no discernible pulse. One side of his face was completely purple; his body had ceased functioning. The EMTs were unable to produce a heartbeat, prompting one of the technicians to inject epinephrine directly into Martel's heart. The injection produced a pulse. The EMTs hurriedly placed Martel into the ambulance and raced to the hospital. The student was in a coma for five and a half weeks, but eventually awoke from the coma.

Some 30 years later, Martel has permanent paralysis on one side of his body and lacks the full use of his right hand, but leads a productive life. He works with an organization called Brain Injury Services and is a member of that group's speakers bureau. He frequently gives talks about his experiences. Once each year, Martel returns to O'Connell at Martin's request to tell students about the blessings in his life and the joys of being a survivor. Martel is fully aware that he owes his life to decisive reactions by both Gayle Connor and the emergency medical technicians. If Connor had not administered CPR, Martel would likely have suffered irreparable brain damage. If the EMT had not administered epinephrine quickly, Martel would not have made it to the hospital alive.

Martel lives each day with a smile, knowing that he is blessed to be alive. When talking with current O'Connell students, Martel takes delight in teasing Martin. For his part, Martin endures Martel's jests with a knowing smile, savoring the strides that Martel has made ever since the day when he was lying lifelessly on the O'Connell track.

Martel accumulates friends easily, many of whom congregate with other brain injury victims and their friends in June of each year for the Bobby Martel Invitational at the Jefferson Falls Mini-Golf Course in Falls Church, Virginia. Martel has plenty of reasons to celebrate, as do his multitude of fans. Friends come to cheer his accomplishments. They come, also, to enjoy his lively sense of humor.

In some ways, Martin identifies with Bobby Martel. Martel nearly didn't make it to age 19. Martin was not expected to reach age five. Having been blessed with the gift of abundant years, Martel approaches each new day with a ready smile. Blessed with that same gift, Martin smiles broadly, particularly when in the company of his friend Bobby Martel.

As an educator, Martin prides himself on his ability to relate to students. He drew on his experiences as wrestling coach to help members of the O'Connell football team understand the importance of a heartfelt apology after they had provoked a fight. He used his insights as a former wrestler to establish common ground with the O'Connell hockey team that had lost sight of the essence of fair play. He called on his own childhood experience to appreciate the remarkable strides that Bobby Martel had made in recovering from a prolonged coma. And as one possessed with an appreciation for comic relief, Martin could privately laud Steve McGraw's creativity in bringing 21 mice to the school, ever thankful that there were not 84.

---

[67] On the morning of September 11, 2001, less than five months after his ordination, McGraw was driving to Arlington National Cemetery to officiate at a military burial service. He took a wrong turn and ended up on a road adjacent to the Pentagon. While he was trying to find his way, he noticed a large American Airlines aircraft flying directly overhead and not more than 100 feet off the ground. McGraw watched in horror as the plane, later identified as the hijacked American Airlines Flight 77, slammed into the Pentagon. McGraw grabbed his prayer book and the oils that he used for anointing the sick, hurdled a guard rail, and stood in front of the burning building. As injured Pentagon workers were hurriedly carried from the building, McGraw moved from one victim to another to offer spiritual help. In the first half-hour after the attack, Father McGraw ministered to several individuals. He was soon joined by other priests and ministers. The clergymen prayed and waited, remaining at the Pentagon until evening approached. Father McGraw continues to marvel at the wrong turn that happened to put him at precisely the right spot. As reported by Angela E. Pometto, "Fairfax Priest Remembers Pentagon Scene on 9/11," *The Arlington Catholic Herald*, 7 September 2006.

[68] The president-principal model was a concept instituted by the superintendent of schools for the Diocese of Arlington. In theory, the president-principal model was intended to bifurcate the school's leadership function into two mutually exclusive spheres. The superintendent envisioned that the president would focus on fundraising and long-term development. The principal was to be responsible for the day-to-day functioning of the school.

Chapter 17
The Leprechaun and the Priest

When asked about his recollections of Dick Martin, Rev. Matthew J. DeForest invariably responds, "Ah, the Leprechaun!" DeForest was a student at O'Connell High School from 1996 to 2000, a period during which Martin served as assistant principal at the school. The child of parents who both were Marine Corps officers, DeForest could be irreverent, even rebellious. As a kindergarten student, DeForest had surreptitiously pocketed all of the colorful push pins that adorned the classroom bulletin board, leaving his teacher, Mrs. Sawyer, without any means of posting pictures for the class. As a high school sophomore, DeForest took on the role of disc jockey in the middle of Patricia McKinley's biology class and began playing songs from the South Park television series at full volume on a tape recorder. Early in his days at O'Connell, DeForest had tagged Martin with the moniker, "the Leprechaun." Martin was short of stature, exactly as a leprechaun was supposed to be. He was also a product of the University of Notre Dame, a school known as much for its fun-loving leprechaun mascot as for its golden dome. And when DeForest walked into English class at the beginning of his junior year and found that his teacher was none other than Martin's daughter, Kerry, it confirmed for him that "the Leprechaun" was a perfect fit. "So this is it," DeForest mused to himself, "this is where the Leprechaun hides his pot of gold." Unbeknownst to DeForest, two other treasures of comparable allure, Kelly and Kimberley, also resided in the Martin family.

More than a century before Matthew DeForest happened upon Kerry Martin in her third floor classroom at O'Connell, Irish poet William Butler Yeats had popularized the legend of the leprechaun.[69] Yeats portrayed the leprechauns as crafty characters, short in stature, who were, by nature, solitary and aloof. Every leprechaun possessed multiple pots of gold and was adept at hiding them. The leprechauns went to great lengths to conceal each pot of gold in a unique and obscure location, the better to foster the notion that their riches were confined to a single pot.

Martin's own "pot of gold," daughter Kerry, remembers Matthew DeForest as a lively participant in classroom discussions and a mostly well-behaved student with a wit that could be, at times, biting. The kid possessed a lively imagination and a penchant for instigating fun. He was a staff writer for the O'Connell school newspaper, *The Visor*; his writing could be exceptional. DeForest's reputation was that of a diligent student, one not noted for being disruptive. His antics would make classmates laugh, and on occasion, that would get him in trouble. He earned his first detention early in his freshman year at O'Connell for talking out of turn in class. There would be other detentions, most of them well-deserved.

Much has changed in the fifteen years since Matthew DeForest last occupied a seat in Kerry Martin's English class. Dick Martin became principal of O'Connell in September 2004. Four years later, "the Leprechaun" retired as principal and took a position in O'Connell's English department. After graduating from O'Connell in 2000, DeForest enrolled in the seminary, intent on becoming a Catholic priest. He was ordained as a priest in June 2009. Two years later, he was appointed assistant pastor at St. Anthony of Padua Church in Falls Church, Virginia.

DeForest regularly presides at the Sunday evening Mass at St. Anthony of Padua. As he looks out from the altar while celebrating the Mass, he often sees Dick Martin occupying a seat near the last row of pews. Martin attends Sunday Mass alone, a solitary figure who prefers to remain in the back of the church. It is a practice that Martin adopted in his days as principal, a measure that helped him avoid unwelcome encounters with parents of O'Connell students.

Time has moved on. Roles have changed. The student has become the preacher. The principal has become an attentive listener. Martin has seen many of O'Connell's former students flourish, none more so than DeForest. In the years since his ordination, Father Matthew has developed into an engaging and dynamic priest with a gift for delivering inspirational homilies. DeForest's words vary from week to week, but the essence of his message remains consistent. "People of hope," he tells the congregation, "must live differently."

One way in which Father Matthew lives differently is in the work he undertakes to nurture his own unique "pots of gold." In the fall of 2011, DeForest took interest in a gentleman named Sean Wawrzaszek, a 45-year old resident in a private condominium known as Merica House. As with the other residents of Merica House, Wawrzaszek was afflicted with cerebral palsy. Wawrzaszek's disability prevented him from manipulating his fingers or articulating words; he depended on a touch-sensitive computer linked to a speech synthesizer to convey his thoughts. With Wawrzaszek's lack of manual dexterity, forming sentences on the computer was a formidable task. Wawrzaszek had to repeatedly cursor through characters and words projected on his monitor to transform his thoughts into meaningful expressions. The process did not lend itself to quick conversations. A routine exchange could take several minutes.

On one occasion, Wawrzaszek, a practicing Catholic, was particularly distressed. He believed there was an effort underway to discourage him from attending Mass at his favorite church. Upon learning of the situation, DeForest paid a visit to Merica House. Talking through his computer, Wawrzaszek asked if it would be okay for him to change religions. It was a question that Wawrzaszek did not pose lightly; his family was steadfastly Catholic. Family tradition notwithstanding, Wawrzaszek wanted a church that would welcome him on Sundays, whether Catholic or not. DeForest spoke to Wawrzaszek at length, with words designed to soothe the anger. After assessing the situation, DeForest proposed a simple solution. "You know," he told Wawrzaszek, "we could do a Mass each month right here at Merica House."

With that simple gesture of caring, a glorious smile came over Wawrzaszek's face, a smile that spoke volumes. In the months after DeForest's conversation with Wawrzaszek, Father Matthew's monthly Masses became a staple at Merica House. The "congregation" included Wawrzaszek as well as fellow Merica House residents Cathy Parr and two sisters, Deirdre Shields and Maureen Shields.

Sean Wawrzaszek passed away, unexpectedly, in August 2013. Nonetheless, DeForest continues his practice of celebrating Mass once a month at Merica House. On each occasion, DeForest delivers a stirring homily for the Merica House residents, sometimes focusing on the joy that came from the magnificent smile of their friend Sean Wawrzaszek or the grace with which Wawrzaszek accepted his physical limitations.

DeForest likes to tell people that "homily material is all over the place." On any given Sunday, his homily material may come from Thomas Aquinas or Mother Teresa, but it is equally likely to come from Sean Wawrzaszek or former pro football player Curtis Martin. In his homilies, DeForest encourages parishioners who are searching for inspiration "to look to the Cross." Echoing the advice once given to him by the rector at his seminary, DeForest reminds parishioners, "When you are out and about, remember to smile."

On a Sunday evening late in 2013, DeForest opened a homily at St. Anthony of Padua Church by playing a recording of Bill Withers' 1972 hit song, *Lean On Me*. DeForest used the song to launch into a reflection on the special ways in which Christians can provide solace and strength to others. From his seat in the last row of pews, Dick Martin listened intently, a man who knows well what it means to lean on others.

DeForest finds more good in the world than bad. He adheres to the belief that if people only dare to dream big, it is possible to change the world "one word, one footstep, one burden at a time." For inspiration, DeForest invokes a prayer attributed to Sir Francis Drake, "Disturb us, O Lord, when our dreams come true because we dream too little, when we have arrived in safety because we have sailed too close to shore."

Martin hears these words from DeForest and smiles. He likes to think that some of the thoughts he hears in DeForest's homilies might reflect the influence of his daughter Kerry, the erstwhile "pot of gold." In her days at O'Connell, Kerry resisted the temptation to dream too little. Years after leaving O'Connell to take a teaching position in the country of Chile, Kerry continues to dream in big ways. And she is comforted to know that at least one of her former students continues to dream big as well.

---

[69]*Irish Fairy and Folk Tales*, edited and selected by W. B. Yeats, Digireads.com Publishing, (Boston, 2010).

Chapter 18
Tissues, Issues, and Lip Gloss

The students sat quietly in Martin's American Dream Revisited class. As is most often the case, girl students far outnumbered the boys. In a typical class of fifteen students, there might be only four or five boys. One of the fundamental differences between girl students and boy students, Martin had concluded, is that girls use a lot more tissue. Martin found that a box of tissues went much faster when he led a discussion on *The Grapes of Wrath* than, for example, when he dissected *The Great Gatsby*. And so in the middle of class one day, perhaps prompted by the thought of Steinbeck's Rose of Sharon gently breast-feeding a dying old man, a girl asked Martin for a tissue. Martin addressed the class, "I'm going to write a book someday," he said, "and it's going to be titled, 'Tissues, Issues, and Lotion.'" "That won't work," a student responded, "You should call it, 'Tissues, Issues, and Lip Gloss.'"

Martin retired as principal at O'Connell in June 2008. He was 67 years old. The job was stressful; four years were enough. Even in retirement, however, Martin continued to teach *The American Dream Revisited*. He found the classroom exchanges to be stimulating. He took delight in the banter with his pupils. So, on a Thursday morning in early December of 2010, Martin stood at the front of classroom 301 as students sauntered in. A penetrating chill seeped through the aging third-floor casement windows. The temperature hovered in the upper 30s.

The students discussed Danny Callahan's wrestling match the day before against two local schools, Bishop Ireton and Pope Paul VI. Danny won the match against Paul VI by five points but lost to his counterpart from Ireton by two.

With the preliminary banter out of the way, the class prepared for a quiz on *The Grapes of Wrath*. With tongue partly in cheek, a student complained about the stress of taking a quiz. Martin tried to be reassuring. "Everyone should get these questions pretty easily," he told the students.

Martin read aloud the first question: *Who is the crazy lady in chapter 22 trying to scare and why?* Callahan raised his hand. The "crazy lady" would have to wait. "Mr. Martin," Callahan asked, "do you have a pen?" Martin halted, then handed over his pen, but it came with a stern warning. "This I have had for 26 years," he told Callahan. "It's fourteen karat gold, don't break it, and don't lose it."

Martin repeated the first question and then moved on to the second: *How did these migrants entertain themselves?*

More questions followed, eight in all. After the students had jotted down their responses and handed them in, Martin turned the questions into a free-flowing discussion of the life of Steinbeck's migrants.

Steinbeck, it was clear, had a fascination with harmonicas:

> A harmonica is easy to carry. Take it out of your hip pocket, knock it against your palm to shake out the dirt and pocket fuzz and bits of tobacco. Now it's ready. You can do anything with a harmonica: thin reedy single tone, or chords, or melody with rhythm chords.[70]

So the migrants made music, especially in the evenings and especially with harmonicas, guitars, and fiddles.

Student Katy Garcia, a junior, was persuaded. She revealed that, after reading Steinbeck's high praise for the harmonica, she had added a harmonica to her Christmas wish list. And if it was true that a harmonica required a lot less learning than a fiddle, as Steinbeck suggested, all the better. "The fiddle is rare, hard to learn," Steinbeck had written. "No frets, no teacher."[71]

Martin led the students through chapter 25 and drew their attention to Steinbeck's final paragraph,

> ...in the eyes of the people there is the failure; and in the eyes of the hungry there is a growing wrath. In the souls of the people the grapes of wrath are filling and growing heavy, growing heavy for the vintage.[72]

It had taken twenty-five chapters for Steinbeck to inject a reference to his chosen title for the book. Grapes had once served as a symbol of the migrants' hopes for a better life. Those hopes had been shattered, replaced by "a growing wrath." It would take another twenty-seven pages for some semblance of hope to be restored. "I'm learnin' one thing good," Ma says midway through chapter 26. "Learnin' it all a time, ever' day. If you're in trouble or hurt or need—go to poor people. They're the only ones that'll help—the only ones."[73]

Martin wanted to be sure that his students took note of the lesson. He had long maintained that *The Grapes of Wrath* was not the easiest of books for students to decipher—or even read. And yet, he had concluded, the graphic lessons that Steinbeck weaves throughout the novel are critical to any age. "Pay attention closely," he instructed his students, pointing out that the only way migrants made progress was by organizing their members to form a united front. *The Grapes of Wrath*, Martin suggested, is all about man's obligation to his fellow man.

Martin thought often of one of his students from years earlier, a kid named Augie Borgess. Borgess had difficulty with books of any complexity, whether it be the weighty *Grapes of Wrath* or a much shorter work such as *The Great Gatsby*. If there were written words, Borgess was going to have trouble, not because he couldn't read, simply because he was adverse to reading. If Borgess was slow to pick up a book, however, he was at least game for a challenge. At Martin's urging, Borgess enrolled in *The American Dream Revisited*. It was a struggle, but Borgess passed the class and, in the process, found that he enjoyed reading. Long after he had graduated from O'Connell, Borgess told Martin, "Now I read all the time."

In later sessions on *The Grapes of Wrath*, Martin would return to the theme of man helping his fellow man. He would take delight in the poignant scene from the closing paragraph, as an exhausted Rose of Sharon, still soaked from a sudden rain, provides sustenance for a dying man:

> She moved slowly to the corner and stood looking down at the wasted face, onto the wide, frightened eyes. Then slowly she lay down beside him. He shook his head slowly from side to side. Rose of Sharon loosened one side of the blanket and bared her breast. "You got to," she said. She squirmed closer and pulled his head close. "There!" she said. "There." Her hand moved behind his head and supported

it. Her fingers moved gently in his hair. She looked up and across the barn, and her lips came together and smiled mysteriously.[74]

In the 1970s, Father McMurtrie had encouraged O'Connell's English teachers to design their own courses. Martin developed a concept for a course that would focus on the great American classics and bear the title *The American Dream*. With McMurtrie's approval, Martin established the course along the lines of a college seminar, with emphasis on daily reading assignments, class discussion, and preparation of analytical essays on each book covered in the course.

Initially, Martin's course centered around three novels, *To Kill A Mockingbird*, *The Great Gatsby*, and *The Grapes of Wrath*. In 1989 when Martin returned for his second tour at O'Connell, he resumed teaching the course under the title, *The American Dream Revisited*. He has taught the course continuously ever since, expanding the subject matter to include books such as *Tuesdays with Morrie*, *The Kite Runner*, *The Blind Side*, and *The Runaway Jury*.

For each work covered, Martin attempts to relate the salient interactions among the characters to everyday situations and current events—so that students can see a link between what happened in 1930 in *To Kill A Mockingbird*'s fictional town of Maycomb, Alabama, for instance, and the ongoing struggles of more modern times.

After completing their study of *The Grapes of Wrath*, Martin and his class took a look at the Great Depression from a different perspective, this time through the eyes of heavyweight boxer James J. Braddock in *Cinderella Man*. Thereafter, they examined *Gatsby*, *The Kite Runner*, and *Tuesdays with Morrie*.

In his lectures, Martin took delight in identifying parallels—in theme, in focus, in attitude. His lectures revealed a fascination with the idea of brotherhood. He preached the same emotions—love and compassion—that motivated Rose of Sharon to provide nourishment for the dying man. Long after his class had put *The Grapes of Wrath* to rest, Martin would find a similar teaching point in the way that friends came to the aid of another dying man, Morrie Schwartz, in *Tuesdays with Morrie*.

Martin drew meaningful contrasts with equal ease. At the same time that Morrie was welcoming visits from friends and colleagues, narrator Mitch Albom's own brother, stricken with cancer, chose to live a secluded life in Spain, well removed from family and friends. "Why?" Martin asked his class. "Was it pride? Was it embarrassment?"

In *The Grapes of Wrath*, whether out of pride or embarrassment, the dying man initially resisted Rose of Sharon's offer of warmth and nourishment. As Martin emphasized to his students, a more enlightened Morrie Schwartz had moved easily beyond the artificial constraints imposed by pride and embarrassment. "Listen, I have to pee," Morrie would announce to friends after he had become too weak to simultaneously stand up and hold the beaker he used for urinating. "Would you mind helping?" he would ask.[75]

In apparent contrast to Mitch Albom's brother, Morrie accepted his approaching death without any sense of embarrassment. "Death is as natural as life," he told Albom. "It's part of the deal we made."[76]

Martin enthusiastically pointed out to his class the choices that Morrie had made, the determination to live "with dignity, with courage, with humor, with composure." As Morrie was educating Albom, Martin was educating his own students.

The other essential lesson, Martin told his students, was to live with love. To emphasize the point, Martin repeated the theme that Morrie had adopted from poet W. H. Auden, "Love each other or perish." Just as Albom had recorded that observation in his notes of September 1995, so too Martin's students highlighted it as a crucial point in their own notes some sixteen years later.

The lessons that Martin conveyed to his class were timeless, as were the insights from *Tuesdays with Morrie* that served as the source for those lessons.

---

[70] John Steinbeck, *The Grapes of Wrath* (New York: Penguin Books, 1999), 328.

[71] *Ibid.*

[72] *Ibid.*, 349.

[73] *Ibid.*, 376.

[74] *Ibid.*, 455.

[75] Mitch Albom, *Tuesdays with Morrie* (New York: Doubleday, 1997), 11.

[76] *Ibid.*, 172.

Chapter 19
Peering Into Eternity

In May 2013, Dick Martin traveled to South Bend, Indiana to attend the 50th anniversary reunion of his graduating class at the University of Notre Dame. Charlie O'Hara, a workhorse halfback on Notre Dame's 1962 football team and, for the previous forty years or so, a Roman Catholic priest, opened the reunion events by celebrating an evening Mass at the Notre Dame Grotto. In his homily during the Mass, O'Hara recalled that he would often retreat to the Grotto during his college years to reflect on whether he might have a calling to the priesthood. He spoke of the Grotto as being "sacred ground." O'Hara called the entire campus "sacred ground" because it was the site where he and his classmates had embarked on their new life so many years ago. For many, it was also the site of their last encounter with Bud Vogel, Denny Phillips and other deceased classmates with whom they had entered the University years earlier.

Taking a page from Charlie O'Hara, Martin wants his students to think of Bishop O'Connell High School as sacred ground, for it too is the site from which they will embark on a new life. Taking a page from Morrie Schwartz, the beloved former professor of Mitch Albom, Martin wants his students to use their full powers of observation when they look out the window. He wants them to appreciate what they see in the same way that Morrie appreciated the subtle changes in the trees and the awesome power of the wind. Martin wants his students to grow, to experience the world fully, and to think beyond excelling in sports or getting into the best college. He has built his philosophy of education on two core principles that Morrie Schwartz would have endorsed: first, the fundamental purpose of schools is to help students grow and, second, nothing, including technology, can substitute for the rapport and influence that a teacher has with his or her students.

In the same way that Morrie Schwartz reached student Mitch Albom with his personality, Martin has used his personality to reach others. From the third floor hallway outside O'Connell's classroom 301, Martin can look out the window and see far into the distance. He can see the changes in the trees and gauge how fiercely the wind is blowing. And if he looks intently, he can see students from the past such as avid reader Augie Borgess, standout wrestler Pat McAteer, future priests Steve McGraw and Matthew DeForest, and countless others whom he has guided in his roles as teacher, coach, and administrator.

Martin has read *Tuesdays with Morrie* more times than he can remember. He pauses over some passages more than others. In particular, the quote that Albom included from Henry Adams, a professor of history at Harvard in the 1870s and the brother of John Quincy Adams, often catches Martin's attention: "A teacher affects eternity; he can never tell where his influence stops."[77]

Morrie Schwartz insisted there was nothing complicated about his formula for showering love on others. "You don't need to have a big talent," Schwartz told Albom. For Schwartz, the simple act of playing cards with a senior citizen or visiting lonely people in hospitals represented an opportunity for loving others.

As the end of life neared, Schwartz made a particular effort to focus on "the essentials." For Schwartz, the essentials boiled down to three relatively simple matters: Have you found someone to share your heart with? Are you giving to your community? Are you at peace with yourself? "The way you get meaning into your life," Schwartz told Albom, "is to devote yourself to loving others, devote yourself to your community around you, and devote yourself to creating something that gives you purpose and meaning."[78]

Mitch Albom once asked his former professor, "How can you ever be prepared to die?" Schwartz responded, "Do what the Buddhists do. Every day, have a little bird on your shoulder that asks, 'Is today the day? Am I ready? Am I doing all I need to do? Am I being the person I want to be?'"[79]

When it comes to Schwartz's "essentials," Martin has largely succeeded. He has raised three daughters who have each made tangible contributions to the lives of others. He has passed on his insights regarding wrestling and the art of competing with grace and honor to the members of his wrestling teams. He has passed on the lessons of life to the students in his literature classes. He has helped to maintain Bishop O'Connell High School as sacred ground in the lives of its students.

If Martin ever seeks any reminder of his impact on high school wrestling, he need only look at the number of coaches that O'Connell's wrestling program has spawned and the number of championships it has won. If he seeks validation of his success as a teacher, he need only think of students such as Vic Bakshi. A 2004 graduate of O'Connell, Bakshi enrolled in *The American Dream Revisited* for his senior elective, lured by Martin's promise of a course that focused on life. In May 2004, with his senior year nearing its end and final grades already a matter of record, Bakshi wrote a letter to Martin. If Martin possessed a trophy case at home, the Bakshi letter would be on prominent display. "The lessons that I will remember," Bakshi wrote, "are the ones that weren't graded, weren't checked, and probably weren't even recognized by anyone other than myself. Most of those lessons, the life lessons, I learned in your class."

Life lessons may not have been the primary attraction when Bakshi decided to sign up for Martin's course. "I figured it would be an easy A," he confessed in his letter. The assumption was accurate. Bakshi got his "A." He also received "great discussions" and other unanticipated rewards. "I enjoyed the discussions in your class more than anything," the letter read. To Bakshi's delight, the discussions focused on practical lessons. "I can honestly say that I really did learn a lot about life and I'm just hoping I don't forget the lessons and learn to apply them every day," he closed.

Over the years, other students in Martin's class have cited comparable learning experiences. Tara Ulepic, O'Connell class of 2014, credited *The American Dream Revisited* with restoring her desire to strive for excellence. "I started the year not really caring about my grades," Ulepic wrote. "The choices I was planning to make were very risky and immature," she stated. Ulepic chose not to pursue those choices because, "through Mr. Martin and his sincerity not only as a teacher, but as a coach and leader, I decided I owed it to myself to strive for … excellence."

Long before Mitch Albom had introduced the world to *Tuesdays with Morrie* and long before Morrie Schwartz had expounded on the role that death plays in refining one's approach to life, Martin had given abundant thought to the impact of the losses that he had experienced over the years—his father's passing in 1957, the death in Vietnam of Bud Vogel, the passing of Martin's brother Jim and his mother Mary Elizabeth, and the deaths of Martin's lifelong friend and classmate Denny Phillips and Superdance founder Maura O'Donnell. Each death served as a reminder that there are no guarantees in life and that the important things should not wait.

Martin lives with certain undeniable regrets. The harshness of his ill-chosen last words to Nancy Rhoades will always be a painful memory. He is well aware that there were situations, at both Bishop O'Connell and Monsignor Hackett, that he should have handled better. The fury of his assault on Mike Garcia serves as a glaring reminder that maturity was slow in coming. Most especially, Martin wishes that there could have been a better resolution of his relationship with his former wife, Chris.

In recognition of Martin's contributions as both teacher and principal, the Bishop O'Connell Parent Teacher Organization established a scholarship fund in Martin's name in 2006. The Richard J. Martin Scholarship Fund awards a scholarship each year to a deserving O'Connell graduate. Students who apply for the scholarship are required to write an essay on the topic of "What O'Connell High School Has Meant To Me."

Martin is gratified and, in a way, amused by the scholarship fund. He thinks he should be the one to write the essay—not to gain a scholarship but to acknowledge his debt to the O'Connell community. He knows, as José Ortega wrote in *The Revolt of the Masses*, that "all life, and consequently the life of history, is made up of simple moments."[80] He knows as well that, as Morrie Schwartz concluded, the simple moments loom larger as one advances in years. Martin thinks of the simple moments at O'Connell—the cough drops dispensed by Father McMurtrie; the friendship extended by fellow teachers Patrice Connolly, Joe Connolly, and Steve Johnson; the wisdom and compassion shown by Al Burch; the visit by his high school coach and teacher,

George Lamprinakos, for Martin's 1993 induction into the O'Connell Hall of Fame.

Over the course of Martin's 50 years as an educator, there have been an abundance of simple moments, all of which have added up to a large life. Martin knows that he has influenced the students at Bishop O'Connell and Monsignor Hackett. He thinks he has seen it all—42 consecutive wins, 21 mice, and more than a few miracles. And if along the way he has affected eternity, so much the better.

---

[77] Albom, *Tuesdays with Morrie*, 21.

[78] *Ibid.*, 127.

[79] *Ibid.*, 81.

[80] Ortega, *The Revolt of the Masses*, 67.

Overtime

"Life is a series of pulls back and forth. You want to do one thing, but you are bound to do something else. Something hurts you, yet you know it shouldn't. You take certain things for granted, even when you know you should never take anything for granted.

"A tension of opposites, like a pull on a rubber band. And most of us live somewhere in the middle."

Sounds like a wrestling match, I say.

"A wrestling match." He laughs. "Yes, you could describe life that way."

So which side wins, I ask?

"Which side wins?"

He smiles at me, the crinkled eyes, the crooked teeth.

"Love wins. Love always wins."

—from *Tuesdays with Morrie*

The 2013-14 academic year marked Dick Martin's 50th year as an educator. He thinks it will be his last. Though he still enjoys the challenge of introducing students to the great works in American literature, he has a busy and fulfilling life outside of the classroom. Other challenges beckon.

To watch Martin in action is to see a man who seems to have absorbed the best that Professor Morrie Schwartz had to offer. As a Eucharistic minister, Martin regularly brings Holy Communion to hospital patients. He delivers food to those in need. He plays golf with former teaching colleagues Bart Steib and Charlie Laniak and goes on extended hiking trips in Maryland and Virginia with Jim Welsford, also a former colleague. Martin has taught reading to illiterate adults. He volunteers his time at golf courses, serving as a starter at one course and a marshal at another. On a trip to Southern California in August 2011 to visit his daughters, he went paragliding high over the Pacific Ocean. Two months later, he traveled to South Bend to watch Notre Dame's football team take on the University of Southern California. The paragliding was a once-in-a-lifetime event, the football game an annual ritual.

Martin's last drink of alcohol came in 1990. Now completely sober for more than 20 years, Martin believes his decision to give up drinking has yielded benefits on many levels. He finds that he is able to live a more energetic and active life. He prides himself, particularly, on being more attentive to the needs of his children and others. The significance of the change did not go unnoticed. His former boss, Al Burch, once said to Martin, "You were so much more fun when you were drinking." Martin's daughters were more approving. Kerry, the youngest, told Martin, "I so respect the depths to which you have changed yourself."

The proud grandparent of four young children named Emma, Grace, Maddy and Griffin, Martin enjoys spending time with his daughters and their families. His oldest daughter, Kelly, earned her undergraduate degree with a double major in psychology and business at the University of Notre Dame and then took a position at O'Connell teaching English and psychology classes. Kelly later moved to Chicago, where she conducted computer training sessions for accounting and tax professionals. She now lives in Encinitas, California, where she is a mother and housewife and a part-time project manager for a middle school. Middle daughter Kimberley received her bachelor's degree in theater and anthropology from the University of Virginia. Kim lives in Charlottesville, Virginia, where she is the director of internet and event marketing for Carter-Myers Automotive. Kerry, the youngest, graduated from George Mason University with a degree in English and then taught at O'Connell for three years before spending another year in Santiago, Chile as a teacher. Kerry currently lives in Burbank, California, where she teaches high school English.

Many of Martin's closest friends from O'Connell have passed away.

Their legacies remain prominent. There is the annual Joe Connolly Classic Golf Tournament, the James W. McMurtrie Football Field, the Steve Johnson Ecology Club, and the Al Burch Memorial Scholarship Fund. Martin treasures the subtle, yet deeply ingrained influence of each individual—Connolly's restraint and calming influence, McMurtrie's talent for inspiring others, Johnson's passion for protecting the environment, Burch's penchant for nurturing those who followed in his footsteps.

Martin treasures, also, the lessons that he has learned from his study of the prominent characters in American literature. In particular, Martin seems to have absorbed every thoughtful nugget that Morrie Schwartz passed on to Mitch Albom.

Like Morrie Schwartz, Martin has wrestled with the tension of opposites… the pull on a rubber band. Like Morrie, Martin holds firmly to the belief that, in the end, love always wins.

Appendix I

Biographical Timeline

February 1, 1941 . . . . . . Dick Martin born in Pittsburgh, Pennsylvania.

1944 . . . . Martin diagnosed as suffering from nephrosis.

1945 . . . . Martin's father makes pilgrimage to Basilica of Saint Anne-de-Beaupre in Quebec, Canada.

1946 . . . . Physicians pronounce Martin cured of nephrosis.

1947-1949 . . . . Martin completes first and second grade at Lincoln Elementary, Mt. Lebanon, Pennsylvania.

1949-1955 . . . . Martin completes third through eighth grades at St. Bernard School, Mt. Lebanon, Pennsylvania.

September 1955 . . . . Martin enrolls at Mt. Lebanon High School.

December 10, 1957 . . . . Martin's father, Dr. James Martin, dies.

June 1959 . . . . Martin graduates from Mt. Lebanon High School.

September 1959 . . . . Martin enrolls at University of Notre Dame.

June 1963 . . . . Martin graduates from University of Notre Dame.

December 1963 . . . . Martin begins employment with Greater Braddock Chamber of Commerce, Braddock, Pennsylvania.

December 1964 . . . . Martin begins employment with Federally-funded Economic Opportunity Program, St. James Center, Pittsburgh, Pennsylvania.

December 1966 . . . . Martin resigns position with Economic Opportunity Program.

January 1967 . . . . Martin begins working as teacher and assistant wrestling coach at South Hills Catholic High School, Pittsburgh, Pennsylvania.

April 1, 1967 . . . . Martin and Mary Christine (Chris) Smith marry.

June 1967 . . . . Martin and Chris relocate to Provincetown, Massachusetts.

September 1967 . . . . Martin begins working as Executive Assistant for Job Corps Program, U.S. Department of Labor, Washington, D.C.

November 1967 . . . . Martin begins as wrestling coach, Bishop O'Connell High School, Arlington, Virginia.

September 1968	Martin begins employment as full-time English teacher at O'Connell High School, in addition to position as coach of the wrestling team.
September 4, 1968	Martin's daughter, Kelly, is born.
December 21, 1970	Martin's daughter, Kimberley, is born.
February 1972	O'Connell's wrestling team wins Virginia State Independent School Tournament Championship.
January 14, 1974	Martin's mother, Mary Elizabeth Martin, dies.
December 1974	O'Connell's wrestling team wins first of its 42 consecutive dual matches.
September 1976	Martin is appointed as director of athletics at O'Connell in addition to coaching duties.
October 30, 1976	Martin's daughter, Kerry, is born.
September 1977	Martin begins as assistant principal for student life at O'Connell, in addition to coaching duties.
January 1978	O'Connell's wrestling team falls to Langley High School, ending streak of 42 consecutive victories in dual matches.
June 1978	Martin resigns as wrestling coach to focus full-time on position as assistant principal for student life.
June 1984	Martin resigns as assistant principal at O'Connell to take position as principal at Monsignor John R. Hackett High School, Kalamazoo, Michigan.
August 1984	Martin begins tenure as principal of Monsignor Hackett High School.
June 1987	Martin resigns as principal of Monsignor Hackett High.
September 1987	Martin begins as principal of Holy Cross Regional School, Lynchburg, Virginia.
June 1989	Martin resigns as principal of Holy Cross Regional School.
September 1989	Martin returns to O'Connell as assistant principal.
September 2004	Martin assumes position as principal of O'Connell under the newly established president/principal model.
June 2008	Martin retires as principal of O'Connell High School, while continuing to teach *The American Dream Revisited*.

Appendix II

Roster of Players

Mitch Albom	Author, journalist, radio and television broadcaster, advocate for the homeless. Graduated from Brandeis University, where he studied under sociology professor Morrie Schwartz, who became the inspiration for Albom's *New York Times* bestseller, *Tuesdays with Morrie*. After college, attempted to carve out a career as a piano player but gravitated toward journalism.
Victoria Anderson	Student at Mt. Lebanon High. Classmate of Denny Phillips and Dick Martin.
Dwayne Andreas	Chief Executive Officer of the Archer Daniels Midland company, the largest processor of farm commodities in the United States.
W. H. Auden	Anglo-American poet. Emigrated from his native England to the United States in 1939. Widely regarded as one of the greatest writers of the 20th century.
Joe Bach	Former lineman on the Notre Dame football team. Was one of the famed Seven Mules on the Fighting Irish 1924 national title team. Had two separate stints as head coach of Pittsburgh's professional football teams, the Pirates in 1935-36 and the Steelers in 1952-53.
Vic Bakshi	Bishop O'Connell High School pupil. Former student in Martin's *American Dream Revisited* course.
Fred Ball	Bishop O'Connell wrestler, 1976-80. Virginia Independent Schools Athletic Association state champion in 1979 (119-pound class) and 1980 (126-pound class).
Phil Baltazar	Bishop O'Connell wrestler during Martin's tenure as coach.
William "Count" Basie	African-American jazz pianist, organist, bandleader and composer during the swing era. Led a big band for almost 50 years beginning in 1935.
Dave Batton	Six-foot-ten forward/center for Notre Dame, 1975-78. Later played professionally in Italy and with the Washington Bullets and San Antonio Spurs.

Angelo Bertelli	Starting quarterback for the University of Notre Dame football team, 1941-43. Won the Heisman Trophy as the outstanding player in college football in 1943, becoming the first Notre Dame player ever to win the Heisman.
Dan Beyer	Deputy to Dick Martin at the St. James Center in Pittsburgh, PA during Martin's tenure with the Federally-funded Economic Opportunity Program, 1965-66.
Ray Blockinger	Martin's classmate at St. Bernard Grade School. Played center on the St. Bernard eighth-grade football team.
Augie Borgess	Bishop O'Connell High School pupil and student in Martin's *American Dream Revisited* course.
Hugh C. Boyle (Rev.)	Catholic priest and long-time bishop of the Diocese of Pittsburgh.
James J. Braddock	World heavyweight boxing champion, 1935-37. Nicknamed the "Cinderella Man," in recognition of his rise from poverty to become heavyweight boxing champion of the world.
Rich Branning	Basketball guard for Notre Dame, 1976-80. Starting point guard for the only Fighting Irish men's basketball team to play in the NCAA Final Four (1978).
Ted Breiner	O'Connell wrestler during Martin's tenure as coach. Virginia Independent Schools Athletic Association state champion in his senior year. Also named most valuable player on the O'Connell football team as a senior. Member of the Bishop O'Connell Athletic Hall of Fame.
Tom Breiner	O'Connell wrestler during Martin's tenure as coach.
Howard "Butch" Breinig	Childhood friend and classmate of Martin. Nicknamed "Tank."
Terry Brennan	Head coach, Notre Dame football, 1954-58. Compiled a record of 32-18.
Thomas Brennan (Rev.)	Roman Catholic priest. Quirky and popular long-time professor of philosophy at University of Notre Dame.
Greg Britto	Lawyer and member of the Virginia Bar. Friend of Martin.

Appendix II

Nick Buoniconti	Captain of the 1961 Notre Dame football squad as a tackle, he converted to linebacker in the pros, playing fourteen seasons with the Boston Patriots (1962-68) and the Miami Dophins (1969-76). Elected to the Pro Football Hall of Fame in 2001.
Al Burch	Long-time baseball coach and administrator at O'Connell. Was coach of the baseball teams that posted a school-record 42 consecutive wins, 1963-65. Served as O'Connell's principal from 1977 to 2004. Member of the Bishop O'Connell Athletic Hall of Fame. During Dick Martin's tenure as assistant principal at O'Connell, students often referred to Burch as "Batman," with Martin cast in the role of "Robin."
Dennis Caffi	O'Connell wrestler during Martin's tenure as coach.
Danny Callahan	O'Connell wrestler. Former student in Martin's *American Dream Revisited* course.
Elizabeth Capetola	Sister of Rev. James W. McMurtrie.
Bill Carpenter	O'Connell wrestler during Martin's tenure as coach. Tri-State champion and O'Connell athlete of the year in 1976. Later served as coach of the O'Connell wrestling team for 29 years. Member of the Bishop O'Connell Athletic Hall of Fame.
Bob Carpenter	O'Connell wrestler during Martin's tenure as coach.
Scott Carpenter	O'Connell wrestler during Martin's tenure as coach.
Bill Cartwright	Seven-foot-one center for the University of San Francisco basketball team in 1977. Played professionally with the New York Knicks, Chicago Bulls and Seattle SuperSonics.
David Cascio	A wrestler at Langley High School, McLean, Virginia.
John Casey	A wrestler at Bishop McNamara High School, Forestville, Maryland.
Miguel de Cervantes	Spain's greatest literary figure. Born in 1547. Author of *Don Quixote*, considered the first modern European novel. Influenced the thinking and writing of José Ortega y Gasset, the intellectual leader of the Spanish Revolution.
Lynn Chandois	Football halfback out of Michigan State University. Played seven seasons for the Pittsburgh Steelers,

	1950-56. Three-time Pro Bowl selection. Named NFL Player of the Year, 1952.
Frank Church	Lawyer and politician. Represented the State of Idaho in the United States Senate from 1957 to 1981.
Mary Elizabeth Clair	Maiden name of Martin's mother.
Roberto Clemente	Hall-of-Fame right fielder for the Pittsburgh Pirates, 1955-72.
Perry Como	Singer and band leader. Native of Cannonsburg, Pennsylvania.
Joe Connolly	Friend of Martin and long-time calculus teacher at O'Connell. Husband of Patrice Connolly. Coached boys and girls tennis teams at O'Connell. Led the boys' team to seven Virginia Catholic championships. Member of the Bishop O'Connell Athletic Hall of Fame.
Patrice Connolly	Religion teacher at O'Connell. Friend of Martin. Wife of Joe Connolly.
Gayle Connor	Physical Education teacher at O'Connell High School during Martin's time as wrestling coach and athletic director at the school.
Pattie Ann Crivella	Classmate of Martin at St. Bernard Grade School. Married Denny Phillips.
Jim Crowley	Left halfback on Notre Dame's football team, 1922-24. One of the famed "Four Horsemen" of Notre Dame, an epithet bestowed by sportswriter Grantland Rice of the *New York Herald-Tribune*.
Angelo Dabiero	Halfback for Notre Dame, 1959-61. Averaged 6.9 yards on 92 carries in his senior year.
Angelo D'Agostino (Rev.)	Physician, psychotherapist, and Jesuit priest. Friend of Martin. Devoted latter years of his life to care of the poor in Kenya. Founded one of the first orphanages for HIV-positive children in Kenya.
Bill Davis (Rev.)	Superintendent of schools for the Diocese of Arlington during Martin's tenure as O'Connell's assistant principal for student life.
James Dean	Hollywood actor of the 1950s who starred in the movie, *Rebel Without A Cause*.
Johnny Dee	Lawyer and collegiate basketball coach. Served as head basketball coach at the University of

Appendix II

	Alabama (1953-56) and the University of Notre Dame (1964-71).
Frank Deford	Writer, author and humorist. Long-time reporter and writer for *Sports Illustrated*. Served as editor-in-chief of the national daily sports newspaper, *The National Sports Daily*, during the period 1990-91.
Matthew DeForest	Student at O'Connell, 1996-2000. Now a Roman Catholic priest in the diocese of Arlington, Virginia. Assigned as pastoral vicar (assistant pastor) at St. Anthony of Padua Church, Falls Church, Virginia.
Hugh Devore	Three-sport star in high school in New Jersey, recruited by Knute Rockne to play at Notre Dame. Career football coach at the collegiate and professional levels. Head coach of the Philadelphia Eagles, 1956-57.
Thomas Dewey	Lawyer and politician. Served as governor of the State of New York from 1943 to 1954. The Republican candidate for President in both 1944 and 1948, he lost to Democrats Franklin Delano Roosevelt in 1944 and Harry S. Truman in 1948.
Pat Donohoe	O'Connell wrestler during Martin's tenure as coach. Virginia Independent School State Champion in senior year.
Howdy Doody	Name used by police as identification when raiding a high school beer party attended by Martin. Howdy Doody was the name of a marionette manipulated by Bob Smith on *The Howdy Doody Show*, a television hit for children, 1947-1960. The marionette's face had 48 freckles, one for each state then in the Union.
Ned Doran	Martin's classmate at St. Bernard Grade School. Started ahead of Martin at quarterback for the 1954 St. Bernard football team.
Bill Earley	Prominent businessman in South Bend, Indiana. For many years, Earley assembled and coached the team of Notre Dame football alumni who would compete against the Notre Dame varsity at the conclusion of the varsity's spring practice season.
Vic Eaton	Quarterback, punter and punt returner for the 1955 Pittsburgh Steelers.

Billy Eckstein	Native of Pittsburgh. Singer and bandleader in the swing era. Friend of sportswriter Bill Nunn.
Tom Fallon	Long-time coach of the University of Notre Dame wrestling and tennis teams.
Ralph Fife	All-American guard at the University of Pittsburgh in 1941. Played professionally for the Chicago Cardinals and the Pittsburgh Steelers. Served as varsity football coach at Mt. Lebanon High School from 1953 to 1966, compiling an overall record of 89-32-5.
Jim Finks	Pittsburgh Steeler quarterback and defensive back, 1949-55. Later served as general manager of the Minnesota Vikings.
Dan Finlay	Marquette University wrestler. Defeated Martin in double overtime in the finals of the 1961 Intercolegiate Individual Independent Interstate (4-I) Tournament.
Edward Fisher	Notre Dame professor of communications arts. International figure and author in the study of movies and films. Juror at the Venice International Film Festival.
F. Scott Fitzgerald	Novelist. Author of *The Great Gatsby*, *Tender Is The Night* and other works.
Mary Flavia (Sister)	Roman Catholic nun and teacher at St. Bernard Elementary School, Mt. Lebanon, Pennsylvania.
Bruce Flowers	Six-foot-eight forward for the Notre Dame basketball team, 1976-79. Played professionally with the Cleveland Cavaliers, 1982-83.
Milton Fogelman	Federal government political appointee. Head of the Jobs Corps for the East Coast. Hired Martin as executive assistant in 1967.
Brian Foley	Worked with Martin at the St. James Center in Pittsburgh, PA during Martin's tenure with the federally-funded Economic Opportunity Program, 1965-66.
Floyd Foley	Head football coach and athletic director at O'Connell, 1971-76. Led O'Connell's football team to the Virginia Catholic League championship in 1973 and 1974. Member of the Bishop O'Connell Athletic Hall of Fame.
Tony Fontana	O'Connell wrestler during Martin's tenure as coach.

Appendix II

Dick Foster	Classmate of Martin at Mt. Lebanon High.
Karen Frye	Student at Bishop O'Connell High School, class of 1985. Friend of Steve McGraw.
Bob Gaillard	Head coach, University of San Francisco basketball team, 1970-78. Later coached basketball at Lewis & Clark College in Oregon for 22 seasons.
Jim Garcia	O'Connell wrestler during Martin's tenure as coach.
Katy Garcia	Bishop O'Connell High School pupil. Student in Martin's *American Dream Revisited* course.
Mike Garcia	O'Connell wrestler during Martin's tenure as coach. Virginia Independent School State champion and St. Alban's Invitational Tournament champion in his senior year.
John Girardot	A student at Notre Dame in the late 1960s, Girardot was scheduled for an on-campus interview with Dow Chemical Co. recruiters on November 18, 1960. A small group of students, who came to be known as the "Notre Dame Ten," protested Dow's presence on campus, disrupting the interviews. Girardot would later express sympathy for the protest.
Otto Graham	Record-setting quarterback at Northwestern University, 1941-44. Played pro football with the Cleveland Browns from 1946 to 1955, competing against Big John Rapacz, Martin's colleague at Monsignor Hackett. Also played pro basketball with the Rochester Royals.
Andrei Gromyko	A statesman who served as Minister of Foreign Affairs for the Soviet Union from 1957 to 1985. Gromyko played a key role for the Soviets in the 1962 Cuban Missile Crisis.
Ralph Guglielmi	Starting quarterback at Notre Dame, 1952-54. Consensus All-American as a senior. Later played professionally, chiefly with the Washington Redskins.
Louis Guimond	Worker who helped to construct the shrine dedicated to Saint Anne, the grandmother of Jesus, in Quebec, Canada. Guimond suffered from rheumatism. He was reportedly cured in 1658 while working on the foundation for the shrine.
John Gutter	Retired Marine Corps officer. Vietnam War veteran. Served on the Bishop O'Connell High School

	staff for more than 25 years, including facilities management and student life positions.
Lionel Hampton	Musician, bandleader and actor. The first jazz vibraphonist. A giant in the jazz world from 1930s to 1960s. Continued to perform professionally until 1991. Friend of sportswriter Bill Nunn.
James Hardy	Six-foot-nine forward for the University of San Francisco basketball team, 1975-78. Post-college, played four seasons of professional ball with the New Orleans/Utah Jazz.
Leon Hart	Three-time All-American end at Notre Dame. Standing six-foot-four and weighing 240 pounds, Hart earned All-American honors three times at Notre Dame. Heisman Trophy winner in 1949. Played eight seasons with the NFL Detroit Lions.
Woody Hayes	Legendary football coach at Ohio State University, 1951-78.
Theodore Hesburgh (Rev.)	Catholic priest. President of the University of Notre Dame for 35 years (1952-1987).
James S. Hirsch	Author of the authorized biography, *Willie Mays: The Life, The Legend*.
Henry Hissrich	Shaler High School wrestling opponent whom Martin defeated to capture the 112-pound district championship in 1959.
Joseph Hoffman (Rev.)	Roman Catholic priest and professor at the University of Notre Dame.
Kevin Holley	O'Connell wrestler during Martin's tenure as coach.
J. Edgar Hoover	The first and longest-serving director of the Federal Bureau of Investigation. Hoover played an instrumental role in the establishment of the FBI in 1935 and served as the agency's director continuously until his death in 1972.
Paul Hornung	Played halfback, fullback, safety and quarterback for Notre Dame (1954-56), while also playing on the varsity basketball team. Winner of the Heisman Trophy in 1956, his senior season. As a professional, helped the Green Bay Packers win four National Football League championships. Elected to both the College and Pro Football Halls of Fame.
Doug Howard	Student and member of O'Connell's varsity foot-

Appendix II

	ball and basketball teams during the 2006-07 academic year.
John Huarte	Notre Dame quarterback, 1962-64. Heisman Trophy winner in 1964. Played professionally for six National Football League teams, 1965-75.
Hubert H. Humphrey	Humphrey was elected to the United States Senate by the people of Minnesota in 1949, becoming the first Democrat to be elected as senator from Minnesota since the Civil War. He remained in the Senate until 1964. From 1965 to 1969, Humphrey was Vice President in the administration of Lyndon Johnson, after which he again represented Minnesota in the Senate (1971-1978).
Mary Ivo (Mother)	Roman Catholic nun. As principal at St. Thomas More Grade School in Arlington, Virginia, hired Martin to be physical education teacher for the 1967-68 school year.
Mike Ingrao	O'Connell wrestler during Martin's tenure as coach. Virginia Independent School State champion and St. Alban's champion, heavyweight class, in his senior year. Named O'Connell athlete of the year, 1972. Later served as a wrestling official and commissioner of the Virginia Wrestling Association. Member of the Bishop O'Connell Athletic Hall of Fame.
Lyndon B. Johnson	The 36th president of the United States. Announced ground-breaking "War on Poverty" during State of the Union address on January 8, 1964. Instrumental in implementing federally-funded educational and recreational programs for youths. Johnson's War on Poverty program funded activities at the St. James Center in Pittsburgh, where Martin served as director for two years, December 1964 to December 1966.
Steve Johnson	O'Connell High School teacher. Martin's colleague and friend. Recycling enthusiast.
Edmund Joyce (Rev.)	Catholic priest and executive vice president of Notre Dame. Arranged for Martin's admission to Notre Dame on probationary status despite Martin's mediocre academic record in high school.
Sonny Jurgensen	NFL quarterback. Member of the Pro Football Hall of Fame. Played for the Philadelphia Eagles from 1957 to 1963 and for the Washington Redskins from 1964 to 1974.

John R. Keating (Rev.)	Roman Catholic priest. Second bishop of the Diocese of Arlington, succeeding Bishop Thomas J. Welsh in 1983. Served in that capacity until his death in 1998.
Cliff Keen	Long-time wrestling coach at the University of Michigan. Coached the U.S. wrestling team at the 1948 summer Olympics in London.
Grace Kelly	Actress who starred in *High Noon* (1952) opposite Gary Cooper, *Mogambo* (1953) with Clark Gable, and *To Catch a Thief* (1955) with Cary Grant. Quit acting at age 26 to marry Prince Rainier of Monaco.
Jacqueline Kennedy	Wife of John Fitzgerald Kennedy and First Lady during the Kennedy Administration (January 1961-November 1963).
John Fitzgerald Kennedy	The 35th president of the United States and first Catholic to occupy the White House. Elected in November 1960, Kennedy held office from January 20, 1961 until his assassination on November 22, 1963. Prior to being elected president, Kennedy represented the State of Massachusetts in the U.S. Senate.
Joseph P. Kennedy, Sr.	Father of John Fitzgerald Kennedy. Successful businessman and statesman. One-time ambassador to Great Britain (1938-40), Kennedy also served as the inaugural chairman of the Securities and Exchange Commission (1934-35) under President Franklin D. Roosevelt.
Kevin Kerrigan	O'Connell wrestler during Martin's tenure as coach. Captain of O'Connell's football and wrestling teams in 1968. St. Alban's Invitational Tournament champion (157-pound class) in his senior year. Attended the University of Notre Dame, where he won the campus boxing championship for three consecutive years, 1970-72. Member of the Bishop O'Connell Athletic Hall of Fame.
Nikita Khrushchev	Leader of the Soviet Union during much of the Cold War, a period of hostile relations between the Eastern Bloc countries, dominated by the Soviet Union, and Western Bloc countries, led by the United States and its NATO (North Atlantic Treaty Organization) allies. Khrushchev was First Secretary of the Communist Party of the Soviet

Appendix II

	Union from 1953 to 1964 and Premier of the Soviet Union from 1958 to 1964.
Jay Kimmit	O'Connell wrestler during Martin's tenure as coach. Selected as high school All-American, 1967-68 season. St. Alban's Invitational champion in his senior year. Member of the Bishop O'Connell Athletic Hall of Fame.
Toby Knight	Six-foot-nine forward for Notre Dame, 1973-77. Later played professionally with the New York Knicks, 1977-82.
Ted Koppel	Hosted the popular ABC-TV late-night show, *Nightline*. Introduced the world to the wisdom of Brandeis University professor Morrie Schwartz after conducting an interview at Schwartz's home in West Newton, Massachusetts.
Edward "Moose" Krause	Collegiate basketball star at Notre Dame during the 1930s. Named Notre Dame basketball coach in 1943. Gave up coaching position in 1949 to become the University's athletic director, a post he held for more than 30 years. Also served as public address announcer at Notre Dame football games.
Joe Kuharich	A native of South Bend, Indiana who went on to play football at Notre Dame. Later became the head coach of the Fighting Irish football team, a position he occupied for all four years of Martin's college career. Left Notre Dame in 1963 after accumulating an overall record of 17 wins and 23 losses.
Bob Kurtzke	O'Connell wrestler during Martin's tenure as coach. Studied as an undergrad at Notre Dame and then attended medical school. Now a prominent neurologist in the Washington, D.C. metropolitan area.
Bill Laimbeer	Six-foot-eleven center for Notre Dame's basketball team, 1975-79. Spent 14 seasons in the NBA, twelve with the Detroit Pistons. In the pros, gained a reputation for physical play and, with teammate Rick Mahorn, formed the core of the Pistons' "Bad Boys."
Pat Laing	Three-year starting pitcher for the Bishop O'Connell High School baseball team (1963-65). Laing won 16 games and lost only one during his high school career and pitched a perfect game

	in his senior season. Led the O'Connell baseball team to a school-record 42 consecutive wins.
Daryle Lamonica	The starting quarterback at Notre Dame for three seasons, 1960-62. Before entering college, turned down a contract to play baseball in the Chicago Cubs organization. Played quarterback in the pros for the Buffalo Bills and Oakland Raiders. With Oakland, his tendency to throw long passes earned him the nickname "The Mad Bomber."
George Lamprinakos	Teacher and wrestling coach at Mt. Lebanon High. Known by the students as "Lampy." Told the 4' 7" Martin, "I don't think basketball is your sport." Encouraged Martin to pursue wrestling as an alternative. Became a father figure for Martin.
Bernard Lange (Rev.)	Roman Catholic priest. Possessed a Ph.D. in biology. Resided at Notre Dame but did not teach classes or conduct research. Full-time occupation was weightlifter. In his prime, claimed to be the fourth strongest man in the world.
Charlie Laniak	Former O'Connell High School teacher. Martin's friend and golfing partner.
Johnny Lattner	Native of Oak Park, Illinois. After graduating from Fenwick High School, enrolled at Notre Dame. Starred at halfback for the Irish, 1951-53, winning the Heisman Trophy in 1953. Played in 1954 for the Pittsburgh Steelers, then served in the U.S. Air Force.
Bill Lawler	O'Connell wrestler during Martin's tenure as coach.
Tom Lawler	O'Connell wrestler during Martin's tenure as coach.
Elmer Layden	Notre Dame fullback, 1922-24. One of the famed "Four Horsemen."
Frank Leahy	Head coach of Notre Dame football, 1941-43 and 1946-53. Won four national championships.
Mike Lind	Notre Dame fullback, 1960-62. Captain of the team in 1962. Known for his intense work ethic and self-effacing ways. Played four seasons in the pros, two with the San Francisco 49ers and two with the Pittsburgh Steelers.
Joseph Lonergan (Rev.)	Pastor of St. Bernard Catholic Church in Mt. Lebanon, the parish to which Martin's family belonged in the 1940s and 1950s.
Joe Louis	Regarded as one of the greatest heavyweight box-

Appendix II

	ing champions of all time. Held the World Heavyweight Championship crown from 1937 to 1949.
Paul Loverde (Rev.)	Roman Catholic priest. Installed as the third bishop of the Arlington, Virginia diocese in March 1999.
Johnny Lujack	Quarterback for the University of Notre Dame football team. Led Notre Dame to the national championship in 1943, then served in the U.S. Navy for the duration of World War II. Resuming his college career after the war, he again led Notre Dame to national championships in 1946 and 1947. A versatile athlete, he lettered in baseball, football, basketball, and track during college and was the Heisman Trophy winner in 1947.
Louis Mack	O'Connell wrestler during Martin's tenure as coach. Died at the age of 40. The wrestling room at O'Connell is named in his honor.
Skip Major	Journalist who covered high school sports for the *Arlington Journal* during Martin's years as O'Connell's wrestling coach.
Mickey Mantle	Hall-of-Fame center fielder for the New York Yankees, 1951-68. Finished his major league career with a batting average of .298 and 536 regular season home runs.
Ted Marchibroda	A native of Franklin, Pennsylvania. Played quarterback for St. Bonaventure University and the University of Detroit Mercy (UDM) in the early 1950s. Was a quarterback for the Pittsburgh Steelers in 1953, 1955-56, and the Chicago Cardinals in 1957. Later served as head coach of the Baltimore Colts, Indianapolis Colts, and Baltimore Ravens.
Bobby Martel	As a sophomore at O'Connell in 1978, suffered a near-fatal episode of pulseless electrical activity (PEA). Made a miraculous recovery after weeks in a coma.
Bill Martin	Older brother of Dick Martin.
Mary Christine Martin	Martin's wife and mother of his three daughters.
James Martin, M.D.	Martin's father, a prominent Pittsburgh-area physician. Formerly chief of staff at Pittsburgh's St. Joseph Hospital and St. Claire Hospital in Mt. Lebanon.

Jimmy Martin	Martin's oldest brother. Preceded Martin at the University of Notre Dame.
"Jungle Jim" Martin	All-American end at the University of Notre Dame, 1950. Played professionally with the Detroit Lions. No relation to Dick Martin and his family.
Katherine ("Dolly") Martin	The first-born of Martin's sisters.
Kelly Martin	The first of Martin's three daughters, born September 4, 1968. Graduated from the University of Notre Dame with a double major in psychology and business. Former English and psychology teacher at O'Connell.
Kerry Martin	Martin's youngest daughter, born October 30, 1976. A graduate of George Mason University. Former English teacher at O'Connell. Received her master's degree in American studies at Pepperdine University.
Kimberley Martin	Martin's middle daughter, born December 21, 1970. Received her bachelor's degree from the University of Virginia with a double major in theater and anthropology.
Mary Elizabeth Martin	Mother of Dick Martin.
Mary Jane Martin	Martin's sister. Second oldest daughter in the Martin family.
Sister Margaret Mary	One-time assistant principal for academics at O'Connell.
Bucky Maughan	Canonsburg, Pennsylvania wrestling star. Competed at 112 pounds in high school. Won 70 consecutive dual matches during four years at Canonsburg High. Went on to wrestle at Moorhead State College (Minnesota) where he was the 1963 NCAA champion in the 115-pound class.
William Mayo	A physician and surgeon and one of seven founders of the famed Mayo Clinic located in Rochester, Minnesota.
Willie Mays	Perennial all-star center fielder for the New York Giants and San Francisco Giants, 1951-1972. Completed his career with the New York Mets in 1973. Hit 660 home runs in the major leagues and compiled a career batting average of .302.
Pat McAteer	O'Connell wrestler during Martin's tenure as coach.

Appendix II

	Named outstanding wrestler at the 1977 Tri-State Catholic Invitational Wrestling Tournament.
Pat "Patmac" McAteer	Father of O'Connell wrestler Pat McAteer. A native of Merseyside, England, he was the middleweight boxing champion of the British Empire, 1956-58.
John McCarren (Rev.)	Roman Catholic priest. Associate pastor at St. Bernard Church during the 1950s and 1960s.
Willie McCorkel	Friend of Martin. Accompanied him to Ocean City, New Jersey for the summer of 1962.
Dan McCown	Classmate of Martin and Denny Phillips at Mt. Lebanon High. Found dismembered frog leg in his salad at lunch after biology lab. Suspected but could never confirm that Phillips was the source.
Michael McGivney (Rev.)	Roman Catholic priest who founded the fraternal and charitable organization known as the Knights of Columbus.
Steve McGraw (Rev.)	Roman Catholic priest. Graduate of O'Connell High School, class of 1984. Spent six years as a lawyer with the Department of Justice before entering the seminary. Serves as parochial administrator of St. Anthony of Padua Catholic Church in Falls Church, Virginia.
Pat McGroarty	Football coach at Pope Paul VI High School.
Joe McGuire	O'Connell wrestler during Martin's tenure as coach.
Brian McInerney	A student at Notre Dame in the late 1960s, McInerney participated in a peaceful student protest against Dow Chemical Co. on November 18, 1969 during one of Dow's on-campus recruiting visits. One of the "Notre Dame Ten," McInerney and his fellow protesters had targeted Dow because it produced the incendiary gel napalm used by the U.S. military as a weapon in Vietnam. The protesters, including McInerney, were suspended from school.
Patricia McKinley	Long-time biology teacher at O'Connell High School.
Alex McMurtrie	Brother of Father James McMurtrie.
Bill McMurtrie	Brother of Father James McMurtrie.
James W. McMurtrie (Rev.)	Roman Catholic priest and friend of Martin.

	Served as principal at O'Connell, 1972-77. Favored Notre Dame sports and the Washington Redskins.
Mary Theresa McMurtrie	Mother of Father James McMurtrie.
Sandy Andreas McMurtrie	Sister-in-law of Father James McMurtrie.
James "Nabi" Michaels	A wrestler at Langley High School, McLean, Virginia. Defeated O'Connell's Freddie Ball in the 105-pound weight class to help Langley topple O'Connell in December 1977 and end O'Connell's consecutive win streak at 42.
Don Miller	Played right halfback for Notre Dame, 1922-24. One of the famed "Four Horsemen." Called "the greatest open field runner I ever had" by coach Knute Rockne.
Marilyn Monroe	Model, actress and singer who was a prominent Hollywood starlet in the 1950s and early 1960s. Born Norma Jeane Mortenson, she changed her name to Marilyn Monroe in the late 1940s to further her film career. Monroe starred in numerous films, including *The Asphalt Jungle* (1950), *Gentlemen Prefer Blondes* (1953) and *Some Like It Hot* (1959). She died under mysterious circumstances in 1962.
John Moran	The older of two brothers who received the most valuable softball player trophies on June 12, 1965 from Willie Mays at the St. James Center awards ceremony. Died on May 4, 1968 while serving in Vietnam with the U.S. Army.
William Moran	Younger brother of John. Like his brother, a good athlete and a talented softball player. Was presented the most valuable softball player trophy by Willie Mays.
Stuart Morrison	A wrestler at Langley High School, McLean, Virginia.
Joe Morrissey	O'Connell wrestler during Martin's tenure as coach. Later served as Commonwealth's Attorney for the City of Richmond, Virginia.
Andy Mould	O'Connell wrestler during Martin's tenure as coach.
Harry Murphy	O'Connell wrestler during Martin's tenure as coach. Captain of Martin's last wrestling team, 1977-78. St. Alban's Invitational Tournament champion at 132 pounds. Named 1978 O'Connell athlete of the year. As wrestling coach at St. Stephen's and St. Agnes

Appendix II

	School, Alexandria, Virginia, was named *The Washington Post* coach of the year in 2000. Member of the Bishop O'Connell Athletic Hall of Fame.
Bill Newlin	As reporter for *The Washington Star*, covered high school wrestling during O'Connell's 42-match consecutive win streak.
Elbert "Elbie" Nickel	Tight end for the Pittsburgh Steelers for eleven seasons, 1947-1957. In 2007, was selected as one of the 33 best players in the 75-year history of the Steelers.
Karl Paul Reinhold Niebuhr	American theologian and commentator on public affairs. Author of the *Serenity Prayer*.
Richard M. Nixon	The 37th President of the United States and the first and only president to ever resign from office. Elected to the presidency in 1972 after a landslide victory over Democrat George McGovern, Nixon left office in 1974 in disgrace after being implicated in efforts to cover up the break-in by Republican operatives at the headquarters of the Democratic National Committee, located in the Watergate building in Washington, D.C.
Bill Nunn	Legendary sportswriter for the *Pittsburgh Courier*. In college, was a talented scorer for the West Virginia State basketball team, receiving tryout offers from the New York Knicks and the Harlem Globetrotters. Served as a scout for the Pittsburgh Steelers for many years.
Brenda O'Donnell	O'Connell student. Died in 1975, at the age of sixteen, due to cystic fibrosis. Her death inspired her sister, Maura, and other O'Connell students to organize a "Superdance" to raise funds for treating children afflicted by the disease and promoting research.
Catherine O'Donnell	Sister of Brenda, Sean, and Maura O'Donnell.
Maura O'Donnell	Sister of Brenda. Graduated from O'Connell with honors in 1976. During four years at O'Connell, earned nine varsity letters in field hockey, softball, basketball, and diving. As a senior, was a Virginia State High School diving champion. Died from cystic fibrosis in 1978 at the age of twenty. Member of the Bishop O'Connell Athletic Hall of Fame.
Sean O'Donnell	Sister of Brenda, Sean, and Maura O'Donnell.

Charlie O'Hara	Notre Dame defensive halfback, 1961-63. Roommate of Denny Phillips in his junior and senior years. Entered seminary after college. Serves as pastor, St. Joseph Catholic Church, Spring City, Pennsylvania.
Thomas "Tip" O'Neill	Long-time U.S. Congressman from Massachusetts and Speaker of the House of Representatives from 1977 to 1987.
José Ortega y Gasset	Spanish philosopher and intellectual leader of the Spanish Revolution in the 1930s. Author of *The Revolt of the Masses*. Served as the source for the personal philosophy of Notre Dame professor Thomas Stritch.
Sandra O'Shea	Long-time biology teacher at O'Connell High School.
Steve Ouellette	Langley High School wrestler. Defeated O'Connell's John Washko on points in the December 1977 O'Connell-Langley match to give Langley a lead it would never relinquish. Langley's victory ended O'Connell's consecutive win streak at 42.
Jesse Owens	Famed U.S. track and field athlete who specialized in the sprints and long jump. Competing in the 1936 Summer Olympics in Berlin, he took home gold medals in the 100 meters, 200 meters, long jump and 4 x 100 meters relay. Friend of *Pittsburgh Courier* sportswriter Bill Nunn.
Mike Pappas	O'Connell wrestler during Martin's tenure as coach. St. Alban's Invitational Tournament champion at 103 pounds as a junior. Runner-up in the Tournament as a senior. Member of the Bishop O'Connell Athletic Hall of Fame.
Buddy Parker	NFL player and head coach. Served as head coach of the Chicago Cardinals (1947), Detroit Lions (1950-56), and Pittsburgh Steelers (1957-64). Refused to allow any of his players to wear uniform number 13.
Cathy Parr	Resident of the Merica House group home in Falls Church, Virginia.
Ara Parseghian	As head coach at Northwestern University (1956-63), his football team defeated Notre Dame four straight times, inducing Notre Dame to hire him as head coach in 1964. Taking over a team that had gone 2-7, Parseghian led Notre Dame to a 9-1

Appendix II

	record. Coached Notre Dame for eleven seasons, 1964-74, winning two national championships.
John Paul II (Pope)	Head of the Catholic Church, 1978-2005. The second-longest serving Pope in history, John Paul II was an influential leader of the 20th century.
Gaylord Perry	Major league pitcher for 22 seasons. Spent the years from 1962 to 1971 with the San Francisco Giants.
Alex Perwich	O'Connell wrestler during Martin's tenure as coach.
Richard "Digger" Phelps	Head basketball coach at Notre Dame, 1971-91. Led the Irish to fourteen seasons of 20 or more wins.
Denny Phillips	A classic student-athlete, excelling in the classroom and on the football field. Named high school All-American and selected for the Pennsylvania "Big 33" team. Was on the receiving end of a 45-yard pass play that allowed Notre Dame to defeat Roger Staubach and Navy in 1962. In high school, allegedly pilfered a frog leg from biology lab and buried it in classmate Dan McCown's salad.
Nick Pietrosante	A two-year starter at fullback for Notre Dame (1957-58), he made a key fumble recovery in the Fighting Irish's 1957 game against the University of Oklahoma that helped Notre Dame end the Sooners' 47-game winning streak. "Even the nuns were astounded," the newspapers proclaimed. Later played nine seasons in the pros, seven with the Detroit Lions and two with the Cleveland Browns.
Mark Pilon (Rev.)	Roman Catholic priest. Served as chaplain at O'Connell during the 1980s.
Gene Pitney	Popular singer-songwriter and musician of the 1960s. His songs were often characterized by a pained tone, as in his 1961 hit, *Town Without Pity*, and his 1962 release, *Only Love Can Break A Heart*.
Bernie Powers	Martin's basketball and football coach at St. Bernard School. Former University of Notre Dame quarterback. Hired Martin to run a federally-funded after-school mentoring, academic, and sports program at Pittsburgh's St. James Center.

Bob Prince	Popular radio and television voice of the Pittsburgh Pirates for 28 years. Introduced the "Green Weenie"—a plastic rattle in the shape of an oversized green pickle—as a good-luck charm at Pirates games.
Raymond Pulaski	Martin's football coach at St. Bernard School when Martin was in seventh grade.
John Rapacz	One-time professional football player and pro wrestler. Stood six-feet-four and weighed 252 pounds. As a wrestler, competed against André the Giant. Later became assistant football coach at Monsignor John Hackett Catholic Central High School, Kalamazoo, Michigan.
Tim Reardon	Classmate of Martin at Notre Dame. Four-time winner of Notre Dame's Bengal Bouts boxing tournament.
John Rebel (Rev.)	Roman Catholic priest. Officiated at the wedding of Dick Martin and Chris Smith.
Marion Redmond	Six-foot-six guard for the 1976-77 University of San Francisco basketball team.
Marlon Redmond	Six-foot-six guard for the 1976-77 University of San Francisco basketball team. Twin brother of Marion. Played professionally for the Philadelphia 76ers and the Kansas City Kings.
Nancy Rhoades	Martin's high school sweetheart.
Greg Rice	An outstanding distance runner for Notre Dame in the 1930s. Specialized in the two-mile run. Stood five-feet-five, gaining him the nickname "Little Dynamite."
Pat Richter	Member of the 1976-77 Bishop Ireton High School wrestling team.
Knute Rockne	Innovative and charismatic head football coach at Notre Dame, 1918-1930. Instrumental in developing the forward pass as an offensive weapon. Delivered famed "Win one for the Gipper" speech to his Notre Dame squad on November 10, 1928, inspiring Notre Dame to a 12-6 victory over a previously unbeaten Army team. Died March 31, 1931 in a plane crash in Kansas.
Fran Rogel	Fullback for the Pittsburgh Steelers, 1950-57. A favorite of Steelers' coach Walt Kiesling, who

Appendix II

	started every game by running Rogel up the middle. The strategy prompted fans to chant, "Hey diddle diddle, Rogel up the middle." Played collegiately at Penn State.
Art Rooney	Dr. Martin's Friday night poker partner and owner of the Pittsburgh Steelers football team. In his youth, was one of the best athletes in Pittsburgh. The Boston Red Sox and the Chicago Cubs each attempted to sign him to play professional baseball. The University of Notre Dame dangled a football scholarship. Rooney elected to attend Duquesne University, where he excelled in boxing. Qualified for the 1920 U.S. Olympic boxing team but did not participate. In 1933, purchased the Steelers, then known as the Pirates, for $2,500. Owned the team until his death in 1988.
André René Roussimoff	Professional wrestler born in Grenoble, France. Giant of a man at seven-feet-four, with weight listed between 424 and 475 pounds. Known professionally as André the Giant. By the age of 12, he stood six-foot-three and weighed 240 pounds. Unable to fit on a school bus, he was driven to school by playwright Samuel Beckett, a friend of André's father.
Eddie Rutkowski	Varsity wrestler and football player at Notre Dame, 1960-62. Friend and wrestling teammate of Martin. Played six seasons in the American Football League with the Buffalo Bills, 1963-68. Later entered politics and was elected to two terms as County Executive of Erie County, New York.
Gerry Sachsel	Notre Dame student and wrestler, three years ahead of Martin. One of the best ever to compete at Notre Dame. Went undefeated in dual matches during his three varsity years.
Jonas Salk	Famed medical researcher and virologist best known for his work in developing the first safe and effective vaccine for the prevention of polio.
John Schmidt	O'Connell wrestler during Martin's tenure as coach.
Morrie Schwartz	Brandeis University sociology professor whose reflections on life and comments on dealing with the prospect of death prompted former student Mitch Albom to write the best-seller, *Tuesdays with Morrie*.

Neil Sedaka	Pop/rock singer, pianist, and composer whose career spanned nearly 55 years. His first song, *The Diary*, was inspired by an encounter with singer Connie Francis. Sedaka saw Francis writing in her diary and asked if he could read what she was writing. Francis refused, prompting Sedaka to speculate about the contents in song. His song, *Breaking Up Is Hard To Do,* reached #1 on the pop charts in 1962.
Bunni Segall	Classmate of Martin and Denny Phillips at Mt. Lebanon High.
Charles Sheedy (Rev.)	Roman Catholic priest. Dean of Arts and Letters at the University of Notre Dame.
Deirdre Shields	Resident of the Merica House group home in Falls Church, Virginia, the sister of Maureen Shields.
Maureen Shields	Resident of the Merica House group home in Falls Church, Virginia, the sister of Deirdre Shields.
Alfred E. "Al" Smith	Smith was the Democratic candidate for president in 1928, the first Catholic to run for the office. Dogged by concerns that the Catholic Church and the incumbent Pope, Pius XI, would dictate his political agenda, Smith lost in a landslide to Republican Herbert Hoover. Before running for the presidency, Smith was elected governor of New York State four times.
Glenna Smith (Sister)	Catholic nun and psychotherapist with Benedictine Counseling Services in Bristow, Virginia. Sister Glenna provided counseling services to Martin.
Jackie Smith	Friend and grade school/high school classmate of Martin. A bruising fullback in football.
Edwin "Duke" Snider	Hall-of-Fame baseball player for the Brooklyn/Los Angeles Dodgers, 1947-59.
Jack Snow	Notre Dame football player, 1962-64. Gained recognition as an All-American in his senior year after coach Ara Parseghian shifted him from flanker to split end. Played with the NFL Los Angeles Rams, 1965-75. After retirement, was an occasional actor in movies and television programs. Father of former major league first baseman J. T. Snow.
Darrell Snyder	O'Connell's head football coach, 1977-82, and 1994-02. Member of the O'Connell Athletic Hall of Fame.

Appendix II

Dick Soisson	Graduate of the University of Notre Dame, 1950. High school football coach in Kalamazoo, Michigan for nearly 50 years, first at St. Augustine High School and later Monsignor Hackett High School. Won more than 200 games as coach.
Willie Stargell	Slugging first baseman for the Pittsburgh Pirates, 1962-82. Member of the Baseball Hall of Fame.
Jimmy Stark	Character played by actor James Dean in the landmark 1955 movie, *Rebel Without A Cause*.
Roger Staubach	1963 Heisman Trophy winner as quarterback at the U.S. Naval Academy. After graduation, served four years on active duty with the Navy, including a tour in Vietnam. Joined the Dallas Cowboys in 1969 and led the team to two Super Bowl wins. Defeated the Minnesota Vikings in a 1975 playoff game, throwing a desperation touchdown pass to receiver Drew Pearson with 24 seconds left in the game. "I closed my eyes and said a Hail Mary," Staubach later told reporters. The comment led to the use of "Hail Mary" as a term of art to describe a pass thrown in desperation by a quarterback toward the end zone at the end of a game.
Ernie Stautner	Born in Germany, emigrated with his family to East Greenbush, New York at the age of 3. Four-year starter at tackle for Boston College, 1946-49. Played fourteen years in the NFL, all with the Pittsburgh Steelers. Selected to play in nine Pro Bowls. Member of the Pro Football Hall of Fame.
Bart Steib	Standout baseball and basketball player for O'Connell, 1960-63. As a senior, played on the 1963 baseball team that began a 42-game consecutive win streak. O'Connell's athlete of the year in 1963. Teacher and coach at O'Connell, 1972-08. Member of the O'Connell Athletic Hall of Fame.
John Steinbeck	American novelist. Published *Of Mice and Men* in 1937. Published *The Grapes of Wrath*, widely regarded as his best novel, in 1939.
Mike Strickland	O'Connell wrestler during Martin's tenure as coach.
Steve Strickland	O'Connell wrestler during Martin's tenure as coach.
Thomas Stritch	Chairman of Notre Dame's Department of Journalism from 1946 to 1970. Served as mentor

	to Martin. With the help of colleague Ed Fisher, established Notre Dame's undergraduate degree program in communication arts. Was influenced greatly by the writings of Spanish philosopher José Ortega y Gasset.
Harry Stuhldreher	Three-time All-American quarterback at Notre Dame, 1922-24. One of Notre Dame's "Four Horsemen."
Michael Taylor (Rev.)	Roman Catholic priest. Former chaplain at O'Connell High School.
Lynn Tecca	Business manager and key advisor for Martin during his tenure as principal at Monsignor John Hackett Catholic Central High School, Kalamazoo, Michigan.
Mother Teresa	Roman Catholic nun who administered to the poor, orphaned, sick and dying in India for over 45 years. Founder of the Missionaries of Charity, an order of nuns operating in many countries of the world. Awarded the Nobel Peace Prize in 1979. Beatified by Pope John Paul II in October 2003 and given the title, "Blessed Teresa of Calcutta."
Dick Teresi	As grade school student, played football for Assumption Elementary School. Later played for the University of Iowa.
Joe Theismann	Notre Dame quarterback, 1968-70. At the insistence of the Notre Dame sports information director, changed the pronunciation of his last name from "Theesman" to "Thighsman," thereby giving Notre Dame an advantage when promoting "Theismann for Heisman." Played twelve years for the Washington Redskins, quarterbacking the team to victory over the Miami Dolphins on January 30, 1983 in Super Bowl XVII.
Brother Theodore	One-time principal and wrestling coach at O'Connell. Hired Martin in 1967 to coach O'Connell's wrestling team.
Dick Tiger	One of the greatest boxers ever to come out of Africa. Won the world middleweight boxing championship in 1962.
Frank Tripucka	Quarterback for Notre Dame, 1945-48. NFL quarterback from 1949 to 1952 with the Detroit Lions and the Chicago Cardinals. Spent 1953-59 in the Canadian Football League. In 1960, signed as an

Appendix II

	assistant coach with the Denver Broncos of the newly formed American Football League. When the Broncos' quarterbacks proved ineffective, Tripucka put on a uniform, becoming the first starting QB for the Broncos. Played four seasons in Denver, 1960-63. Father of former Notre Dame and pro basketball player Kelly Tripucka.
Harry S. Truman	The 33rd president of the United States (1945-1953).
Julius Tucker	Owner of Tucker Freight Lines, a trucking company based in South Bend, Indiana until its purchase by Central Transport of Sterling Heights, Michigan in 1984. Though not formally affiliated with Notre Dame, Tucker was an enthusiastic supporter of the University and exercised particular influence in matters involving Notre Dame athletes.
Tara Ulepic	Bishop O'Connell High School pupil. Former student in Martin's *American Dream Revisited* course.
Johnny Unitas	Legendary quarterback for the Baltimore Colts, 1956-72.
Harry Van Trees	Bishop O'Connell wrestler, 1976-80. Virginia Independent Schools Athletic Association (VISAA) state champion at 132 pounds in 1980. Head wrestling coach at Oakton High School, Vienna, Virginia, for fourteen years.
Bobby Vinton	Well-known pop singer in the 1960s. Native of Cannonsburg, Pennsylvania.
Sister Maria Virginia	An Immaculate Heart of Mary (IHM) nun. Assistant principal for academics at Bishop O'Connell High School during Father James McMurtrie's tenure as principal.
Harold "Bud" Vogel	Classmate and friend of Martin throughout grade school, high school and college. Member of football teams at all levels of school, playing tight end for St. Bernard School, Mt. Lebanon High, and Notre Dame.
Nick Walz	Long-time equipment manager for Notre Dame athletics.
John Washko	O'Connell wrestler during Martin's tenure as coach.
Sean Wawrzaszek	Resident of the Merica House group home in Falls Church, Virginia.

Lee Wells	Classmate of Martin at St. Bernard School and Mt. Lebanon High School.
Jim Welsford	Friend and former colleague of Martin.
Thomas J. Welsh (Rev.)	Catholic priest. Installed as the first bishop of the Arlington Diocese in 1974. Later served as bishop of the Diocese of Allentown, Pennsylvania.
Bob Williams	Played quarterback for Notre Dame under head coach Terry Brennan, 1956-58. Led the Irish to a 7-0 victory over the University of Oklahoma on November 16, 1957, ending the Sooners' 47-game winning streak. Drafted by the Chicago Bears in 1959 but chose to enroll at the University of Pittsburgh Medical School.
Donald "Duck" Williams	Six-foot-two shooting guard for Notre Dame, 1974-78. Was the team's primary scorer in his junior season. Played professionally for the Utah Jazz.
Darryl Wilson	High school wrestling opponent of Martin. Nicknamed "the Squirrel." Their match, billed as "The Squirrel vs. The Beaver," ended in a 1-1 draw.
Dick Wilson	Pan-American champion wrestler for Toledo University in the 1960s. Competed at 123 pounds.
Steve Yeager	Senior at Mt. Lebanon High School during Martin's freshman year of high school.
Matt Zecony	As grade school student, played football for Assumption Elementary School. Later played for the University of Iowa.
Fritzie Zivic	Former world welterweight boxing champion (1940-41). Lived near the Martin household in Mt. Lebanon. Went 158-64-9 for his career, with 80 knockouts.

About the Author

FRED DAY is a lawyer engaged in private practice in Falls Church, Virginia. He is a graduate of Providence College in Providence, Rhode Island. He holds a master's degree in political economics from the University of Albany, State University of New York, and a law degree from George Washington University, Washington, D.C. His previous books include *Dream Team: Saints and Gentle Souls From the World of Sports* (2007), *Sports and Courts: An Introduction to Principles of Law and Legal Theory Using Cases From Professional Sports* (2005), and *Clubhouse Lawyer: Law in the World of Sports* (2004).